URBAN ELITES AND MASS TRANSPORTATION

URBAN ELITES AND MASS TRANSPORTATION

THE DIALECTICS OF POWER

J. ALLEN WHITT

PRINCETON UNIVERSITY PRESS • PRINCETON, NEW JERSEY

Published by Princeton University Press,
41 William Street, Princeton, New Jersey
In the United Kingdom: Princeton University Press,
Guildford, Surrey

All Rights Reserved

Library of Congress Cataloging in Publication Data will be
found on the last printed page of this book

Publication of this book has been aided by a grant from
the Paul Mellon Fund of Princeton University Press

This book has been composed in Linotron Times Roman

Clothbound editions of Princeton University Press books
are printed on acid-free paper, and binding materials are
chosen for strength and durability

Printed in the United States of America by Princeton
University Press, Princeton, New Jersey

For Clyde McCoy Whitt, my father,
and in memory of Bess Ellen Whitt, my mother.

CONTENTS

CHAPTER FIVE

CHAPTER SIX

LIST OF TABLES AND FIGURES

TABLES

ACKNOWLEDGMENTS

Many people contributed to the creation of this book. Foremost among them are Harvey Molotch and G. William Domhoff, whose support, insights, and criticisms were of the highest value. I also gratefully acknowledge the expert assistance of Richard Appelbaum, William Chambliss, Richard Flacks, David Gold, Joyce Rothschild-Whitt, and Michael Useem. Basil G. Zimmer provided welcomed and dependable moral support. Chris Sonderegger did a superb job of typing the manuscript.

LIST OF ABBREVIATIONS

BAC	Bay Area Council
BART, BARTD	Bay Area Rapid Transit system
CED	Committee for Economic Development
CR	*Composite Report* on transportation, 1962
CTC	Citizens' Transportation Committee
FSC	Freeway Support Committee
GM	General Motors Corporation
IPT	*Improving Public Transit in Los Angeles* report, 1967
IRT	Institute for Rapid Transit
LAT	*Los Angeles Times*
MTC	Bay Area Metropolitan Transportation Commission
NCL	National City Lines
PBHM	Parsons, Brinckerhoff, Hall, and Macdonald (engineering firm)
PBQD	Parsons, Brinckerhoff, Quade, and Douglas (formerly PBHM)
PBTB	Joint venture of PBQD, Tudor Engineering, and Bechtel Corporation
PCL	Pacific City Lines
RRT	*Regional Rapid Transit* report, 1956
SBNP	*Santa Barbara News Press*
SCRTD	Southern California Rapid Transit District
SFC	*San Francisco Chronicle*
TARDAC	The Tuberculosis and Respiratory Diseases Association of California
UCMT	United Cities Motor Transit
WOGA	Western Oil and Gas Association

URBAN ELITES AND MASS TRANSPORTATION

This book is about politics and power in contemporary American society. It contributes to our understanding of who the powerful are and how they operate to get their way. It shows how public policy, private planning, and even the form of our cities can be shaped to serve the interests of those with predominant power. To study these issues the book focusses on a crucial subject which touches our daily lives, which has had enormous influence in determining the conditions of our urban existence, and will continue to play a substantial role in shaping the form and character of metropolitan regions. The subject is transportation. Transportation is important in itself, but is even more important as a perspective from which to view politics and power in our society.

This book approaches the problem of understanding power in a unique way. First, the book does not simply present one perspective, the usual way to study power; rather, the book compares three different models of political power with one another in order to determine which can best explain the empirical events observed. Each step in the analysis is governed by a detailed comparison between what each of the models would predict and what is actually found. To compare the models the book presents a series of hypotheses from each theoretical model and tests how well each hypothesis is supported by the subsequent evidence. Thus the approach is more comparative and systematic than is usually the case in works that examine politics and power.

Secondly, this book is unique in that it develops and applies a model of political power—the class-dialectical model (Whitt, 1979a)—to an area in which it has rarely been applied: the local or regional level. The whole arena of so-called "community power" has been (for reasons that will directly be explained) the virtually exclusive domain of the other two models, elitism and pluralism. Of these two, pluralistic approaches have been most common. The dialectical model, however, has essentially never been used at the level of the community, nor has it been presented in the research literature (see Aiken and Mott, 1970; Bonjean et al., 1971; Hawley and Wirt, 1974; Polsby, 1980). This lack of attention to the dialectical model has been unfortunate since the model appears to be an effective alternative to both pluralist and elitist models.

Thirdly, this book can be read as a detailed example of how to analyze power at the local level and of how to go beyond the immediate confines of the community and relate local power and political events with similar relationships and processes at the national level. As the analysis unfolds, it will become clear that additional insights may be gained by going beyond pluralist and elitist techniques and asking different questions and using newer methods. In the end, this work is also, therefore, a suggestive paradigm for research methods following from the dialectical perspective.

During the last two decades, American social science research on political power has stirred a well-known debate, generally conceptualized as pluralism versus elitism. This has eclipsed consideration of the dialectical model. This is ironic since, as an explicit political model, it has the longest historical roots of the three. Its clearest origin is found in the work of Karl Marx, although elements of the model may be traced back as far as the early Greeks. In recent years, the dialectical model has experienced a vigorous and elaborate development in the hands of contemporary neo-Marxists. This development has been especially robust within European sociology, political science, and philosophy, but has also begun to influence work in other parts of the world, including the United States. However, the dialectical model has yet to make its presence felt in the field of community power.

There are probably two main reasons for this disregard of the dialectical model as a guide for empirical research at the local level. First, there has been a theoretical and methodological polarization in the field due to the dramatic pluralistic/elitist debate. This polarization has encouraged researchers and critics to collapse categories and to treat the class-dialectical and elitist models as equivalent. For example, in the new edition of his book, *Community Power and Political Theory*, Nelson Polsby (1980), one of the leading figures in the field, makes no distinction between elitist and Marxian models, instead treating both as "stratification theory." Yet elitist and Marxian models are quite different. This confusion on the part of a major scholar reflects the general confusion in the field. I would argue that this blurring of important distinctions between the two models has confused and oversimplified the theoretical issues, thereby retarding the development of political theory. Secondly, a great deal of the pluralist/elitist debate has grown out of, and has likewise generated, empirical studies of political power at the community level. However, researchers who have used the dialectical model have usually focused on the national or international level, leaving the whole area of community studies to the pluralist and elitist approaches.[1] Since the study of community power (in the United States at least) became the traditional testing-ground for supposedly general models of political power, the class-dialectical model has been largely overlooked by political researchers in the United States. A major goal of this book is to begin to remedy that neglect by specifying and assessing the class-dialectic model, along with the better-known elitist and pluralist models.[2]

The relative explanatory power of the three models is assessed by applying them to a crucial area of public policy: urban transportation politics. The rise to dominance early in this century of the private automobile caused profound changes not only in how we travelled but also in our patterns of social life, the use of land, the shape of our cities, the structure of our economic system, and

---

[1] As Alford (1975:150-52) points out, the class model generally has been concerned with the societal context of action, while the pluralist and elite models have tended to look at the individual and organizational contexts, respectively. Therefore, the latter two models have been more readily applicable at the level of community power analysis. I am arguing that the class-dialectical model can and should be applied to the community as well.

[2] I use the term "class-dialectic" for a specific reason. It is intended to call attention to two of the essential features of the model: it is based on a class analysis and it assumes a dialectual conception of history and class relations. (The meaning of dialectual will be explained in Chapter One.) Other writers, also working within the general Marxian tradition, use such terms as class-conflict, class-struggle, class, or Marxian to describe their models. Not all of these models, however, contain what I see as the two essential features described above, particularly the dialectical component.

the social opportunities and limitations we confronted. More recently, burgeoning problems brought by mass use of the automobile have made evident the need for alternatives to the private automobile. Calls for new and improved public transportation systems have been one important response to traffic congestion, urban sprawl, central city decline, the immobility of those without autos, air pollution, the increasing costs of land clearance and highway construction, and the decreasing availability and increasing cost of motor fuel. Cities in the United States have been upgrading their public transportation systems and a few, such as Washington, D.C. and San Francisco, have recently built expensive new subway and surface rail systems. The enormous range of auto-related urban problems and the costly public transit systems being proposed and constructed make urban transportation a fertile area for political analysis. Not only are crucial theoretical issues involved, but also many major political, economic, and social interests are at stake. The theoretical and practical salience of transportation issues is made even more prominent by a central conclusion of this research: these new systems of urban transportation are not likely to solve the problems they were presumably designed to alleviate. The analysis to follow will make clear why this is so.

This book then is about politics. My first task has been to define and clarify the three existing political models. This is necessary in light of the continuing confusion regarding these models. Secondly, each model is used to derive a general set of hypotheses telling us what we would expect to find if the model in question is correct. Next the cases in urban transportation politics are examined in detail to assess which of the three sets of hypotheses appear best able to account for the empirical results. Finally, the book closes by drawing out the broader theoretical and practical implications of the findings of this study.

Throughout, this work has been guided by the conviction that empirical case studies can move beyond mere description and assume general meaningfulness and utility only under the beams of systematically placed theoretical floodlights. With well-defined hypotheses derived from each of the theoretical political models, social scientists can begin to utilize case study materials from a variety of institutions and settings in a cumulative fashion. Progress in political theory, practical understanding of political phenomena, and appropriate generalizing from research findings all depend on systematic analytical methods. This book is an attempt to contribute to those ends.

CHAPTER ONE

THE PLURALIST, ELITIST, AND DIALECTICAL MODELS

As one would expect, the intellectual and historical roots of the three political models considered here are quite varied. The pluralist model is rooted in classical liberalism, that philosophical doctrine stressing maximum individual freedom and limited and democratic government. The writings of James Madison and Alexis de Tocqueville are representative. Within the present century, the main shapers of pluralist thinking have included Arthur Bentley (1908), David Truman (1953), and V. O. Key (1959). Elitist theory is grounded in the work of Italian scholars Vilfredo Pareto (1935) and Gaetano Mosca (1939), and German sociologists Max Weber and Robert Michels (1915). Drawing mainly from Weber, C. Wright Mills (1956) has been the leading early articulator of elite theory within the United States. The class-dialectic model is based largely on the work of Karl Marx, with later contributions by numerous theorists.

The discussion of these models represents a distillation of a large amount of literature. It is an abstract, brief way of highlighting the most salient similarities and differences among these three perspectives. The purpose is not to review fully the literature on which each of these models is based, nor to discuss subtle differences, ambiguous cases, and so on. Rather, the goal is to present the essential, defining characteristics in a clear and straightforward manner. Although it is possible to classify these perspectives in other ways and to emphasize somewhat different aspects of each,[1] the categorization in Table 1 is the most useful

[1] Thus, Alford (1975) refers to "paradigms" instead of models, and labels them pluralist, elite, and class. Although my own classification was developed inde-

one for our purposes. The table shows the theoretical character-istics of the pluralist, elitist, and class-dialectical models. In order to put flesh on the bones of this abstract categorization and to make the models more concrete and intelligible, each model will be illustrated by briefly discussing the works of two or three writers. The focus will be on United States' sociology and political science of the post-World War II era, for it was during this period that specific research methods for empirically testing each of the models within the United States context were first systematized and applied. Since the elitist model was the first to be fully spelled out in this regard, it is best to begin there.

The Elitist Model

The elitist model holds political power to be concentrated in the hands of elites who occupy the top position in large and increas-

pendently, there are strong similarities. There are, however, at least two major differences between my scheme and Alford's. First, his aim is to categorize the paradigms relating the "relations between the *state* and the society" (emphasis added). I am not directly concerned with the state, but with how one discovers the locus of power in the society or community. Second, my analysis holds that the concept of the dialectical nature of power (stemming from the existence of systemic contradictions) is central to the class-dialectical model. Alford does not present this as a feature of his class paradigm.

Esping-Andersen et al. (1976) have developed a classification of four "per-spectives," again concerning conceptions of the functioning of the state. These they call the pluralist, instrumentalist, structuralist, and political class perspectives. This classification varies from my own (for reasons that will be explained) but parallels it quite closely, although in this case too my analysis was developed independently. Here they do stress the dialectical nature of power, with class political struggle seen as both limiting dominant class actions and producing modifications in the structure of the state. The main purpose of the work is to demonstrate that it is possible to think of the state not simply as an instrument of a ruling elite or as determined by systemic contradictions, but as "an object of class struggle" in its own right (Esping-Andersen et al., 1976:190). However, for purposes of this work roughly what they call the structuralist and class per-spectives will be treated as one category, the class-dialectic. The similarities between the two perspectives are many, and such a distinction is not necessary for the present analysis that is concerned not with the state, but with comparing the class-dialectic model on the one hand with the pluralist and elite models on the other.

Table 1. Characteristics of Models

	Pluralistic	Elite	Class-Dialectic
Basic units of analysis	Interest groups	Institutional elites	Social institutions; social classes
Essential processes	Interest group competition	Hierarchical dominance by elites	Imperatives of social institutions; class domination and conflict
Basis of group power (resources)	Many bases: organizational, governmental, economic, social, personal	Institutional position, common social background, convergent interests	Class position; degree of class consciousness and organization
Distribution of power	Dispersed among competing, heterogeneous groups	Concentrated in relatively homogeneous elites	Held by dominant class, but potentially available to subordinate classes
Limits and stability of groups' power	Unstable; limited by democratic value consensus, shifting strength among organized interests and by cross-cutting allegiances	Stable, no identifiable limits to elite domination	Historically contingent; generally stable, but limited by class conflict and contradictions within and among social institutions
Conception of role of the state	State is a broker, able to preserve some autonomy by balancing competing interests	State has little, if any, autonomy; captive of elite interests	State serves interests of dominant class in order to act to preserve basis of class hegemony

ingly centralized institutional hierarchies. Elites tend to be unified in purpose and outlook because of their similar social backgrounds and because of a convergence of interests arising from their positions within dominant social institutions. The goals of elites are reflected directly in the actions of the state which has little, if any, autonomy relative to elite goals and interests. Elites almost invariably get their way whenever important public decisions are made, and social conflicts, when they occur, are managed by elites in such a way as to produce outcomes favorable to their interests. As a consequence, there are no clearly identified limits to elite power and the distribution of power is essentially stable. Each of these points will be discussed in more detail.

The best-known commentator on the elite is C. Wright Mills. Mills (1956) argues that institutional elites in the United States—in this case those in business, the military, and politics—are increasingly able to exercise decisive power in the society. He writes:

> The power elite is composed of men whose positions enable them to transcend the ordinary environments of ordinary men and women. . . . For they are in command of the major hierarchies and organizations of modern society. They rule the big corporations. They run the machinery of the state and claim its prerogatives. They direct the military establishment. They occupy the strategic command posts of the social structure in which are now centered the effective means of the power and the wealth and the celebrity which they enjoy.   (Mills, 1956:3-4)

As our economic, political, and military institutions have grown they have become far more centralized and powerful according to Mills. This places enormous powers in the hands of those persons who happen to be at the top of each of the hierarchies, those positions that he calls the "command posts of modern society" (Mills, 1956:5). Other institutions are dwarfed by comparison: "No family is as directly powerful in national affairs as any major corporation; no church is as directly powerful in the external biographies of young men in America today as the military establishment; no college is as powerful in the shaping of momentous events as the National Security Council" (Mills, 1956:6).

Mills contends that power is even more centralized by the existence of shared political interests and personal similarities among the political, economic, and military elites. Their similar institutional positions place them in the same social and political group: "The people of the higher circles may also be conceived as members of a top social stratum, as a set of groups whose members know one another, see one another socially and at business, and so, in making decisions, take one another into account" (Mills, 1956:11). They have similar social backgrounds, having graduated from the same elite schools and holding memberships in the same exclusive social clubs. In these schools, clubs, and elite families they get to know one another and develop shared attitudes, tastes, and worldviews. They come to think of themselves as special.

This experiential and psychological resemblance is one basis, argues Mills, for social unity and positional interchangeability among these elites. They tend to think alike, to act alike, and to see other elites as being like themselves. They often move from one institutional hierarchy, such as the military, to another, such as business or politics.

Further, Mills contends that the three institutional hierarchies have many coinciding interests so that there are few checks and balances operating among business, military, and political elites.

The shape and meaning of the power elite today can be understood only when these three sets of structural trends [i.e., the decline of political democracy, the ascendancy of the military, and the rise of a permanent-war economy] are seen at their point of coincidence: the military capitalism of private corporations exists in a weakened and formal democratic system containing a military order already quite political in outlook and demeanor. Accordingly, at the top of this structure, the power elite has been shaped by the coincidence of interest between those who control the major means of production and those who control the newly enlarged means of violence; from the decline of the professional politician and the rise to explicit political command of the corporate chieftains and the professional warlords; from the absence of any genuine civil service of skill and integrity, independent of vested interests (Mills, 1956:276).

This set of structural coincidences has blurred the distinctions among the military, the state, and the economy, particularly so between the latter two institutions. The state and the corporate economy "cannot now be seen clearly as two distinct worlds," Mills writes (1956:274). Business and government have become so intertwined that "it has meant the ascendancy of the corporation's man as a political eminence" (Mills:1956:274). Thus, the state does not act against the interests of the power elite because those interests are now the interests of the state: "the political directorate, the corporate rich, and the ascendant military have come together as the power elite, and the expanded and centralized hierarchies which they head have encroached upon the old balances and have now relegated them to the middle levels of power" (Mills: 1956:296).

It is a somber and pessimistic view of power that Mills sets forth. Most of us live a life far removed from the mighty institutional levels of power. According to the Millsian view, the state is in thrall to the corporate chieftains and the military warlords; their destructive rule is unopposed. It is a chilling picture that offers little hope, certainly, for the ideals of equality and democracy: "In so far as national events are decided, the power elite are those who decide them" (Mills, 1956:18). For Mills, the rest of us are subjects of power, not exercisers of power.

Mills' analysis concentrates mainly upon the national levels of power. A more local view of power—at the community level— had been set forth by Floyd Hunter (1953) a few years before Mills wrote. Hunter was more empirically oriented than Mills, devising a research strategy that later became known as the reputational method for studying power. Focusing on Atlanta, Georgia, he used four community organizations (i.e., the Community Council, the Chamber of Commerce, the League of Women Voters, and newspaper editors) as sources of names of top civic, business, political, and social leaders. A panel of judges who were knowledgeable about community affairs were then asked to rank the top ten leaders in each field. He found a high degree of consensus regarding who those top leaders were. Interviews were conducted with these leaders and sociometric studies were carried out to ascertain the extent to which they knew and interacted with each other (Hunter, 1953:262-71).

Hunter concludes that a relatively small group of elites decide most important matters in the community. He divides these leaders into four groups based on their relative power in local affairs. The "first-rate" leaders are "industrial, commercial, financial owners and top executives of large enterprises" (Hunter, 1953:109). Persons such as top public officials and small business owners occupy the second-rate level of power. In the third-rate level are found "selected organization executives" and newspaper columnists, for example. Small business managers and professionals, among others, are found in the fourth-rate (Hunter, 1953:109).

The top leaders tend to "interact among themselves on community projects and select one another as leaders" (Hunter, 1953:74). They are organized into several "crowds" or cliques and they tend to take active roles in community events affecting their interests (Hunter, 1953:78). Business leaders are the most powerful group, and government generally serves their interests: "It is true that there is no formal tie between the economic interests and government, but the structure of policy-determining committees and their tie-in with the other powerful institutions and organizations of the community make government subservient to the interests of these combined groups" (Hunter, 1953:102).

In a later work, *Top Leadership, U.S.A.*, Hunter (1959) extends his research to the national level. Again, he arrives at similar conclusions about the elite:

> Continuing to utilize the model of a community power structure in my interviews, I found certain common elements among the top leaders, whom I began to look upon as a national power structure, as they look upon themselves. I have already mentioned the facts that they knew each other, that they could rate each other in a status scale, and that they tended to include and exclude others from their company.

. . . They represented a cross-section of national civic life, and active recruiting into the circuit goes on continuously to fill vacancies, geographic and otherwise. For the most part they tended to know certain persons in Congress and other national government policy posts. . . . Importantly, they knew the patterns of the policy-making process and generally agreed on the content of such patterns (Hunter, 1959:175).

Hunter also sounds a new note here, pointing out the pivotal role played by the corporation in political life in the United States: "From empirical observation it seems reasonable to say that the corporate enterprises are the most potent single forces on the American scene. They reach into every cranny of American life, and their patterns of operations parallel and intertwine with every American institution. Through selected members they collectively control the political machinery at all levels of government, when control is necessary to their functioning" (Hunter, 1959:252).

Mills and Hunter, then, present the basic model of elite power. From their perspective, a relatively small elite, perched in the major institutions of American society, determine the major decisions at both the local and national levels. They hold the preponderant share of political and economic power. There is no reason to believe that they will be less powerful in the future or that the society will become more effectively democratic.

Recently elitist writers Kenneth Prewitt and Alan Stone (1973) have pointed out that while modern elitist theory generally shares all of the characteristics just discussed, there are two schools of thought concerning the normative aspects of elite rule. One school holds that "rulers exploit and manipulate the ruled for personal benefit." Such rule is socially repressive for the society and is therefore undesirable. On the other hand, the second school sees elites as performing necessary and socially beneficial tasks. They are the main source of organization and guidance for the society as a whole: "And if the rulers enjoy many special advantages, these are only the just rewards for the special skills they bring to the task of governing and for the efforts they expend on behalf of the entire society" (Prewitt and Stone, 1973:5).

The work of Prewitt and Stone also clearly shows why elite

models assume that power is quite stable and why change, if it happens at all, is gradual. Elites are seen as inevitable in all societies. As Prewitt and Stone (1973:5) note, "every society can be divided into the small number who rule and the larger number who are ruled." Secondly, it is the character of the elite that determines the direction and character of the society. Social change comes about when elites change. This "circulation of elites" to use Mosca's and Pareto's phrase, happens slowly. "Most of history is not revolutions," say Prewitt and Stone (1973:22-23), "but rather the day-in, day-out performance of important tasks by elites and the modest but significant changes in the composition of the ruling groups."

Most recently, elite theorist Thomas Dye (1976) has produced an important volume devoted to an extensive analysis of the American institutional elite. The national elite, he argues, are "the individuals who occupy positions of authority in large institutions" (Dye, 1976:6). The institutional bases of elite power which Dye examines are industry, finance, utilities, government, the news media, law, foundations, civic organizations, and universities. Dye's work holds special interest for us because he directly addresses the issue of the degree of elite consensus within the elite stratum. Noting that those adopting a pluralist model contend that differences of opinion and interest divide elites, Dye states the elitist counterthesis that these differences tend to be over specific policy issues, that there is overarching agreement on fundamental values, that "the range of disagreement among elites is relatively narrow, and that disagreement is generally confined to means rather than ends" (Dye, 1976:169). Thus, elite theorists emphasize elite unity and consensus while pluralists emphasize fragmentation and conflict. This question of elite unity will be a central focus of this present study.

THE PLURALIST MODEL

The work of Mills and Hunter formed the basis for the model of elite power. As a response to this model, Robert Dahl (1961) was the first to formulate a systematic counter-view of power, the pluralist model. Dahl challenged many of the assumptions, methods and conclusions of researchers on the elite, arguing that political power is actually much more decentralized and democratic than elitists contend.

The pluralist model (Table 1) starts with interest groups as the basic feature of organized political life. The power (or influence as most pluralists prefer to call it) of private groups is based mainly on the effective political organization of voluntary associations, but also is a function of such individual qualities as the political strategies and leadership abilities of party and group leaders. A key concept is competition. Competitive relationships among the many diverse interest groups that make up society, along with the diverse allegiances held by group members, have the effect of dispersing power over a wide range of organized groups. This distribution of power is also essentially unstable since interests and alliances are typically short-lived, and new groups and coalitions are continually being created and organized as old ones decline. There are limits on the power of any one group. This is true by virtue of the necessity for compromises with other groups and because of the existence of a basic value consensus which stresses adherence to generally-accepted democratic norms and values. Although influenced by the demands of organized interest groups, the state is able to serve its own independent ends and to achieve substantial autonomy by operating as a broker or balancing agent among the competing groups.

Dahl's most influential work is *Who Governs? Democracy and Power in an American City* (1961). Like Hunter (1953), who had first studied power at the local level in Atlanta, Dahl chose to study the local power structure of New Haven, Connecticut. Conceding that New Haven had once been ruled by an elite of wealth and social standing, Dahl argues that this oligarchy was gradually replaced, first, by the "entrepreneurs" or self-made businessmen, and then by the "ex-plebes," that is, rising members of the working class or lower middle class (Dahl, 1961:11). These far-reaching changes in political power were brought about by larger changes in the structure of local society. At first, political advantages and resources were cumulative: wealth, social status, education, public office, and political power tended to cluster in the same groups and individuals. The rise of mass political parties that were forced to compete for the votes of large numbers of ethnic peoples and immigrants helped to change all that: "What the immigrants and the ex-plebes had accomplished, however, was a further split in political resources. Popularity had been split off from both wealth and social standing. Popularity meant votes; votes meant office; office meant influence. Thus the ex-plebes completed the transition from the old pattern of oligarchy based upon cumulative inequalities to new patterns of leadership based upon dispersed inequalities" (Dahl, 1961:51).

Dahl, like other pluralists, stresses the role of voluntary associations and political parties as counterweights to the power of wealthy and propertied elites, or the "Economic Notables" as he calls them (1961:67-68). In a pluralistic society such as our own, people and groups are quite heterogeneous, displaying great variation in ethnic background, religion, skills, education, style of life, values, tastes, income level, and so forth. This social pluralism gives rise to political pluralism: people have diverse interests, ideologies, and concerns. Not everyone values the same thing or has equal interests in attaining or defending it. "Political heterogeneity follows socioeconomic heterogeneity" (Dahl, 1961:59). Pluralists contend that people join groups that share their specialized interests. Voluntary associations are numerous and represent a wide range of political philosophies and goals. Out of the competition of the political parties and other voluntary associations comes a dynamic and vigorous expression of varied points of view, insuring that everyone can join a group that will represent their own interests and that will engage in efforts to influence the political system. These facts, together with the sheer numbers of nonelite individuals, mean that "the Economic Notables, far from being a ruling group, are simply one of the many groups out of which individuals sporadically emerge to influence the policies and acts of city officials" (Dahl, 1961:72). Not only are the notables outnumbered, but they, like everyone else, have sometimes conflicting interests: "the Notables tend to participate only marginally in politics. Frequently, as we have seen, they live elsewhere. Then too their most important economic and social goals are not often *immediately* at stake in local decisions, particularly given the prevailing system of beliefs. They are busy men with full-time occupations'' (Dahl, 1961:78).

Therefore, the picture of political power that Dahl paints is considerably more democratic and optimistic than that painted by Mills. Here, masses of people organize into groups and political parties to defend their most important interests. The competition from these diverse interest groups has pushed the old elites from the center of the political stage, elites who themselves have been internally weakened by divided loyalties and differences in points of view. Although the system does contain significant inequalities of influence, a rough kind of democracy is maintained. The power of the wealthier, more politically skilled, better organized, or more manipulative is constrained finally by the existence of a widely shared democratic creed: ''wide consensus on the democratic creed does have two important kinds of consequences. On the one hand, this very consensus makes occasional appeal [by professional politicians] all but inevitable, for the creed itself gives legitimacy to an appeal to the populace. On the other hand, widespread adherence to the creed limits the character and the course of an appeal. It insures that no appeal is likely to succeed unless it is framed in terms consistent with the creed. . . . Blatant inconsistencies are likely to be exposed'' (Dahl, 1961:324-25).

Another major attempt by a pluralist to counter the ''Hunter-Mills thesis'' (Rose, 1967:XIV) appeared in print six years after Dahl's work. In *The Power Structure* (1967), Arnold Rose summarizes the extant literature on pluralism and draws on his personal experiences as a member of the Minnesota legislature. He argues for what he calls a ''multi-influence hypothesis,'' as opposed to ''the economic-elite dominance'' model of Mills and Hunter (Rose, 1967:3). Rose summarizes his findings as follows:

> Segments of the economic elite have violated democratic political and legal processes, with differing degrees of effort and success in the various periods of American history, but in no recent period could they correctly be said to have controlled the elected and appointed political authorities in large measure. The relationships between the economic elite and the political authorities has been a constantly varying

one of strong influence, co-operation, division of labor, and conflict, with each group influencing the other in changing proportion to some extent, and each operating independently of the other to a large extent. Today there is significant political control and limitation of certain activities of the economic elite, and there are also some significant processes by which the economic elite use their wealth to help elect some political candidates and to influence other political authorities in ways which are not available to the average citizen. Further, neither the economic elite nor the political authorities are monolithic units which act with internal consensus and coordinated action with regard to each other (or probably in any other way); in fact, there are several economic elites, which only very rarely act as units within themselves and among themselves, and there are at least two . . . political parties which have significantly differing programs with regard to their actions toward any economic elite and each of these parties has only a partial degree of internal cohesion. (Rose, 1967:493)

Thus, like Dahl, Rose presents a picture of shifting political power alignments, the general dominance of political authorities over economic elites, lack of elite internal cohesion, and political parties with a large and independent measure of influence.

These themes have most recently been restated in the work of Nelson Polsby, another pluralist scholar of great influence. The second edition of *Community Power and Political Theory* (Polsby, 1980) is devoted to an extended critique of elitist studies (what he calls "stratification theory") and a defense and reassertion of pluralist methods and theories. Polsby defines the pluralist model as specifying: "dispersion of power among many rather than a few participants in decision-making; competition or conflict among political leaders; specialization of leaders to relatively restricted sets of issue areas; bargaining rather than hierarchical decision-making; elections in which suffrage is relatively widespread as a major determinant of participation in key decisions; bases of influence over decisions relatively dispersed rather than closely held; and so on" (Polsby, 1980:154).

Thus, in the pluralist view, there is no rule by power elites. There is a competition for influence among organized interest groups, with no one group able to consistently dominate the others. Public policy emerges as a result of this complex calculus of ever-changing coalitions. As a consequence, public policy is seen not as the product of a self-serving ruling elite, but as the result of competing ideals, goals, interests and compromises in a plural society. It is argued, therefore, that a rough level of democracy prevails. The chief practical danger is, from the pluralist perspective, not that a ruling oligarchy will arise, but that no one will be able to govern effectively. Political fragmentation and the proliferation of narrow interest groups may lead to policy paralysis and social chaos. Many present-day pluralists believe this is now happening in our society. Rather than power which is concentrated and policy-effective, power is seen, in this neopluralist vision, as so dispersed as to be ineffective in doing what needs to be done.

THE CLASS-DIALECTICAL MODEL

Although it has points in common with both the pluralist and elitist models, the class-dialectical model represents an alternative conception of power with crucial differences from both. The major differences concern, first, the institutional context of political activity; second, the analysis of class-based politics; and third, the concept of the dialectic.

The class-dialectic model holds that political processes must be understood in terms of the institutional structure of society (e.g., the economy, the legal system, the state) and in terms of the relation of social classes to one another. The organization of the basic institutions of society (especially the economy) has crucial implications for not only the general character of the society but also for how classes relate to each other and how political power is exercised. The structure of social institutions places restraints and limits on the behavior of groups within the society. In order to comprehend politics, then, one must understand how the imperatives of social institutions shape the actions of classes and individuals. Dialecticians argue that to focus only upon the immediate decisional and behavioral aspects of politics (as do most pluralists and researchers on the elite) is to fall into the trap of what Lukes (1974:22) calls "methodological individualism." One must be aware not only of the possibility of suppression of political issues by dominant classes (Bachrach and Baratz, 1962), but also of the strategic possibility of allowing the bias of social institutions to determine political outcomes with no observable decisions or actions, as such, being required of dominant political actors. The class-dialectic model argues that one must understand the logic and biases of social institutions as well as the observable political behavior of social classes and individual actors. It is asserted that there is a mutually reinforcing relationship between social institutions and dominant classes: dominant classes act to preserve those institutions that are the basis of their own dominance, or "hegemony." According to the class-dialectic view then, institutions shape behavior (of both dominant and subordinate classes) and the dominant class shapes institutions. Thus, one cannot be fruitfully studied without the other.

The class-dialectic model holds that capitalist societies are characterized by the presence of a dominant class that controls the means of production. This control is the basic resource for power in the society. With it comes the ability to carry out ideological hegemony (Miliband, 1969) and generally to manipulate the societal context in which political contests are waged. Other bases of power are the degree of class-consciousness and the extent of class political organization. The state functions to serve the interests of the dominant class by preserving the bases of class hegemony. However, class-dialectical theory sees power as potentially available to the subordinate classes if they become sufficiently class-conscious and politically organized to wrest control or to challenge the control of the means of production. Thus, it is maintained that the power of the dominant class is not absolute. This is even more true because (1) there are not only interclass conflicts, but also intraclass conflicts among capitalists, and (2) there are contradictions within the economic and class structure producing disruptions that may limit the ability of the dominant class to act.

It is this dialectical conception of power, of the relations between social classes, and of history, that is the most important difference separating the elitist and class-dialectic models of power (although as was pointed out, the two models are often erroneously confused with one another). More will be said about the dialectic later.

The class-dialectical conception of power is more complex than either the pluralist or elitist models. The model will be illustrated by looking at the work of two researchers, in this case James O'Connor and Roger Friedland.

O'Connor's *The Fiscal Crisis of the State* (1973) sets forth a political model with some superficial parallels to both pluralist and elitist models. He writes: "The first and most powerful influence in the national government is the capitalist class—owners and controllers of the monopoly corporations and state contractors. The members of this class have organized themselves along interest-group *and* class lines (competitive capital organizes itself mainly along interest-group lines)" (emphasis added; O'Connor, 1973:66). Here there is both the emphasis on the domination of the state by a small segment of the society—in this case by a class rather than by institutional elites—and the pluralist emphasis on interest-group politics. The similarities end there, however. O'Connor takes these ideas of domination of the state and interest-group politics and places them in a different theoretical context which gives them a whole new meaning. In addition, he uses conceptual categories and research methods that depart radically from other models.

As in other dialectical analyses, the central stress is upon understanding the operation of the political-economic system as a whole. Political, economic, and social phenomena are seen as closely interconnected: they cannot be comprehended independently. Second, social classes are the units of analysis. Third, the political-economic system is held to be fundamentally contradictory in its operation.

Although O'Connor's analysis illustrates the essential characteristics of the dialectical model, not all proponents of the model would find his particular approach useful. In fact, there is controversy surrounding his specific method of analysis. What follows, then, is an example of one analysis that is dialectical in nature. As in the case of elitist and pluralist models, details in models vary.

O'Connor's analysis starts with a tripartite division of the economy into the monopoly, competitive, and state sectors. The competitive sector is the home of small business and interest-group politics; the monopoly sector is the home of large-scale capital and more class-conscious capitalist politics. The state or public sector is organized by the government but includes state contractors as well as public agencies. It is the dynamic and complex interaction among these three sectors of the economy that O'Connor examines.

Essentially, O'Connor argues that the relations among the three sectors are contradictory, posing significant problems for the functioning of the economy, the state, and the capitalist class. These contradictions stem from still more fundamental contradictions. "Our first premise," says O'Connor (1973:6), "is that the capitalistic state must try to fulfill two basic and often mutually contradictory functions—*accummulation* and *legitimation*." The function of accummulation, that is the creation or maintenance of societal conditions favorable to the profitable growth of capital in the private economy, and the function of legitimation, or the creation or maintenance of conditions promoting social harmony instead of social conflict, pose a delicate problem for the state: "A capitalist state that openly uses its coercive forces to help one class accummulate capital at the expense of other classes loses its legitimacy and hence undermines the basis of its loyalty and support (and hence its legitimacy). But a state that ignores the necessity of capital accummulation risks drying up the source of its own power, the economy's surplus production capacity and the taxes drawn from this surplus" (O'Connor, 1973:6).

In order to further the interests of the capitalist class by maintaining accummulation and legitimacy, the state must make expenditures. These expenditures are either in the form of "social capital" or "social expenses." Social capital corresponds to the accummulation function and includes all of those expenses needed to ensure profitable operation of the economy. There are two subcategories of social capital: "social investment" and "social consumption." According to O'Connor,

Social investment consists of projects and services that increase the productivity of a given amount of labor power and, other factors being equal, increase the rate of profit. A good example is state-financed industrial-development parks. *Social consumption* consists of projects and services that lower the reproduction costs of labor and, other factors being equal, increase the rate of profit. An example of this is social insurance, [accident, illness, death, retirement, unemployment insurance, etc.] which expands the reproductive powers of the work force while simultaneously lowering labor costs. (O'Connor, 1973:7)

Together, then, these two subcategories of social capital aid the process of accummulation by increasing the productivity of labor and by lowering its costs of reproduction.

The other major category of capital expenditures, social expenses, consists of all expenses required to promote the relatively smooth and harmonious functioning of society—that is, those efforts of the state aimed at legitimation. In contrast to social capital (which is indirectly productive because it aids the expansion of surplus value) social expenses are not productive. "The best example," says O'Connor (1973:7), "is the welfare system, which is designed chiefly to keep social peace among unemployed workers."[2]

As the requirements of profit and social peace are often at odds with one another, so are outlays of social capital and social expenses. This contradictory process accounts for a host of economic, political, and social crises. O'Connor discusses two main kinds of crises: "First . . . although the state has socialized more and more capital costs [i.e., the society as a whole, or workers as a group, must ultimately pay the costs of production, air pollution, tax write-offs for industry, etc.], the social surplus (including profits) continues to be appropriated privately. . . . The socialization of costs and the private appropriation of profits creates a fiscal crisis, or 'structural gap,' between state expenditures and state revenues. The result is a tendency for state expenditures

---

[2] A similar perspective on what might be called the "social control" functions of welfare is advanced by Piven and Cloward (1971).

to increase more rapidly than the means of financing them" (O'Connor, 1973:9). In other words, although the society as a whole must pay many of the costs of production, it is not the society but the private sector (particularly the monopoly sector) that disproportionally benefits by the profits generated. Benefits get "bottled up" there. Since, in O'Connor's view, the state must try to maintain both this accummulation process and ensure social harmony, and since the state does not make a profit but must rely on taxes, the state cannot make ends meet. A budget deficit and a fiscal crisis necessarily result.

> Second . . . the fiscal crisis is exacerbated by the private appropriation of state power for particularistic ends. A host of "special interests"—corporations, industries, regional and other business interests—make claims on the budget for various kinds of social investment. . . . Organized labor and workers generally make various claims for different kinds of social consumption, and the unemployed and poor . . . stake their claims for expanded social expenses. Few if any claims are coordinated by the market. Most are processed by the political struggle. Precisely because the accummulation of social capital and social expenses occurs within a political framework, there is a great deal of waste, duplication, and overlapping of state projects and services. (O'Connor, 1973:9)

What is more, "Some claims conflict and cancel one another out. Others are mutually contradictory in a variety of ways" (O'Connor, 1973:9-10). Thus, the whole is a "highly irrational process from the standpoint of administrative coherence, fiscal stability, and potentially profitable private capital accumulation" (O'Connor, 1973:10).

Since O'Connor's analysis holds that capitalist production is a fundamentally irrational and contradictory system, these irrationalities and strains are felt, he argues, throughout the society. In contrast to the pluralist and elitist models, it is the impact of this institutional context of political action to which the class-dialectic model particularly sensitizes us. The elitist model indicates that elites almost invariably get their way, the pluralist model that they rarely get their way. The class-dialectic model suggests that the ruling class is generally well-served by the institutions of capitalist society, but that the class does not have the capability of invariably having things its way because of the web of contradictory needs with which it must contend. While it may generally rely on societal institutions for support and benefit, this reliance is not without its difficulties, risks, instabilities, and costs. Contradictions sometimes restrain the actions of the ruling class, as O'Connor's analysis attempts to make clear.

Other insights that may emerge from a class-dialectic analysis are found in Roger Friedland's *Class Power and the Central City: The Contradictions of Urban Growth* (1976). While O'Connor is concerned with analyzing the relationships and contradictions among classes and institutions in the United States as a whole, Friedland specifically focuses on central cities. He wants to show how national class power (as manifested in both capitalist and working class organizations) is linked to local class power in central cities. Again, central themes are (1) systematic analysis, (2) social classes, and (3) inherent contradictions in the political economy. The major thesis of Friedland's work "concerns the attempts of national corporations and labor unions to manage the contradictions of urban growth" (Friedland, 1976:1). Briefly, the argument runs as follows. (A somewhat more detailed examination of relevant aspects of Friedland's work is found in the final chapter of this book.) The decline of central cities in the United States poses significant problems for both capitalist class organizations and working class organizations, that is, for both corporations and labor unions. Profitability of corporate investments declines and the strength of central city union employment is reduced. These class-based organizations are thus presented with a number of dilemmas:

> How to sustain accummulation in the central city in the face of changing spatial organization of production and consumption? How to maintain local programs to stimulate central city economic growth in the face of an increasingly poor and non-white resident population for whom the benefits of this economic growth were very limited? How to maintain corporate and labor union political domination in the face of

an increasingly politicized non-white population whose communities were frequently disrupted by the central city growth programs? (Friedland, 1976:2)

Attempts to solve these problems take the form of policies designed to stimulate new capital investment in the central city (e.g., urban renewal, metropolitan region planning, new transport systems, and so on) and policies aimed at political pacification of poor and minority central city residents (e.g., welfare expansion, poverty and Model Cities programs, neighborhood city halls, and urban manpower programs). Many of these programs and goals have been inadequate and contradictory. For example, Freidland argues that urban renewal had the effect, on the one hand, of bolstering central city accummulation while, on the other hand, it simultaneously undermined the legitimacy of urban governance by destroying black communities and displacing thousands of poor people: "Central city growth programs had politicized the black community, while social control programs [such as the War on Poverty and Model Cities] failed to depoliticize it. The result was the urban revolts of the 1960's" (Friedland, 1976:556). In his analysis Friedland (1976:557) finds, for instance, that "riot intensity [is] . . . positively related to the level of residential urban renewal [within a city], the type of renewal most likely to displace large numbers of black people." Class actions designed to preserve the urban foundations of class-based organizations thus led to the implementation of policies with inherent contradictions, contradictions which generated a new round of problems and challenges. Here we see once more the essential characteristics of a class-dialectical analysis.

DIFFERENCES AMONG THE MODELS

There are several important differences among the pluralist, elitist, and class-dialectic models. First, the elitist and class-dialectic models use larger units of analysis (institutional elites; institutions and social classes, respectively) than does the pluralist model (interest groups and individuals). Second, the elitist and class-dialectic models hold that power is much more concentrated (in elites; in ruling or dominant classes) than is true in the pluralist model, which sees power dispersed among a multitude of competing interest groups. Third, differences concerning the role of the state are clearest between the pluralist and elitist models: in the pluralist model the state has autonomy, in the elitist model the state does not. Although the class-dialectic model does indicate that the state serves the general interests of the dominant class, it is not possible to classify in a simple way the model's representation of the issue of state autonomy. There is a debate among proponents of the dialectic concerning how much autonomy the state has and by what means the state is able to serve dominant class interests.[3] Finally—and perhaps most importantly—the pluralist model indicates that power relations are quite unstable, while the elitist model presents a very stable picture of such relations. The class-dialectic model conceives of power as much more stable than in the pluralist model, but less stable than the elitist model.

This latter point is closely tied to the concept of the dialectic. Although it is rooted in the works of Aristotle and other pre-Socratic philosophers, the dialectic is associated mainly with Hegel and, particularly, Marx. Marx substantially modified Hegel's use of the dialectic, transforming it from an idealistic conception of history to a materialistic one (Zeitlin, 1968:89-94). Following Appelbaum (1978) in most respects, I shall use the term dialectic to refer to a theoretical model with the following three characteristics: (1) It is wholistic, that is, it sees specific phenomena in

---

[3] The first view regarding state autonomy is close to the power elitist position: the state acts directly in the interests of the ruling class and will not take actions that damage the interests of that class or any large segment of it. Thus there is little or no state independence from ruling class interests and goals. The second view of the state holds that the state must have a certain amount of autonomy if it is to avoid getting captured by specific groups of powerful capitalists. Should this happen, the state would not be able to serve class interests in general, instead falling prey to narrow interests and intraclass disputes. This view is closer to the pluralist position regarding state autonomy, however the pluralist position would not say that the state serves capitalist interests. The first view also tends to argue that capitalists are capable of organizing as a class without the need of state assistance, while the second view maintains that the state is an essential feature of capitalist social organization and domination.

terms of the larger context of interconnected institutions and historical events. (2) It holds that inherent contradictions exist within and among social institutions, contradictions that serve as endogenous engines of social change. Contradictions result, it is argued, from the unplanned and irrational nature of capitalist institutions. The actions undertaken, and the institutions created, to accomplish one goal inevitably produce as a side effect unsought consequences, often of an undesirable nature (from the standpoint of the initiator). The practical effect of contradictions is to generate actions and policies that may operate at cross purposes, to produce social strains and conflict, and to undermine and limit effective action and institutional functioning. (3) It is historically contingent. That is, it is not a deterministic nor a voluntaristic model, but one based on concrete analysis of historical events. It does not aim to be entirely abstract nor universalistic in its application. As the times vary, so must specific aspects of the model. The essentials, however, remain. The specific class-dialectic model presented in this book is designed to comprehend politics in a corporate capitalist society (the United States), at a certain time (the late twentieth century), and under certain social conditions (e.g., the decline of central cities, dependency on the private automobile, the fiscal crisis of the state, etc.). Minor theoretical modifications would have to be made in order to apply the class-dialectic model to other capitalist societies, to our society at another time, or under a different set of historical circumstances. This is so since it is argued that the substantive content of class-based behavior changes as conditions change. Yet classes, class interests, and contradictions per se continue to exist.

This is not meant to imply that pluralist and elitist models are oblivious to historical conditions or to the institutional context of political events. Nor do these models fail to notice problems such as conflicts, unanticipated consequences, and inefficiencies in carrying out social policies. However, within these models such phenomena are generally regarded as being of secondary, incidental importance and are not given central prominence in theory or research. It is in only the class-dialectic model that a theoretical rationale is provided and attempts are made to treat systemic analysis, contradictions, and historical contingencies as basic principles.

GENERATION OF HYPOTHESES

The foregoing discussion of the three competing models of political explanation was necessary in order to demonstrate the characteristics of the two currently dominant models of pluralism and elitism and to lay out the alternative but largely neglected class-dialectic approach. The remainder of this book will aim to assess empirically the relative explanatory potential of the three competing models with the more specific goal of discovering if any insights may be gained through a consideration of the class-dialectic model. In order to do this, each of the models must be used to create general hypotheses to guide the coming investigation. All of these hypotheses should be understood to apply to contemporary society in the United States.

PLURALIST HYPOTHESES.   If the pluralist model is correct, the study of an important political issue should reveal (1) the active involvement of numerous interest groups, (2) divergent goals and interests among the groups, (3) a vigorous, competitive relationship among the groups, (4) interests and alliances that shift over time, and (5) political outcomes that consistently favor no particular group over any other.

POWER ELITIST HYPOTHESES.   If the power elitist model is correct, the study of an important political issue should reveal (1) a high degree of elite involvement, (2) general convergence of interest among elites, (3) elite unity and dominance on the issue, (4) stability of political allegiances, and (5) outcomes that consistently favor elite interests.

CLASS-DIALECTIC HYPOTHESES.   If the class-dialectic model is correct, the study of an important political issue should reveal (1) biases of social institutions that favor outcomes beneficial to dominant classes; (2) evidence of latent class conflict (divergent in-

terests) or observable class conflict over the issue, perhaps including intraclass conflicts among the dominant class, but
accompanied by attempts to achieve class unity and cohesion; (3)
political alliances and stability of power relations that are historically contingent, reflecting the need to respond to inter- and
intraclass conflicts and structural crisis; and (4) outcomes that
usually favor dominant class interests, but may also reflect the
power of opposing classes and the limitations imposed by structural contradictions.

The goal here is not to test these hypotheses in the formal sense.
Rather, the burden of this study is to analyze a set of case studies
in the specific issue-area of transportation, to weigh the relative
usefulness and validity of the three models for understanding
political processes at the community level, and to provide guides
for further theoretical elaboration and research.

METHODS OF RESEARCH AND SELECTION OF ISSUES

In addition to the prime question as to which of the two approaches
is more accurate in depicting political reality, the pluralist/elitist
debate has also focused on the issue of the research process.
Contention has surrounded: (1) the research methods to be used,
and (2) the criteria to be used in selecting a political issue for
study. Bachrach and Baratz (1962), for example, have argued that
the pluralist decisional method is biased in that it does not allow
for the possibility of deliberate suppression of issues. "Nonde-
cisions" by elites entirely escape the decisional method. Also,
Walton (1970) has shown that the kind of power structures discovered in community studies appears to be partly an artifact of
the specific methods utilized, with decisional methods tending to
uncover pluralistic structures, and reputational methods finding
elite power structures.

The strategy employed in this book will be as follows. Since
there is little agreement in the field as to what constitutes an
"important" issue, and no clear consensus as to the most appropriate method for doing research, issues were chosen and methods
utilized that appeared to satisfy the criteria clearly acceptable to

at least pluralist methodological requirements. If it is true that the use of pluralistic criteria should bias results toward pluralistic findings, these are the most conservative criteria we could have chosen. The following two caveats must be kept in mind when interpreting this study's results. First, should support for the pluralist model emerge, it cannot be ruled out that this is simply an artifact of the study design. Secondly, should findings support either the elite model or the class-dialectic model, we may have considerable confidence in the results, since any biases in research methodology are in the pluralist direction.

One pluralist writer has clearly spelled out the criteria to be used in conducting research on political issues. This study attempts to follow Nelson Polsby's (1970:301) specifications: "First, the researcher should pick *issue-areas* as the focus of his study. Second, he should be able to defend these issue-areas as being very *important to the life of the* community. Third, he should study actual *behavior,* either at first hand, or by reconstructing behavior from documents, informants, newspapers and other appropriate sources. . . . The final recommendation is of the same order: researchers should study *the outcomes* of actual decisions within the community" (emphasis added).

The issue-area for this study is public transportation politics. The question of the importance of an issue-area under investigation is crucial. In the case of transportation, several grounds exist for saying that the issue is important. The specific decisions examined here (see Table 2) involved the allocation or potential allocation of large amounts of public monies among various competing transportation uses. All of these electoral decisions had implications for the construction of facilities that would have had considerable impact on patterns of transportation flow and land use, and on land values and economic activity in large urban areas. The BART (Bay Area Rapid Transit) system campaign of 1962 in San Francisco authorized the construction of an expensive new rail public transit system for the Bay Area. Proposition A on the California ballot of 1968 proposed to build a BART-like but more expensive system for the Los Angeles area, as did the similar Proposition A of 1974. Proposition 18 of 1970 would have allowed some of the enormous sums of money that were tied up in the California

Table 2. Summary of California Transit Elections

Issue	Date	Area	Proposal	Financing	Contributions		Outcome
					For	Against	
BART	Nov. 1962	Bay Area	rail	$792 million bond issue to be financed out of property taxes	$203,000 from business	none	passed
Prop. A.	Nov. 1968	L. A.	rail & bus	$2.5 billion bond issue to be financed by sales tax	$458,000 with 86% from business	$25,000 from five contributions	failed
Prop. 18	Nov. 1970	Calif.	divert 25% of highway funds	none required	$18,000 in small contributions	$348,000 from highway lobby	failed
Prop. 5	June 1974	Calif.	divert 5-25% of highway funds	none required	$203,000 with 99% from business	$1,700 from auto club	passed
Prop. A.	Nov. 1974	L. A.	rail & bus	sales tax to match federal funds	$563,000 with 94% from business	none	failed

NOTE: This table, drawn from "Can Capitalists Organize Themselves?" by J. Allen Whitt, is reprinted from *Power Structure Research* (SAGE FOCUS EDITION, Vol. 17) G. William Domhoff, Editor, copyright 1980, pp. 97-113 by permission of the Publisher, Sage Publications (Beverly Hills/London). Previously in *The Insurgent Sociologist*, Fall, 1979.

highway trust fund to be used to support the construction of alternative transit systems. While Proposition 18 failed to pass, the similar Proposition 5 of 1974 was successful. These were all far-reaching and important decisions. Many groups had material interests and stood to gain or lose a great deal. These were, in short, not merely "symbolic" issues, but "instrumental" ones that would "convey benefits to particular groups" (Edelman, 1967:2). In addition to these reasons, it should be noted that pluralists themselves treat transportation issues as important: Polsby (1970:298) asserts that importance, and Banfield (1961) uses the Chicago Transit Authority as the basis for a decisional case study. Therefore, it appears that Polsby's first and second recommendations are met by selection of this issue-area.

The two final recommendations by Polsby, that actual behavior and decisional outcomes be studied, are met by the research design. The research methods employed here are similar to those used by Banfield (1961) with some essential modifications. As in Banfield's study, the decisions analyzed here were reported in the news media and constituted matters of public controversy. In fact, all five issues were electoral campaigns. Whereas Banfield based his study on the one urban area of Chicago, this study broadens the definition of community to include the political boundaries of the state of California. The definition is broadened to allow the inclusion of electoral campaigns that were not restricted to large cities (as were Proposition A of 1968 and Proposition A of 1974, both in Los Angeles), or to urban regions (BART campaign of 1962 in the San Francisco Bay Area), but also involved statewide issues (Proposition 18 of 1970 and Proposition 5 of 1974). Together these campaigns constitute a coherent issue-area of interrelated transportation decisions affecting California and its major urban areas: they were the most important public decisions concerning transportation in the state between 1962 and 1974. This broader definition of community should pose no problems for pluralist theorists since the inclusion of a larger polity and a geographic and social area of such diversity would be expected to increase rather than decrease interest group plurality (see McConnell, 1966).

A more important departure from the Banfield method was to

supplement interview data and media analysis with an examination of campaign contribution data. Media coverage was used to provide an initial list of persons and organizations reported to be active in the transportation campaigns. These people were contacted, interviewed concerning their roles in the campaigns, and asked to provide names of other active organizations and people. More interviews were then conducted. After several dozen interviews, it was clear that there was general agreement as to what groups and leaders had been active on both sides of the issues. Interviewees included government officials, business leaders, voluntary and civic association members, trade association officials, investigative reporters in the media, and political campaign organizers. This information was then checked against records of actual campaign contributions, a technique not used by most decisional researchers, but definitely fitting Polsby's suggestion that actual behavior be studied.

Fortunately for this study, California is somewhat atypical in that corporate contributions are legal and are recorded with the California secretary of state. Many other states prohibit such contributions or limit the amount a corporation may contribute. California provided a nearly unique opportunity to study corporate contributions in detail. Contributions data are very important because they clearly show active, material involvement in electoral campaigns, and they provide a means of checking the validity of media and interview accounts identifying support and opposition. Using campaign contribution data as a means of studying the political process is an underutilized research technique, in spite of the general recognition of the significant impact of money in elections (see Alexander, 1976). Used together, these three sources of data (media accounts, interviews, and contributions) provided a consistent and comprehensive picture of active supporters and opponents of the issues studied.

The most important departure from previous methods used in community and issue-based power studies, such as those used by Banfield, is the incorporation of a longitudinal study of several related public decisions over a considerable period of time (in this case, twelve years). Instead of studying only one decision occupying a relatively brief span of time, this historical, multi-decision approach made it possible to discover the dynamics of political involvement and to isolate patterns of political behavior not apparent over short intervals, as during one political campaign.

All three political models are alike in that they acknowledge that powerful groups with special interests may come to dominate certain political arenas for periods of time. However, the models differ on the permanence and significance of such special interest domination. Pluralists contend that the power of special interests will eventually be challenged by the rise of competing centers of power, such as other firms in the marketplace, organized voluntary associations, political parties, or governmental action. In one particular version of pluralist theory, Galbraith (1956) coins the term "countervailing power." A plurality of interests and groups therefore is seen as insuring that no specific set of narrow interests will long hold sway. Elitist and dialectical theories, on the other hand, provide much less clear expectations about both special interest politics and its outcome. First, these two models do not assume that an analysis of politics at the level of interest groups is the most fruitful approach; instead they use elites and classes, respectively. Second, elitist and class-dialectical theories—to the extent that they are concerned with interest groups—generally see these groups as reflections of broader elite or class interests. Within this framework then, elitist and dialectical theories tend to posit interest groups as reflecting relatively stable elite or class interests, interests that are fairly permanent and not much influenced by countervailing forces. In other words, pluralists are typically much more sanguine than elitists and dialecticians regarding the effectiveness of countervailing power among interest groups.

In light of these differences among the models, there seemed to be reasons for supposing, a priori, that the issue-area and specific cases selected for study would provide a rich source of data for explanation by the three models and might, in fact, constitute a crucial test, particularly for the differences between the pluralist model on the one hand and the elitist and class models on the other. A number of writers have given accounts of a powerful "highway lobby" operating at the national and state levels which has been generally successful in promoting legislation and public policies favorable to automobile-oil-highway interests and in blocking development of effective alternative systems of urban transportation (Buel, 1972; Kelley, 1971; Leavitt, 1970; Mowbray, 1969; Snell, 1974). Oil companies, automobile manufacturers, automobile clubs, heavy construction firms, tire and rubber producers, insurance companies, and related interests have been identified as making up the national and state highway lobbies. The state of California is said to have one of the country's most powerful and effective lobbies (Simmons, 1968). Yet in spite of this well-documented historical power of highway interests in California, it began to appear in the 1960s and 1970s that pluralistic expectations of countervailing power were beginning to be fulfilled. A competing and potentially powerful interest group seemed to be in the making, a group that might challenge the power of the highway lobby and perhaps eventually help to break the state's overwhelming dependence on automobiles as the mode of urban transportation. In the state, as was true nationally, there had been much discussion in the 1960s and early 1970s of the destructive aspects of the automobile on urban areas, and citizens' groups and urban politicians were advocating modern transport systems for California's cities. Most importantly, a decision had been made in San Francisco in 1962 to build the first wholly new transit system in any American city in over half a century. At that time, the BART system was said to be the most expensive privately engineered project in the history of the United States. Generating hundreds of millions of dollars worth of construction work and requiring huge quantities of costly, high technology components, BART was clearly a boon to transit industry suppliers and contractors. A logical question to ask from the standpoint of the pluralist/elitist debate would be: Was the rise of BART an indication of a nascent rapid transit interest group in California (and possibly in the country as a whole) that would countervail against the great economic and political power of the highway lobby? What was the nature of the political forces that produced the plans for BART? What are the implications for the three models? Initially, this study began as an attempt to answer these questions.

Before the BART case is examined, some general comments are called for regarding the series of five case studies to follow.

The analysis in the remainder of this work will proceed as if we are peeling an onion: as one layer is stripped away, another will appear beneath it. The case studies represent the first layer, the outer skin of the onion. These cases must be fully understood and appreciated before the next layer can be removed and analysis continue at a deeper level. Each successive layer will add to our understanding and we eventually will begin to see patterns emerge. In the final core analysis, it is these patterns that will be of central concern.

It is now necessary to deal with the surface layers of the onion: the transit case studies must be presented in detail. To prepare for later analysis, the reader is asked to pay attention to the following aspects of these cases: (1) the nature of each transit proposal; (2) the interests that initiated, supported, or opposed each proposal; (3) the likely impact of the proposals; and (4) how each was to be financed. Table 2 is a summary of these aspects.

The next chapter will start at the beginning: an examination of the history of the crucial BART system and a look at the political forces that brought it into being.

CHAPTER TWO

BART AND THE GENTLEMEN ENGINEERS

> Basic to the recognition of symbolic forms in the political
> process is a distinction between politics as a spectator
> sport and political activity as utilized by organized groups
> to get quite specific, tangible benefits for themselves.
> —Murray Edelman, *The Symbolic Uses of Politics*

In November of 1962, voters in the San Francisco Bay Area approved a $792 million bond issue to finance the Bay Area Rapid Transit (BART) system. The Bay Area thus became the first metropolitan region in the United States to build a wholly new mass transit system since Philadelphia completed its subway almost sixty years previously (Bazell, 1971:1125). Pointing out that BART represented the most expensive privately engineered project in United States history, supporters proclaimed the new system a bold step forward in the development of efficient, modern systems of urban mass transportation. It was asserted that BART would help solve Bay Area traffic congestion problems, would provide valuable transportation services for the poor, would reduce local air pollution, and would stimulate the economy and generate jobs. In January 1972, *Consulting Engineer* published an article entitled "BART Makes Tracks to the Future" that began with a panegyric to the system: "Conceivably, it is the first stamp that the 21st century has laid upon public transportation. The San Francisco Bay Area Rapid Transit System (BART) gives just that suggestion. It is a marvel of technique, virtuoso in concept, versatile as the Renaissance, and as streamlined as a bullet."

Whatever technical characteristics BART may possess that are capable of inspiring the praise of engineers (and there are important differences of opinion on this issue even among engineers), I shall argue that BART has largely been a social failure. It has not fulfilled the publicly proclaimed vision of its promoters. BART has not materially improved the mobility of the Bay Area population, especially the lower-income population. Nor has it significantly improved the urban environment in terms of either aesthetic factors or patterns of urban land use. The system does not do much to lessen the congestion of major traffic arteries. The principle reason that it does not do these things is because BART is not designed to challenge the dominance of the private automobile in the Bay Area. This failure, I shall argue, was not an accident. Rather, BART was designed to serve other goals, goals that are not in conflict with the continuation of automobile dominance. Essentially, these goals were the preservation and growth of the central city and the protection of corporate investments there. Moreover, the prime initiators and supporters of BART were the giant corporations located in downtown San Francisco. There was very little involvement by citizens' groups and there was no opposition to BART by California's famous highway lobby because it was realized that BART was a supplement to the private automobile, not a replacement for it. The system was to be financed out of bonds and property taxes, not out of the highway trust fund. To demonstrate these points it is necessary to look briefly at the history of pre-BART transportation issues in the Bay Area before examining the BART issue itself.

PRE-BART PLANS AND PROBLEMS

It has been pointed out that the San Francisco area is in some ways ideal for public transportation systems. The topography is organized into natural "transportation corridors" by the mountains and the local bodies of water. Not surprisingly, several proposals for such systems have been aired since the turn of the century, most of the pre-World War II plans focusing on a subway system for the downtown San Francisco business district (Zwerling, 1972:30).

The biggest impetus for a mass transit system came during World War II. The Bay Area was the location for important military facilities and defense industries. The stepped-up war production and the influx of thousands of workers produced severe problems in the Bay Area, a chief one being transportation. There were massive traffic jams and delays in the movement of materials and people (Scott, 1959:244-49). The situation became so acute by the spring of 1943 that a subcommittee of the House Committee on Naval Affairs launched an investigation of the Bay Area problems. The eventual report concluded that:

> The lack of adequate and properly coordinated transportation facilities in the San Francisco Bay area is undoubtedly the primary factor in the failure to obtain the highest degree of efficiency from the available labor supply. . . . This same lack is unquestionably having an adverse effect upon the procurement of the additional migrant labor that is so badly needed. Because of traffic congestion and delays, thousands of workers are forced to put in 12 or 13 hours a day in order to work 8 hours. The peculiar geographical situation in the Bay Area probably makes the transportation problem more acute than in any other section of the country. (Quoted in Scott, 1959:255)

Significantly, because of these and other problems, the subcommittee recommended that no further war industries be brought into the Bay Area (Scott, 1959:255). Local transportation problems had reached crisis proportions, at least from the point of view of Bay Area industry and government.

At the close of the war, the federal government urged the states to establish reconstruction commissions to aid in economic conversion to peacetime. California's State Reconstruction and Re-Employment Commission created the San Francisco Bay Region Council to guide post-war development in the area (Shipnuck and Feshbach, 1972:6). Although the Bay Region Council was funded by the state during its first year, in 1945 the council incorporated as a private, nonprofit organization, changing its name to the Bay Area Council (BAC).

It was soon made clear that the BAC was a business organization. As a former BAC chairman and head of the Bank of America explained, "The larger business-industrial firms with interests extending throughout the Bay Area region were the moving spirits in forming the Council" (Quoted in DeFreitas, 1972:13).

When the BAC went private, Bank of America, American Trust Company, Standard Oil of California, Pacific Gas and Electric, U.S. Steel, and Bechtel Corporation each pledged $10,000 annually to support the BAC (Sundeen, 1963:71; Bollens, 1948:115).

Describing itself in its literature as a "research-based, action-oriented body developing and articulating the responsible business viewpoint on important [Bay Area] regional issues," the council has maintained its big business membership throughout the years. A study of the BAC done in the early 1960s, for example, although not identifying companies by name, observes: "Nineteen of the thirty [BAC] trustees represent corporations which, at the end of 1960, were among the 84 largest corporations with headquarters located in San Francisco, or the 52 largest corporations with headquarters located in the Bay Area outside of San Francisco. . . . Fifteen of the nineteen corporations have their headquarters in San Francisco" (Sundeen, 1963:98-100). Of the twenty-seven Bay Area corporations ranked in the *Fortune 500* industrial and financial firms in 1970, twenty-three were represented on the BAC Board of Trustees.

Moreover, the BAC appears to be an organization of corporations rather than an organization of corporate executives. For instance, when one compares the membership of the BAC board of trustees in 1972-73 with the membership in 1974-75, one discovers that nine people who are listed on the 1972-73 board do not appear on the later list. Analysis indicates, however, that these drop-outs reflect the departure only of individuals, not of corporations. Of the nine corporations represented by these men, seven are still represented, but by new faces, on the 1974-75 board. Corporate links tend to be maintained even though people come and go.[1]

From its very first meeting in late 1944, the BAC evidenced a great deal of interest in Bay Area transportation matters. In that first meeting, the vice-chairman of the group listed the major

---

[1] Analysis based on lists of BAC trustees obtained from the council. The seven companies that reestablished connections were Fibreboard, Lockheed, United Air Lines, FMC, Fireman's Fund, Crocker National Bank, and Bank of California. The *Oakland Tribune* and Memorex failed to reestablish connections (within the two-year period).

problems facing the Bay Area. As stated, they were aviation facilities, transportation of all types, sewage disposal, bridge and highway development, coordination of regional factual data, public works, and foreign trade.[2]

In the ensuing years, the BAC has done much more than discuss and research such issues. As BAC literature proclaims, "The Council attempts to be instrumental in initiating—not merely reacting to—public policy." The council has been especially active in the field of transportation. Major campaigns have included proposals for new bridges across the bay, the creation of a Golden Gate Authority (similar to the New York Port Authority), and, of greatest interest for our purposes, the creation of a rapid transit system for the Bay Area (Sundeen, 1963:143-69).

The BAC was the prime mover in convincing the California legislature to establish the San Francisco Bay Area Rapid Transit Commission in 1951 to study transit problems in the nine Bay Area counties and to develop a master rapid transit plan for the area (Zwerling, 1973:15). Speaking before the Committee for Economic Development (CED) in 1966, BAC President Stanley E. McCaffrey told of the role of the BAC: "Some years ago, in 1951 . . . we joined with others in establishing a committee to study the possibilities of establishing a system of rapid transit in the Bay Area to help meet our growing problems of transportation. This committee resulted in the creation of a Rapid Transit Commission by the State Legislature."[3]

The BAC's push for rapid transit continued beyond the planning stage into the BART bond campaign in 1962. As the general manager of the BAC explained to me in an interview: "We were very heavy in some of the early planning and were, I think, quite heavy in working toward the passage of the bond issue." The BAC was indeed heavily involved in the bond campaign, as I shall discuss at greater length later.

During the time that the BAC was working to establish a rapid transit system for the Bay Area, there were other local and national historical events that also helped to pave the way for such a system.

[2] San Francisco Bay Region Council, "Minutes of First Meeting," December 8, 1944, p. 2. Quoted in *Sundeen* (1963:70).

[3] "The Bay Area Story," BAC pamphlet, undated.

Since 1923, the San Francisco Bay Area had been served by an effective system of electric trolleys operated by the Key System Transit Company. Shortly after the BAC had begun to talk about Bay Area transportation problems, the Key System was acquired (in 1946) by National City Lines. This was a fateful occurrance, for National City Lines represented automobile and bus interests, interests that wished to eliminate electric trolleys from the streets of American cities.

Bradford Snell (1974) has extensively documented the connection between companies such as National City Lines and automobile interests, particularly General Motors Corporation (GM), but also Firestone Tire and Rubber Company, Standard Oil of California, Mack Truck, and Phillips Petroleum. The goal of these interests, Snell argues, was to suppress alternative modes of transportation that would compete with motor vehicles. Historically, these companies had an economic interest in substituting buses for rail passenger transportation and, more recently, in displacing buses and rail freight by automobiles and trucks. Snell's position is that the enormous economic power of the automobile industry has resulted in vast market leverage that has allowed diversification into fields of transportation other than automobiles. A crucial example is the massive conversion of American urban electric transportation systems to bus (and automobile) systems. In 1932, GM established United Cities Motor Transit (UMCT) for the purpose of acquiring electric streetcar companies, converting them to GM bus operations, and reselling them to local concerns with the agreement that only GM bus replacements could be purchased. (GM had, and still has, Snell charges, a near monopoly on city bus production in the United States.) This was done in three small cities before GM was censured in 1935 by the American Transit Association for its activities. In 1936, GM dissolved UMCT and combined with Omnibus Corporation. The first major accomplishment of the pair was the acquisition of New York City's streetcar system and its conversion to GM buses. The practical and symbolic importance of this action is emphasized by Snell: "The massive conversion within a period of only 18 months of the New York system, then the world's largest streetcar network, has been recognized subsequently as the turning point in the electric railway industry'' (Snell, 1974:30).

Simultaneously with the New York conversion, GM and Greyhound in 1936 formed National City Lines, Inc. (NCL). Two years later, GM and Standard Oil of California organized Pacific City Lines (PCL). The object of these holding companies was the same as that of the earlier United Cities Motor Transit: to acquire, convert to buses, and resell urban electric transit systems. Upon resale, provision was made to preclude reconversion to electric operation: contracts were written that prohibited the purchase of ''any new equipment using any fuel or means of propulsion other than gas'' (Snell, 1974:31). Exclusive contracts were also written with several suppliers of motor vehicle products. The findings of the United States Court of Appeals, Senate Circuit, in 1951 (United States vs. National City Lines, Inc., 186, F.2d:562-574) are instructive. On April 9, 1949, National City Lines, Pacific City Lines, General Motors, Firestone Tire and Rubber Company, Standard Oil of California, Mack Truck Company, Phillips Petroleum, and Federal Engineering Corporation were indicted for conspiring to gain control of public transportation services in a number of cities for purposes of eliminating competition in the sale of buses, petroleum products, tires and tubes. In addition, they were indicted for ''having conspired to monopolize part of the interstate trade and commerce of the United States, to wit, that part consisting of the sale of buses [sic], petroleum products, tires and tubes used by local transportation systems'' controlled by National and Pacific (United States vs. National City Lines, Inc., 186, F.2d:564). The defendants were acquitted of the first charge and found guilty on the second count. For all practical purposes, the charges were the same. On a later appeal, the United States Court of Appeals, Senate Circuit, judge noted:

> There is no dispute that the City Lines [National and Pacific] defendants and the suppliers [General Motors, Mack, Standard, etc.] entered into various oral and written arrangements in accord with which the latter purchased preferred stock from the former, at prices in excess of the prevailing market prices, amounting in total cost to over nine million dollars

and that the money received from the sales of such stock was used by City Lines defendants to acquire control or substantial financial interest in various local transportation companies throughout the United States. (186, F.2d:565)

The court, in an exemplary show of leniency, saw fit to fine GM $5,000. The treasurer of GM, who had played a key role in the operation of PCL, was fined the sum of $1 (Snell, 1974:32).

Yet at the time of the conviction and token fine, General Motors had been involved in the dismantling of more than one hundred electric transit systems in forty-five cities, including not only San Francisco and New York, but Philadelphia, Baltimore, St. Louis, Oakland, Salt Lake City, and Los Angeles (Snell, 1974:32).

It is difficult, if not impossible, to know just how much the nationwide demise of electric trolley systems was due to these particular corporate activities. The traditional counter-assumption is, of course, that private automobiles and buses won out over electric trolleys because the former were more technologically advanced, efficient, and popular with consumers. From this perspective, increasing automobile dominance was inevitable and socially progressive. It is not the goal here to try to decide this complex issue. Rather, the Snell analysis should stand as a useful antidote to the conventional wisdom on this matter, especially in light of the continued existence of many electric trolley systems in cities outside the United States. Within the United States, it is clear that corporate interest group power did play a role in shaping at least the short-term fate of public transit systems.

Once the San Francisco Key System was taken over by National City Lines, the process of converting the existing streetcar lines to bus lines began (Zwerling, 1972:28). Ridership of the trollies had been declining and the change to buses appeared to hasten the trend. Buses were noisier and had to contend with automobile traffic. Patronage continued to fall as the East Bay tracks were ripped up and schedules and maintenance were cut. This "modernization" culminated in 1958 with the removal of the rails from the San Francisco Bay Bridge (Barnes, 1973:18).

It is ironic that at the same time that Bay Area electric transit was in its death throes, a popular revolt against local freeways was gathering momentum. Beginning in 1957, with protests against the unpopular Embarcadero Freeway, and continuing over the next seven years, citizens' groups protested several freeway projects in San Francisco. Reacting mainly to the social disruption and aesthetic damage done by urban highway construction, numerous civic organizations and homeowners' groups engaged in vigorous and sustained opposition to these projects. Popular pressure encouraged some members of the San Francisco Board of Supervisors to introduce a resolution in 1959 that directed the mayor and city officials not to cooperate any further with the state Division of Highways on plans for new San Francisco freeways (*San Francisco Chronicle*, Jan. 23, 1959:1). A few days later the full Board of Supervisors voted unanimously to stop construction of seven of the ten freeways planned for the city (Liston, 1970:45). The freeway revolt continued in late 1964 when the supervisors voted against the proposed Golden Gate Park freeway extension (*SFC*, Oct. 14, 1964:1). The anti-freeway position was reaffirmed in 1967 when the San Francisco City Planning Commission rejected the idea of any new freeways for San Francisco (*SFC*, Feb. 16, 1967:1).

The demise of the Key System Transit Company and the virtual cessation of freeway construction in San Francisco undoubtedly helped to galvanize interest in a rapid transit system for the Bay Area. However, these were not the most important factors that influenced decisions for such a system. To reiterate: the Bay Area Council's concern with rapid transit development considerably antedated both the conversion of the Key Lines and the rise of the freeway revolt. BART was a BAC product.

In his presentation to the Committee for Economic Development, BAC President McCaffrey spoke of the council's devotion to regional economic growth: "We work with banks, railroads and utilities and other business groups, as well as with local chambers of commerce and industrial development associations in endeavoring to develop the kind of business climate which will be conducive to the growth of existing industry and which will be attractive to new industry." This is an important statement. In fact, I shall argue that it provides the key for understanding not only the basic motivation behind the creation of BART, but also illuminates attitudes and processes that profoundly influence the shape and substance of our cities and that play crucial roles in determining the nature of urban politics.

The above statement is indicative of the almost unanimous concern of business with the promotion of urban growth. This concern is an understandable outgrowth of both the character of our economic system and the attributes of our metropolitan areas. As Molotch notes: "The American metropolis is not a deliberate social experiment or aesthetic expression. It is the coincidental outcome of the capitalist market process—where land is merely a commodity to be bought, sold and exploited like any other. American cities have been merely arenas within which money could be made and the land of the city itself has become a part of the money-making process" (Molotch, 1975:438). One can begin to understand the dynamics of this process by conceiving of "the urban settlement's analytic unit, a given parcel of land, as representing not just a physical resource but *a specific human interest*" (emphasis in original; Molotch, 1975:439). The people or corporations who own land or who have land-related interests see their well-being as somehow linked to that parcel of land. The general goal is to increase one's own wealth by enhancing the land's profit potential. According to Molotch, "this means that there is a struggle going on: each landowner is trying to attract the sorts of land users—builders, bankers, factories, or whatever—that will bring profit. Generally speaking, the more intensive the development, the higher the profitability of the land associated with that development. The rub comes from the fact that a finite amount of development is going to take place, making each landowner a competitor with every other in the continuous quest for a scarce resource: development" (Molotch, 1975:439).

This competition for development has the effect of constantly intensifying land use with a region, creating an "urban growth machine." Competition goes on at several levels: (1) Regions compete with other regions (and nations) for growth. Thus, there is the struggle between the so-called sunbelt and snowbelt. (2) Cities compete with other cities. For example, one of the major motivating factors—as will be seen in the next chapter—behind the two proposals for BART-like systems in Los Angeles was the desire by elites in that city to keep up with San Francisco in the competitive race for growth. (3) Cities compete with their suburbs, and (4) different areas of the city compete with each other. In other words, a number of competitive struggles are going on simultaneously, with competition at one level being nested within competition at the next level. I shall argue that one of the most crucial struggles, from the standpoint of understanding urban politics, is that which takes place between central cities, on the one hand, and less central areas of the city, suburbs, and competing metropolitan regions, on the other hand. In short, there is what I would call a powerful "central city growth machine" operating within the larger urban growth machine identified by Molotch.

Business groups such as the Bay Area Council espouse centralized urban growth, particularly in downtown San Francisco. In the first place, many of the businesses represented on the BAC own large blocks of land and expensive buildings in downtown San Francisco whose value would increase with rising land prices. Standard Oil of California, for example, maintains its huge world headquarters in the heart of the city. Banks and other financial firms have direct interests too since they hold millions of dollars in mortgages on central city offices. Banks have often been at the forefront in central city growth projects, as in the case of New York City's World Trade Center, which was conceived and financed by the city's large banks (Leinsdorf and Etra, 1973:141). Other businesses, in addition to having material vested interests in property, could profit with the arrival of new business and customers in the city. Big, central city retailers in San Francisco such as Emporium-Capwell fall into this category. Downtown stores have been particularly hurt by the rise of suburban shopping centers and feel that improved consumer access to the city would improve their competitive position. In spite of the tendency of some businesses (particularly industries) to seek suburban locations, there remain others that still view central city location as a crucial business resource. This is especially true of businesses whose primary function is administrative or financial (e.g., corporate headquarters, insurance, banks, etc.). The importance of financial firms to the San Francisco economy (and in the BAC) is indicated by the fact that the city is often called "The Wall Street of the West." For these firms, centralized location is seen as facilitating direct communication and face-to-face contracts among business leaders, thus promoting efficiency and personalized business relations among the members of the business community. This phenomenon is not limited to San Francisco. Ewen makes much the same point in her study of Detroit: "The expansion of the Detroit area and the greater complexity of commerce and industry there make even more imperative a centralized location where decision-makers can meet, make contacts, and maintain immediate communications. The possibility of rapid transit systems that would do in the coming decades for local area travel what the 'executive jet' has done for national travel provides the basis for continued expansion regionally and continued centralization" (Ewen, 1978:234-35). Another result of centralization is to provide a basis for regular interaction and social cohesion among important segments of the business community. As will be shown, social cohesion is of considerable value and concern within the world of big business.

It is my argument that (1) the large businesses in downtown San Francisco were the principle forces behind the creation of BART, and (2) the paramount goal was to preserve and extend the economic development of downtown San Francisco. Evidence for these two propositions is set forth in the remainder of this chapter.

After World War II, there was concern among San Francisco business and civic elites, not only over the war-time crisis in transit, but also over the effects on the city of booming suburbanization. Zwerling observes: "San Francisco's civic leaders were convinced that if nothing were done to prevent it, their city would decay for many of the same reasons that other major American cities were decaying. Expanding networks of high-speed public roadways enabled people to move out of central cities into suburban areas. Furthermore, as low-density suburbs began to emerge, retail businesses and light industry began to leave the urban core to take advantage of new markets and lower costs" (Zwerling, 1973:15). The same process that had encouraged suburbanization—the growth of automobile usage—was now making access to the central city difficult. San Francisco elites had perhaps arrived earlier than the *Wall Street Journal* at the conclusion that heavy reliance on the automobile had generated air pollution, traffic, disruption of homes and jobs, "and roads that often detract from business growth, rather than enhance it (*Wall Street Journal*, July 24, 1970, p. 6)." Important people in San Francisco began to see the sweeping dominance of the automobile-highway system as a fetter on further concentrated urban and business growth.

As previously mentioned, the BAC played an important part in getting the California legislature to establish the first body to study Bay Area transportation. In 1953 the San Francisco Bay Area Rapid Transit Commission made its preliminary report to the legislature. The findings included the conclusion that the Bay Area could not solve its transportation problems by automobile alone and that a coordinated system of mass rapid transit was needed. The commission warned: "Good mass transportation made the centralized big city possible and good mass transportation is *essential to preserve it*" (emphasis added).[4] Commenting on the report, a California senate committee echoed this concern: "The impact of traffic strangulation and congestion on downtown properties is being felt with alarming effect. It has brought about decentralization of business . . . and a consequent decrease in the volume of business conducted by downtown establishments."[5]

The commission requested and was granted additional funds to develop a master transit plan for the Bay Area. In November of 1953, the commission hired the firm of Parsons, Brinckerhoff, Hall, and Macdonald (PBHM) to conduct studies. PBHM was a New York-based engineering-consultant firm whose founder had developed New York City's subway system (Zwerling, 1972:34).

Transit Study Reports

In 1956, PBHM presented its report to the commission. This document, *Regional Rapid Transit (RRT)*, became the basic plan-

[4] Conclusions of the study cited in Zwerling (1972:33-34); quote cited in *Mass Rapid Transit, Answer to Traffic Congestion in the San Francisco Bay Area*. Report to the California Legislative Senate Interim Committee on San Francisco Bay Area Metropolitan Rapid Transit Problems (Sacramento: State Printing Office, 1953), p. 23.

[5] As above, from the Interim Committee report, p. 23.

ning document for BART.[6] Once again, there was heavy emphasis
on the problems of decentralization for the central city. Sum-
marizing the report's findings, PBHM states: "The dominant
question for the Bay Area is whether to accept the stagnation and
decline of interurban transit and to prepare for drastic decentralization and repatterning of its urban centers to meet the avalanche
of automobiles that will result—or whether to reinvigorate interurban transit so as to sustain the daily flow of workers, shoppers,
and visitors on which the vitality of these urban centers depends"
(RRT:1). The report goes on to note that "prosperity of the entire
Bay Area will depend upon the preservation and enhancement of
its urban centers and subcenters," a task requiring a new transit
system (RRT:1).

The desire for central city location by certain businesses and
the implications for urban transit were pointed out:

> Those firms which still require a central location because
> they need to be in close proximity to other firms and acces-
> sible to the labor and consumer market of the entire region
> will unquestionably continue to seek locations at the regional
> center—they will, that is, if improvements in the transpor-
> tation system increase accessibility. . . . Certain types of
> commercial activities are clearly centrally oriented; and we
> can expect that the concentrations of major financial insti-
> tutions, specialized professional offices, corporate establish-
> ments in San Francisco and Oakland will be even larger in
> the future than they are now. (RRT:18)

Later, when the commission made its final report to the legislature in 1957, the theme of economic centralization was continued. Transportation had to provide the means "of fulfilling the
accelerating demand for single-family houses in dispersed suburban areas and of preserving and enhancing at the same time the
urban concentration of employment and commerce where the means
to earn that standard of living must largely focus."[7]

---

[6] Regional Rapid Transit: A Report to the San Francisco Bay Area Rapid Transit
Commission, 1953-1955 by Parsons, Brinckerhoff, Hall, and Macdonald (Engineers) (New York 1956).

[7] San Francisco Bay Area Rapid Transit Commission Report to the Legislature
of the State of California, December 1957, p. 76.

With the presentation of its report, the commission was dissolved. That same year, the legislature created the San Francisco
Bay Area Transit District (BARTD) composed initially of five
(Alameda, Contra Costa, Marin, San Francisco, and San Mateo)
of the nine Bay Area counties. Other counties could later join if
they wished to do so (Zwerling, 1972:39). In May of 1959, the
district hired three engineering firms to develop a rapid transit
plan for the region. The firms were: the authors of the previous
Regional Rapid Transit report, Parsons, Brinkerhoff, Quade, and
Douglas (formerly Parsons, Brinckerhoff, Hall, and Macdonald),
of New York and San Francisco; Tudor Engineering of San Francisco; and the Bechtel Corporation of San Francisco. This joint
venture became known as PBTB (Zwerling, 1972:39; Liston,
1970:57).

As will be pointed out later at greater length, the decision by
the district to hire private firms to develop plans for BART, rather
than to build an "in-house" engineering group to do the job, was
a consequential choice. Over the next five years PBTB conducted
engineering and other studies and produced the second major
BART planning document, the *Composite Report* (*CR*), issued in
May 1962.[8]

The *Composite Report* followed the assumptions and lines of
analysis contained in the *Regional Rapid Transit* report, and once
again the emphasis was on economic growth and centralization.
The report however, shows even more clearly that the system was
not conceived so much in terms of a means for improving transportation, but more in terms of a tool for shaping the future growth
of the region. As they are listed in the *Composite Report*, here
are the presumed "Specific Benefits of Rapid Transit" in the Bay
Area:

1. *Preservation and enhancement of urban centers and sub-*
   centers
2. *Increased property values*
3. *Help to prevent disorganized urban sprawl*

---

[8] *The Composite Report: Bay Area Rapid Transit*, May 1962 by Parsons-Brinck-
erhoff-Tudor-Bechtel; Smith, Barney & Co.; Stone and Youngberg; and Van
Beuren Stanbery.

4. Improved employment conditions
5. Improved access to social, cultural, and recreational opportunities
6. More efficient transportation expenditures since less will be required for automobile-related expenditures
7. Low cost public transportation
   (emphasis added; *CR*; 82:83)

The salience to the planners of centralized urban growth is explicitly stated here. Moreover, if the order of presentation of goals has significance, it is clear that what are normally thought to be the public benefits of mass transit (improved access and traffic flow, lower cost, etc.) were conceived as subsidiary to growth.

It is also apparent from the planning documents that a rail system was the preferred choice for the Bay Area. As Zwerling notes: "It appears that all the principles were agreed on the solution—rail rapid transit—prior to the first real study of the region's transportation requirements. The State of California and the nine Bay Area counties . . . were thinking in terms of a rail system. The San Francisco Bay Area Transit Commission was thinking about a rail system. Indeed, the consulting firm [PBHM] hired to determine the need for and feasibility of a rail system was a firm whose transit expertise rests on rail systems" (Zwerling, 1972:44). PBHM's *Regional Rapid Transit*, for example, quotes with approval a 1955 report of the Toronto Transit Commission to the effect that land values and building construction have been stimulated in that city by the construction of the Yonge Street Subway (*RRT*:106). In the second planning document, the *Composite Report*, the engineering consultants explicitly recommend a rail system for the Bay Area (*CR*:4-6).

Given the goal of shaping the growth of the region, it is not surprising that a rail system was seen as the proper choice. It was expected that a rail system, in contrast to a more flexible system, would produce growth at predictable locations. In the words of BART's director of planning: "The thing about a bus line is that it can be moved. But a rail transit stop will be there day after day, and this allows for [real estate] development" (Bazell, 1971:1125). Growth would occur along transit corridors, but especially at the downtown terminus where lines from the suburbs converged. Members of the Bay Area Council held this view. Former BAC member Robert Nahas told me: "So the areas you can expect to grow will be downtown San Francisco . . . and it should stimulate apartment house growth and . . . residential growth out in the suburbs." In another interview, BAC General Manager, Angelo Siracusa, predicted that BART will promote "growth and development," "appreciation of property values," and higher densities, saying that "I think there will be some very, very strong impacts."

One of the most important men behind BART was Adrien Falk, vice-president of S & W Fine Foods, president of the California Chamber of Commerce, an early trustee of the Bay Area Council, and the first chairman of the BART District. Falk, in an interview with *Bay Guardian* reporter Burton H. Wolfe, explained his vision of future centralization in San Francisco: "Certain finance, banking industries, want to be centralized, want to have everyone near each other. They don't want to have to go one day to Oakland, the next day to San Jose, the next day to San Francisco. . . . I believe there is a renaissance of our big cities taking place. BARTD will make it possible to bring all the people in here. The new construction it will generate will be a great improvement for San Francisco."[9]

Roger Lapham, Jr., another member of BART's board of directors, predicted: "The end result of BARTD is that San Francisco will be just like Manhattan."[10] When asked by Wolfe whether it was desirable for San Francisco to become like Manhattan, Lapham replied: "It's not a question of whether it's desirable, but what's the practical matter. As a practical matter you can't have 18 different banking and insurance centers. You have to concentrate them with all the various services around them. The people who run these centers want all their services, the people they work with—advertisers, attorneys, accountants—around them. It's a complete part of the way we do business in this country."[11] "Suppose some people in San Francisco don't want their city

[9] Burton H. Wolfe, *The Bay Guardian*, June 18, 1968, p. 5.
[10] *Ibid.*, p. 1.
[11] *Ibid.*, p. 5.

converted into a Manhattan?'' Wolfe persisted. Lapham stated, ''Then let them go someplace else. But don't keep complaining about it, because that's what is *going* to happen, and nobody can stop it (original emphasis).''[12]

Such images of the virtues and inevitability of growth were not limited to the BAC and BART directors. Louis W. Riggs, president of Tudor Engineering Company (one of the three joint venture firms that planned BART) stated that: ''it will take a strong mass transportation system to provide a back-bone for high-density urban development. . . . New high-rise development will take place all along BART lines and property around station sites particularly will acquire exceptional location value.''[13] In an address to the Institute for Rapid Transit, a spokesman for the Ranchers' Exploration and Development Corporation added: ''The first economic asset of . . . [BART] is its effectiveness as a tool for economic development for the region. The rapid system will create a leverage for economic growth which simply would not exist without it.''[14]

Belief that BART would generate growth in San Francisco was widespread among the members of the business community. All interviewees, when questioned in interviews about BART's impact, expressed this opinion. For example, a Bank of America executive talked of the rise of new construction directly related to BART; a vice president of Wells Fargo Bank said that BART was essential to ''maintaining economic life in the community''; a Southern California Edison Company executive stated that BART will ''help . . . [the Bay Area] grow in a way that's going to be meaningful to the economic pocket book of industry, business, and the wage earner.''

The idea of mass transit as a tool for growth also extended beyond the Bay Area business community. An administrator of the Institute for Rapid Transit (the industry's trade association) told me that rail systems would serve to ''revitalize'' the central business districts of cities in the United States. His boss at that

[12] *Ibid.*

[13] Louis W. Riggs, address to Engineering Foundation Conference, April 27, 1971. Reprint from Tudor Engineering Company.

[14] Kenneth D. Lawson speech to Institute for Rapid Transit, May 10, 1963.

time, Dr. William J. Ronan,[15] president of IRT and head of the New York Metropolitan Transportation Authority, has spoken of the need "to proceed with urban public transportation investment in order to shape [urban] development" (Kizzia, 1974:41).

This conception of transit as a means of growth rather than as a means of movement was also shared by political leaders of the country. Shortly before the BART bond election, President Kennedy, in a major policy address to the United States Congress, said, "Our national welfare . . . requires the provision for good urban transportation with the proper use of private vehicles and modern mass transport to help shape, as well as serve, urban growth."[16] Over a decade later, President Nixon, creator of the Urban Mass Transit Administration, was reported to have said: "the Department of Transportation is not a particularly flamboyant place, but its programs can change the face of the country."[17] The senior editor of *Architectural Forum* also recognized this crucial fact when he wrote: "BARTD is more than transportation—it is the largest single act of urban design currently underway in the U.S." (Bailey, 1966:59).

THE BART BOND CAMPAIGN

The 1962 campaign to make BART a reality reveals the heavy involvement of the largest of the San Francisco businesses. The campaign also is an example—as the epigraph at the beginning

[15] Ronan is in a position to know much about urban mass transit and big city growth. He is a past president of the Institute for Rapid Transit, and head of the New York Metropolitan Transit Authority. During the confirmation hearings for Vice President Nelson Rockefeller, it was revealed that Rockefeller had given Ronan a $550,000 "gift" (*LAT*, Oct. 8, 1974:11). Ronan described himself as "an advisor to the Rockefeller family (*LAT*, Oct. 11, 1974:16)." It is interesting to note that Nelson Rockefeller and David Rockefeller, chairman of the Chase Manhattan Bank, have been involved in real estate development in lower Manhattan. David Rockefeller was instrumental in getting the city of New York to build a new subway line into that area (*LAT*, July 22, 1973:1: *LAT*, Oct. 11, 1974:16).

[16] Message to Congress, April 6, 1962. Quoted in Meyer *et al.* (1965:1).

[17] Quoted in *Mass Transit*, June 1974, p. 21.

of this chapter suggests—of what Murray Edelman calls "symbolic politics," the politics that serves to reassure the public at large that some social need is being met while conveying specific, material benefits to a smaller, organized group. BART was publicly promoted as a cure for traffic congestion, while the main concern of its supporters and planners was the creation of profitable patterns of urban economic development.

The question of whether to build BART was presented to the Bay Area voters in November of 1962. Approval of the ballot measure would authorize the San Francisco Bay Area Rapid Transit District to issue $792 million worth of general obligation bonds for the purpose of constructing a 75-mile rail (subway, surface, and elevated) rapid transit system for the region. The interest on the bonds was to be financed out of local property taxes.

Although the San Francisco Bay Area Rapid Transit District had started out with five of the nine Bay Area counties as members, by the time of the election San Mateo and Marin had opted out of the program, leaving only three counties (Alameda, Contra Costa, and San Francisco) to participate in the vote (Zwerling, 1973:55-56). Thus, the system was only to include one-third of the counties in the Bay Area. To make matters more difficult for BART supporters, California law required a 66 2/3 percent affirmative vote to approve the BART bonds. Alan K. Browne of Bank of America was one of those who worked hard to get a vote by the three county area rather than county-by-county. He was also instrumental in getting the state legislature to reduce the needed BART vote from 66 2/3 percent to 60 percent. As it turned out these were crucial actions, for the BART issue would not have passed had it not been for these changes.

Supporters of the BART bond issue (known as Proposition A on the three-county ballot) organized a campaign committee called Citizens for Rapid Transit, whose top members, significantly, were all San Francisco bankers. It was chaired by Mortimer Fleishhacker, Jr., a director of Crocker Citizens Bank. The other two members were Carl F. Wente, chairman of Bank of America, and Kendric B. Morrish, vice president of Wells Fargo Bank. The campaign committee was organized by the so-called "Blyth-Zellerbach Committee," after BARTD president Adrien Falk requested them to do so. Falk also hired Henry W. Alexander to manage the pro-BART campaign.[18] Alexander, in an interview, described the Blyth-Zellerbach Committee as a group of the top level management of leading area companies, "the Establishment in San Francisco." The Executive Director of the San Francisco Planning and Urban Renewal Association (a private group organized by the Blyth-Zellerbach Committee and also funded largely by big business), when asked by letter about the membership of the Blyth-Zellerbach Committee, responded: "The B-Z Committee was formed in 1959 to further the economic and aesthetic development of San Francisco . . . I am not certain I am free to disclose its membership other than to say that most of the large companies headquartered in San Francisco make up its membership of 18." BART campaign manager, Henry Alexander, pointed out to me that the B-Z Committee and the Bay Area Council had overlapping membership. Bazell, writing in *Science* magazine, comments on the committee's composition and role: "For several years before the 1962 BART election a group of civic leaders conducted a well-financed campaign to promote rapid transit. Variously known as the Blyth-Zellerbach Committee or the 40 Thieves, the groups included the heads of such San Francisco-based corporate giants as the Bank of America and the Pacific Gas and Electric Company. Without their campaign, it is unlikely that Bay Area residents would have approved BART" (Bazell, 1971:1126). Members of the BAC agree on the effectiveness of the campaign; BAC General Manager Siracusa said that the BAC was "quite heavy" in working for the passage of the bond issue. In BAC literature, BAC President McCaffrey has stated that the organization "played an important part in helping achieve the favorable vote of approval by the voters."

Although the statements of business leaders and the BART planning documents emphasize urban growth as a major objective of BART, the public campaign for BART promoted the system as a cure for traffic congestion. Typical newspaper ads for BART by the Citizens for Rapid Transit hailed BART as "the low-cost cure for the traffic mess," and "the best traffic cure we can get—

[18] Burton Wolfe, *The Bay Guardian*, June 18, 1968, p. 2.

for the least money!'' Such a message would have obvious appeal to the thousands of Bay Area commuters who were weary of morning and afternoon traffic jams on the major traffic arteries between San Francisco and its suburbs.

The BART bond issue was widely endorsed by the San Francisco business community, civic groups (such as the League of Women Voters), governmental organizations, and the press. There were, however, a few groups who went on record as opposing the measure. These groups were virtually all based outside of San Francisco in the East Bay. The Chambers of Commerce of some small East Bay cities (e.g., Bryon, El Cerrito, and Pittsburg) as well as the city councils of such communities opposed BART. The same was true of newspapers in these communities. The most significant group against the bond issue was probably the San Francisco Labor Council. Other labor organizations supported BART. The labor council's opposition was apparently rooted in the belief that BART would benefit workers from the East Bay more than those in San Francisco.

In spite of the stand of these groups, there was virtually no organized opposition to BART. The Civic League of Improvement and Associations ran an ad that was against the taxes needed to support BART (*SFC*, Nov. 5 1962:22). The Central Council of Civic Clubs and the San Francisco Labor Council jointly ran an ad that objected to BART for several reasons: high cost; the BARTD board was appointed instead of elected; insufficient BART service to many residential and industrial areas; increased taxes; questions as to the technical efficiency of the system; and service to only three of the nine Bay Area counties (*SFC*, Nov. 5, 1962:18).

Within the Bay Area business community there was scattered opposition, also mainly from outside San Francisco. One of the chief reasons that San Mateo County dropped out of the BART District prior to the election seems to have been the objections there of large landowners such as the owner of a large, new suburban shopping center (Zwerling, 1972:54). According to interviewees, he feared that BART might take his customers into San Francisco to shop. As Zwerling notes, ''The most articulate and active opponent [of BART] was Robert J. Nahas, an East Bay developer, past President of the Oakland Chamber of Commerce, and a highly respected civic leader'' (Zwerling, 1972:61). Nahas felt that rail transit was an outdated concept and that the cost of BART was not worth its benefits. In an interview with me, Nahas said that BART would generate dense development and would not solve traffic problems.

The most important fact about Nahas is that he was a trustee of the elite Bay Area Council, and he resigned his position in disagreement over BART. Nahas complained to me: ''I heard this whole plan being developed in the Bay Area Council, and I felt that it was not equitable, it was not practical. I didn't like the way it was sold, and I just had to do something about it.'' Nahas spent some of his own money in opposing BART, through making speeches, engaging in debates, and other activities. He could find little support from other members of the business community. Part of Nahas' objection was that ''San Francisco was always going to be the principal beneficiary of BART.'' As he put it, ''I'm more closely allied with the East Bay . . . and the East Bay is going to pay [through property taxes] for most of the cost.'' In the interview, he went on to charge: ''The principal purpose of BART—it was promoted by people who are interested in downtown San Francisco, the office buildings in downtown San Francisco. And for those who go into downtown San Francisco and the financial district, or close to Market Street and who live fairly close to a BART station, it's fine.'' Thus, as the Molotch (1975) perspective would predict, regional business rivalries and competition for urban development appear to have played roles in producing some of the opposition to BART.

In addition, a few other businesses were mildly opposed to BART. Southern Pacific Railroad was ''a little less than enthusiastic'' about BART, I was told by a former California State Chamber of Commerce official, past general manager of the Western Oil and Gas Association (WOGA), and first general manager of BART. The basis of the Southern Pacific opposition seems to have been that Southern Pacific—like many railroads—wants out of the business of transporting people. BART, it was felt, would require a subsidy and would therefore establish an undesirable precedent from the railroad's point of view. In the end, however, Southern Pacific took a neutral position. Also, some elements of the highway lobby (the California State Automobile Association and a few oil companies) at first were against BART. However, according to a Bank of America executive, there was no active opposition by these elements.

Unfortunately for purposes of research, there is no official public record of the campaign contributions for and against the BART bond measure. At the time of the local election in 1962, there was no legal requirement that campaign committees file lists of contributors. Therefore, other means must be used to identify contributors to the BART campaign.

Shortly after the election, a civil suit was filed against the San Francisco Bay Area Rapid Transit District. The plaintiffs were Robert L. Osborne and three others. Osborne, the principal person behind the suit, was an Oakland city councilman and East Bay manufacturer. The suit charged that fixed rail is an obsolete, century-old concept; that BART stations would be too far apart to encourage riders; that better and more efficient transit systems were rejected by BARTD; that the ultimate cost of the system would be much greater than $792 million; that BARTD's contract with PBTB was an open-ended, illegal contract that would result in engineering fees rising without limit; that the joint venture engineering firms were not impartial because they were friends of the powerful Bechtel family; that BART had made false promises about the nature of its service (e.g., virtually silent operation, no standees, etc.); and that an illegal, close working relationship existed between the Citizens for Rapid Transit Committee and BART public officials.[19] (As will later be seen, many of these charges appear to have been true.) The suit also charged that the main purpose of BART, as set forth in BARTD legislation, was the "preservation and enhancement of . . . [the Bay Area's] urban centers and subcenters." This, it was charged, was not a proper function of the California legislature.[20]

Our interest in the suit is the light it throws on campaign con-

[19] Wolfe, *The Bay Guardian*, July 19, 1973, p. 6.

[20] "Transcript of Proceedings." Robert L. Osborne, Dewayne E. Boblitt, Stanley E. Nunn, and Junior G. Gertsch, Plaintiffs, *vs.* San Francisco Bay Area Rapid Transit District, *et al.*, Defendants, Contra Costa County Superior Court, Department no. 7. December 1962, no. 87332.

tributions for BART. In the course of the suit, a deposition was taken on March 25, 1963, from Carl F. Wente, chairman of the Bank of America, and chief fund-raiser for the Citizens for Rapid Transit. In the deposition, Wente told about his methods of soliciting contributions: "Yes sir, I solicited [Edgar] Kaiser [of Kaiser Industries], and I told Kaiser at the time, 'You are interested in this for several reasons. First place, you are interested from a civic standpoint, it is a good thing for the city. You have your office here. You are in the cement business, you are in the steel business, you are in the aluminum business, you are in the engineering business, you are in all kinds of—your outfit ought to be interested in this from every conceivable angle.' " When Kaiser objected that the $25,000 contribution Wente was asking for was too much, Wente replied, "Relatively, that is small considering the size of the billion dollars worth of work, let's be frank. You fellows are going [to make a killing?]—there is potential there."

In addition to the $25,000 Kaiser donation, Wente revealed a partial list of contributors to the BART campaign. They included many of the firms that had had, or would have, BART contracts and who stood to make large profits. The PBTB group was well represented: Parsons, Brinckerhoff, Quade and Douglas—$5,000; Bechtel Corporation—$15,000; Tudor Engineering—$2,500. Other contributions included: Westinghouse Air Brake—$12,000; Standard Oil of California—$10,000; Bethlehem Steel Corporation—$12,500. These contributions represent approximately $82,000, or less than half of the total ($203,218) reported by Wente. Wente did not reveal the source of the remaining money, but it is safe to assume it came from large San Francisco businesses, such as those represented on the Blyth-Zellerbach Committee and the Bay Area Council. They were clearly interested in BART. As one former business executive commented to me: "The business community, they don't put up money for a campaign unless it's going to be rewarding to their interests and to the interests of the community." When I asked him about the role of the Blyth-Zellerbach Committee, he told of the groups' high status in the business community and its leading part in the campaign: "Well, the Blyth-

Zellerbach Committee, that was the finance committee. That's the $205,000 [sic] . . . Those are two great big names, see. Dave Zellerbach, then head of Crown Zellerbach . . . and Charlie Blyth of Blyth and Company, one of the great investment bankers and a very dear and old friend of mine. They spearheaded this . . . they're the most highly respected men in the community.''

Other than the two anti-BART newspaper ads previously mentioned, there is no evidence of contributions against BART. Organizations and money were overwhelmingly on BART's side. Thus, it can be seen that BART was essentially a creation of the large corporations in downtown San Francisco, and that the main goal of those businesses was to stimulate and shape the economic growth of the Bay Area in profitable ways. However, BART was symbolically sold to the voters as a solution to traffic congestion, this message apparently touching sympathetic chords in a sufficient number of voters.

The ballot for the election in November 1962, was a long one: there was the gubernatorial race between Pat Brown and Richard Nixon, twenty-five California propositions, twenty-five elective offices, and eleven local propositions (including Proposition A, the BART measure) (*SFC*, Nov. 5, 1962:19). BART passed by a narrow margin of 1.2 percent. The affirmative vote was as follows: Contra Costa County, 54.2 percent; Alameda County, 59.7 percent; San Francisco County, 66.9 percent (Zwerling, 1972:62). As previously mentioned, Bank of America executive Alan Browne's successful efforts to get a vote by region instead of by county, and the reduction in the needed affirmative vote from two-thirds to three-fifths, made a great deal of difference: without either change or with only a reduction in the needed vote, BART would have passed only in San Francisco County; with only the provision of a unified three-county vote, BART would have failed in the entire district; with both of the changes, BART was successful in the whole district. Obviously, the San Francisco County vote provided BART's winning margin. It was a close call for BART's supporters, but authorization for the construction of the BART system had been given. The actual construction of BART was to require more than a decade to complete.

BOOM AND BUST: A SHORT CRITIQUE OF BART

The passage of the BART ballot measure allowed general obligation bonds for constructing the system to be sold. The first bond sales were made a little over a year after the voters' approval of the system. The sales were handled by John M. Peirce, who was at that time financial director for the district. According to Peirce, banks and financial institutions considered these bonds sound investments: they were tax exempt and guaranteed payable out of property tax revenues. In spite of this, Peirce pointed out in the interview that "there has to be a certain amount of selling [promotion of the bonds]." In addition to emphasizing the tax exempt and guaranteed status of the bonds, Peirce also sought to "encourage" banks to buy the bonds by taking the proceeds of the bond sales and reinvesting them in time deposits with the purchasing banks. Bonds were sold in blocks via competitive bids among syndicates of banks. According to Peirce, all banks in San Francisco purchased bonds, including, of course, those banks (Bank of America, Crocker Citizens, and Wells Fargo) whose representatives made up the organization (Citizens for Rapid Transit) that had campaigned for BART. These bankers, like most other business supporters of BART were interested in promoting Bay Area growth.

What has been BART's role in promoting growth in the region? This is a question that is difficult to answer with assurance. Part of the difficulty lies in the fact that BART is fairly new and its long-term impact on patterns of urban growth is not yet fully evident. Secondly, there is the problem of the lack of an adequate "control" condition, that is, of a means for assessing how much of the growth that has occurred in San Francisco would have taken place without BART.

Professor James E. Vance, Jr., of the Geography Department at the University of California at Berkeley, is a student of transportation matters and was an early opponent of BART. He explained his position to me. He believes that "Manhattanization" is a general process in American cities, and that BART cannot be seen as the sole factor promoting growth in San Francisco. Other cities, Vance argues, have tall buildings without having mass transit, and the downtown high-rises in San Francisco came before the completion of BART. Vance does concede that downtown San Francisco has continued to grow as a center for finance and administration and that these functions can probably not be decentralized.

In *The Urban Transportaion Problem*, Meyer, et al. also deemphasize the growth-inducing potential of transit: "Transit availability . . . does not seem to be a sufficient condition for creating density or downtown growth, nor does it seem to be a major deterrent to the development of new employment opportunities in the suburban ring. Other factors [e.g., income of population, family characteristics, communication technology, etc.] seem much more important" (Meyer et al., 1965:54). They conclude: "With or without transit, American cities have been decentralizing (Meyer et al., 1965:360)." Like Vance, they realize that it may be impractical to decentralize certain financial, commercial, and executive centers.

One of the authors of *The Urban Transportation Problem*, Martin Wohl, was an early critic of BART. Wohl's major criticism of BART is that the system is "inflexible" and cannot respond to current trends toward decentralization. "BART," he charged in an interview with Burton Wolfe, "is a 19th Century system with a few modern embellishments to make it appear futuristic."[21]

The question of the desirability of centralization versus decentralization is a point of debate between city planners and transit experts. According to William L. C. Wheaton, dean of the College of Environmental Design at Berkeley: "Virtually all city and regional planners want to strengthen central business districts. Central banking, financing and the like are naturally centered downtown." Wheaton agrees with Wohl that decentralization is "the wave of the future" for American cities, but notes that if even a fraction of future growth is in the central business districts, mass transit will be a necessity.[22]

Much more critical of systems like BART is Professor William L. Garrison of the University of Illinois, formerly head of the

[21] Wohl, quoted in Wolfe, *The Bay Guardian*, December 24, 1968.
[22] *Ibid.*

Transportation Center at Northwestern. He maintains that rail transit is not a good substitute for automobiles and stresses the need for alternatives to both cars and rails:

> The mass rail transit system is a dog and we had better get away from it. . . . Mass rail transit systems like BART perpetuate living and working in very densely populated areas. They are designed to continue the process of constructing massive high-rise buildings in central downtown districts and compelling people to commute long distances to get to work. . . . Hence, the majority of the people in our field ["total transportation"] are now seeking alternatives to mass transit as well as the automobile.[23]

The crucial question, of course, is not the opinion of transit experts, but what business elites in San Francisco thought would happen as a result of BART's construction. They expected growth. Whatever the nuances of conviction among the academic community regarding the exact relation between rail transit and growth of the central business district, there was little doubt within the BART hierarchy and among the business community about the assumed connection. An anticipated dramatic increase in land values was touted by BART officials and the engineers: "Documents issued by the BART public relations office and Parsons, Brinkerhoff, Tudor, and Bechtel extoll the 'fact' that property values have risen ten-fold in Toronto after rapid transit construction. The statement apparently comes from an address by a past president of the Toronto Real Estate Board in which he stated 'Properties *doubled* and *tripled* in value and sometimes increased as much as *tenfold*' " (emphasis in original; Lewin, 1974:19). Apparently, this provocative idea gained great currency and acceptance among Bay Area business elites, even though it was based on a myth. The University of California BART Impact Study found in its key informant interviews that: "nearly everyone interviewed had some awareness of the Toronto experience and held the opinion that the subway there had caused a 'boom' in land value and construction. A factor of ten was often cited. Yet

---

[23] *Ibid.*

there is essentially no documentary evidence for the Toronto case, and there is nothing to relate the transportation to the land use pattern. Participants in the development process talk a lot to each other, and information which often has little more substance than rumor is acted upon and, in effect, becomes fact."[24] Certainly among the business community this belief that rapid transit causes development might result in a "self-fulfilling prophecy" (Merton, 1968:475), leading to private investment decisions that, in fact, produce growth. This may well have been the case in San Francisco where a great deal of high-rise office construction occurred between the approval of BART in 1962 and its completion in 1974. Whether, as Vance maintains, this construction would have happened anyway is not clear.

It is quite clear, however, that the San Francisco business community was ardently supportive of growth and that important segments of that community perceived a direct link between BART and downtown development. The most manifest and lucid expression of this notion is an advertisement that appeared in *Fortune*. It was sponsored by the Greater San Francisco Chamber of Commerce (Zwerling, 1972:58) and is entitled "Bay Area Rapid Transit: A Building Boom in the Billions" (*Fortune*, 1970). In heady terms, the piece begins: "Even without a train running, rapid transit already has made an impact. BART—as the system has been dubbed—triggered a building boom in the billions of dollars. . . . The Bay Area has underway a billion dollar-plus commercial, industrial and residential face-lifting centered chiefly in San Francisco and extending to other BART station locations." The ad features smiling pictures of prominent San Francisco business leaders, such as the presidents of Bechtel Corporation, Pacific Telephone and Telegraph Company, Standard Oil of California, and the chairmen of Wells Fargo Bank, Bank of America, and Kaiser Industries. Numerous quotes from other big businessmen are included, quotes saying that the development potential was "explosive," that BART "solidifies San Francisco's core city position," and so forth. Inventorying new construction, the ad

[24] Institute of Urban and Regional Development, *BART Impact Studies, Final Report Series* (University of California, Berkeley, 1973), pt. III, vol. 2, p. 3.

proudly announces: "BART already holds a major place in the corporate thinking of such giants on the San Francisco scene as Bank of America, Wells Fargo Bank, Crocker-Citizens Bank, Bank of California, Transamerica, Pacific Telephone Co., Pacific Gas and Electric Co., Crown Zellerbach Corporation, Potlatch Forests Inc. and many others. It has formed the basis for much new corporate office building, including among others Pacific Insurance Company, Del Monte Corp., and Transamerica." Other recent San Francisco buildings include the Wells Fargo Building (a key BART stop), the Crocker Citizens Building, the world headquarters of the Bank of America, and the Rockefellers' high-rise Embarcadero Center.[25] The ad also notes, "In San Francisco, a revised zoning code opened the South of Market area for intensive development to match the North of Market area. . . . The Yerba Buena project, extending South of Market between Third and Fourth Streets, covers eighty-seven acres." (For a moving account of the impact of this "urban renewal" project on the low-income residents of that area, the reader is referred to Hartman's 1974 study of the Yerba Buena Center.) An optimistic view of the future prevails. The January 1972 issue of *Consulting Engineer* remarks that "since 1962, investors have put nearly $1 billion into planned new buildings, and there is more to come" (Cohen, 1972).

Land values in San Francisco have increased, but not as much as the "Toronto" myth would indicate. The actual Toronto experience seems to have been a 58 percent increase in assessments adjacent to the subway compared to a normal increase of 25 percent for the period 1952-62.[26] Increase in land values along BART lines seems to closely parallel the actual Toronto experience: a 5 percent annual increase near BART, 3 percent elsewhere (*SFC*, Feb. 11, 1973). It is not clear whether the increase in land values adjacent to BART stations represents a net social gain or whether this increase has been at the expense of other sites in the city or metropolitan area. In other words, BART may have merely redistributed growth instead of generating new growth. In this

[25] Wolfe, *The Bay Guardian*, June 18, 1968.

[26] *Transit in Toronto*, Toronto Transit Commission, rev. ed., 1971, p. 35. Quoted in Lewin (1974:20).

case, some property owners would have gained at the expense of others. In spite of this, the Institute of Urban and Regional Development reports that "BART has undoubtedly triggered a speculative environment in the land market of the region."[27] The general manager of the Bay Area Council, Anthony Siracusa, agrees, telling me that "right after the bond issue was passed, there was a great deal of speculation in land."

In sum, it has been shown that there was widespread expectation within the business community that BART would help the urban area to grow, particularly San Francisco's central business district. Business leaders in turn made decisions that did produce growth. It is a moot point as to whether BART "caused" this growth. One could as easily argue, for example, that BART and the building "boom" were both the consequence of the favorable and expectant attitudes of business leaders toward the attainment of urban growth: BART and many of the high-rises, in fact, were being built simultaneously.

The central question, however, is not whether BART itself caused growth. Rather, the point is that BART was designed primarily to serve the goal of city growth and to defend property investments in the central city. Mass transit systems such as BART are not the only means of promoting growth and defending business interests in the central city. Historically in the United States, other forms of transportation such as marine harbors and ports, railroads, airports, and highways have been used too. The BAC had noted the importance of other forms of transportation in its initial meeting in 1944. Through the ensuing years, the BAC has been a major backer of the development of harbor facilities, airports, bridges, and highways in the Bay Area (Sundeen, 1963:143-69). BART was not seen as a substitute for those other facilities, nor was it planned to be such. One of BART's chief planners was Louis W. Riggs, president of Tudor Engineering Company (a member of PBTB). Riggs certainly does not envision BART as a significant challenge to the automobile. In an address to an engineering group, he predicted: "Automobile traffic will con-

[27] Institute of Urban and Regional Development, *Econometric Studies*, vol. I, pt. III, p. 48. Quoted in Lewin (1974:20).

tinue to grow here, as the result of the very nature of metropolitan development in an automobile age. . . . So we will continue to need *massive highway construction* and street improvement programs'' (emphasis added). More significantly, Riggs' assessment matches that of the Bay Area Metropolitan Transportation Commission (MTC), a group created by the California Legislature in 1970 to study transportation needs in the area. In 1973, the MTC produced its *Regional Transportation Plan* calling for both new freeways and improved transit service. In the Summary of the Draft Environmental Impact Report on that plan, the MTC notes, "The Regional Transportation Plan [including BART] will not seriously change the dominance of the automobile" (Metropolitan Transportation Commission, 1973:13).

Not only does BART not challenge the automobile, it may even encourage automobile usage. Rothschild notes that "most of the transit systems being planned [in the U.S.] *support* the present pattern of highway transportation: *they make it easier to own an automobile.* . . . They will make the commuting journey from suburb to office to suburb easier and more pleasant. They will serve inevitably to encourage the creation of more and further distant suburban dormitories, and to reinforce a pattern of urban development and land-use based on a general use of automobiles" (emphasis added; Rothschild, 1972:28). The MTC report admits that the current Bay Area transportation plan will cause urban development "to continue in the old pattern: broader and broader commuter suburbs, denser and denser high-rise office centers" (MTC, 1973:9).

Another reason that systems such as BART will not challenge the automobile is that they may cause just enough improvement in highway traffic flow to permit more intensive use of roads. This was the argument, at least, that former Secretary of Transportation John Volpe used before the Automobile Manufacturers Association. Transit, Volpe said, might help to unclog roads, adding, "there's not much . . . hope of expanding your sales if the average motorist looks upon driving as a chore rather than as efficient, pleasant means of transportation" (*Wall Street Journal*, June 24, 1970:32). The same argument about traffic reduction had been used some years before by Kenneth D. Lawson, a spokesman for the Ranchers Exploration and Development Corporation. Discussing the economic benefits of BART, he said: "The large diversions of automobile passengers to Rapid Transit at the choked traffic gateways will also permit freer flowing and faster moving automobile travel along the major arteries." The major planning document for BART, *The Composite Report (CR)*, states that "The State Department of Public Works also has indicated that *efficient operation of its freeways* will depend on the reinvigoration of interurban transit in the Bay Area" (emphasis added; *CR*, p. 80). Earlier, the Regional Rapid Transit report had assumed the continued growth of roads and cars in the Bay Area, noting that "1990 may well be the date when every garage will be outfitted with two cars" (*RRT*, p. 18). It was specifically acknowledged that BART was "intended to operate as a *complement* to a system of freeways, expressways, and arterial highways in an area where automobile ownership per capita is very high (emphasis added; *RRT*, p. 69). Whether or not this hope for traffic reduction is reasonable (and there is evidence that it is not, as will shortly be pointed out), such statements certainly do not assume antagonism between transit and autos.

Another reason that BART does not challenge the automobile lies in the number and kind of people that the system will serve. The nature of this service also involves the issue of social equity.

It is doubtful that BART can really be called a "mass" transportation system, for it was designed to serve a special clientele. After observing the exhibits at Transpo '72, Rothschild commented on the elite nature of the new rapid transit systems: "Public transportation could be used to redistribute wealth and opportunity, and to redesign cities. But the suburban tramlines as conceived at Transpo would not be likely to have this effect. . . . The message is: Mass tramlines can be profitable—when they are installed for the benefit of people whose time and psychic virility have a high dollar value" (Rothschild, 1972:28).

BART is essentially a radial, interurban railway system that links the suburbs and outlying towns with downtown San Francisco. Such a system does not adequately serve the urban travel needs of most people, especially lower-income, minority, and working people. Let us see why this is so.

Writing in the mid-1960s, Meyer et al. point out that radial commuting patterns are increasingly less important: "Another important postwar phenomenon is the increasing prevalence of cross-haul [across outlying areas of the city] and reverse commuter [from central city outward in the morning, from suburb to center in afternoon] trip patterns in urban areas to the point where non-CBD trips are now more than twice as numerous as those to and from the CBD. . . . The CBD-oriented, corridor pattern remains important only in a few of the largest cities, notably New York, and even then accounts for far less than a majority of regional trips" (Meyer et al., 1965:361-62). A disproportionate amount of the cross-hauling and reverse commuting is accounted for by low-income (often black) workers who live in ghettos near the central business district, or who live in segregated pockets of the city and must get to other suburban areas where many of their jobs (in construction, industry, etc.) are located (Meyer, et al. 1965:166-67). A radial system like BART is of little benefit to these people, because cross-haul needs are not served and because radial lines are spaced more widely as they approach the edges of the city, often making access to suburban work sites difficult. Moreover, much of the transit demand of low-income people is local. "In general, users of high-speed, long-distance rail commuter systems are among the wealthier classes of society" (Kain and Meyer, 1970:81). The poor rely disproportionately on local, downtown bus systems and, ironically, on expensive taxicabs (Kain and Meyer, 1970:81). An interurban rail system does not serve these local transit functions.

Professor James Vance, of the Geography Department at Berkeley, speaking to me of the basis of his opposition to the BART proposal, said: "This was an exceedingly selfish proposal. It was basically a proposal to spend a great deal of money to provide a high-class commuting system for . . . that minute fraction of the population that were in . . . administrative and fiscal activities in downtown San Francisco. . . . It didn't provide useful transportation in minor parts of the city." Despite the avowals of BART officials that the system would be of service to low-income people, BART does not go near the largest black ghetto in San Francisco, Hunter's Point. On the other hand, small, upper-middle class, suburban communities such as Orinda and Lafayette have BART stations. These well-to-do commuters are well-served by BART. As Wohl comments: "Downtown is increasingly becoming the headquarters for the more prosperous workers, and it seems that BART was especially designed to serve these workers, not the poor who probably need it most, and not the masses who represent the bulk of San Francisco's and Oakland's population."[28] Speaking of the effects of the Regional Transportation Plan (including highways and BART), the MTC concludes, "The system will continue to give the best service to the people who have the advantage already: car-owners, commuters, the affluent, suburbanites" (MTC, 1973:10).

Not only does the design of BART mean that most of the public will not be served, but the system is financed in such a way as to cause those very people who will derive the least benefit from BART to bear a disproportionate share of the costs of constructing and operating BART. The system is supported by a property tax within the three-county district. In addition, when BART ran into financial difficulties in the late 1960s, the California legislature (at the urging of San Francisco business leaders, such as a Wells Fargo executive I interviewed) voted a one-half cent sales tax in the district to subsidize BART (Bazell, 1971:1128). Both property and sales taxes are widely recognized as being heavily regressive (e.g., Hunt and Sherman, 1972:145), meaning that the poor pay more than their share to support the system.

A system that does not serve the bulk of automobile users cannot effectively solve the problem of traffic congestion. When BART opened its transbay service on 16 September 1974, officials on the Bay Bridge between Oakland and San Francisco reported that they could see no effects on Bay Bridge traffic levels, but AC Transit and Greyhound (transit companies that operate buses across the Bridge) reported reductions in their business (*SFC*, Sept. 17, 1974:5). A later report by the state Department of Transportation confirms this: BART has taken only about 6 percent of the daily vehicular traffic off the Bay Bridge. Moreover, 75 percent of BART riders have switched from another form of transit, buses.

[28] Quoted in Wolfe, *The Bay Guardian*, November 1, 1968, p. 12.

Thus, only 25 percent of BART's users had formerly commuted in automobiles (*LAT*, Oct. 6, 1974:2). This is a far cry from the estimate in the *Composite Report* that "61 percent would be diverted from automobiles" in 1975 (*CR*, p. 81). The general manager of the Bay Area Council conceded to me that BART is "not going to take traffic off the Bay Bridge," saying that the bridge will always be at capacity. Anthony Downs' Law of Peak-Hour Traffic Congestion states that additional highway construction cannot solve traffic congestion since auto ownership far exceeds highway capacity. Any marginal, short-term reduction in traffic on a highway merely encourages others to drive that route in the future. Soon, both the old highway and the new are operating at above capacity (Downs, 1970:189). The same reasoning applies to BART's effects on major traffic arteries in the Bay Area: BART will allow more people from suburban areas to ride transit and to drive, filling roads to capacity once again. Total traffic will likely increase. But traffic reduction was never the primary goal of BART. As we have seen, this symbolic goal may have attracted voters to support bonds for BART, but those who first conceived and implemented BART had more material goals in mind.

CONCLUSION

BART will not challenge the dominance of the private automobile, for it was not designed to do so. BART will not increase the mobility of the poor and thus help to redistribute life chances, for it was not designed to do so. BART was the creation of the large businesses in downtown San Francisco, and the principal aim of these businesses—in addition to supplementing the auto-highway system with an elite commuting system between San Francisco and its suburbs—was to promote urban development in predictable and profitable ways and to defend property values in the central city. The influence of such prestigious and powerful business groups as the Bay Area Council and the Blyth-Zellerbach Committee was evident at all stages of BART's development. Not only did they initiate the early transit studies that eventually led to

BART, they also played leading roles in getting BART approved by the voters.

There was even involvement in the construction of BART. One of the most prominent members of the BAC, in fact its president during the time of the BART campaign, was Stephen D. Bechtel, head of the largest construction company in the world, the Bechtel Corporation. The Bechtel Corporation was one of the three joint venture firms that designed BART. There is evidence that Bechtel Corporation exercised more influence than the other two firms in the BART decision-making process, and perhaps even more than the official BART board of directors itself.

In July 1972, the members of the Bay Area delegation to the California legislature asked the office of the California legislative analyst, A. Alan Post, to conduct an investigation of BART. The system had been plagued with technical problems, delays, questions about management capabilities, and financial difficulties. The legislative analyst conducted extensive investigations into the operations of BART and produced a series of three reports during the next two years. The final report concluded that, although the construction of the system was formally under the supervision of the public officials of the Bay Area Rapid Transit District board and management, there was really very little public control of the process:

> We firmly believe that in large measure the problems are attributable to *controllable* factors which were and continue to be the responsibility of the district Board of Directors and district management.
>
> In our review of the district's administration during the past two years we have concluded that nearly every aspect of the district's administration, from contract design, contract award and contract supervision to the daily management of operations and maintenance, has suffered from *a lack of direction and control on the part of the board and management* (emphasis added).[29]

[29] *Analysis of BART's Operational Problems and Fiscal Deficits, with Recommendations for Corrective Action*, Legislative Analyst (State of California, March 19, 1974), p. i.

The roots of this lack of public control over BART go back to 1962 when the district board decided to hire private engineering firms to design the system, instead of putting together an "in-house" engineering staff to do the job. Rather, the joint venture firms (PBTB) were given the job. James Cooney, a principal author of the legislative analysts' reports on BART, told me that investigations showed that PBTB was given a contract that "virtually tells them to design the system, let the major contracts, and to supervise the system." PBTB, said Cooney, had been formed by Bechtel Corporation, and "BART through the years totally relied on Bechtel to do everything . . . Bechtel took more and more control . . . over what was going on." Private control displaced public control.

Contracts with private subcontractors were often written by PBTB on a "cost-plus" basis that provided no incentive for economizing. There were massive "cost overruns," loosely written contracts, and technical failures. PBTB (which had contributed money to the BART bond campaign) started out in 1962 with a contract to manage the system, the contract then estimated to ultimately cost $56.3 million. By late 1972, the cost of that contract was estimated to have risen to $142 million, a 152 percent increase.[30] Total cost for the BART system was projected to be approximately $1.5 billion, a 50 percent increase over the *Composite Report* estimate (Lewin, 1974:17).

The story of BART's numerous financial, technical, safety, and managerial problems would itself constitute a separate chapter. Suffice it to say, there is abundant evidence that private engineering interests (especially Bechtel) virtually captured the BART design and construction process, and that this lack of public control played a crucial part in the generation of the system's problems. The decision of the BART board to allow private firms to manage the system also extended the influence of members of such business groups as the Bay Area Council directly into the "nuts-and-bolts" of BART's design and construction.

It is too early to yet decide with certainty which of the three

[30] *Investigation of the Operations of the Bay Area Rapid Transit District with Particular Reference to Safety and Contract Administration*, Legislative Analyst (State of California, November 9, 1972), pp. 53-54.

political models presented in Chapter One is best supported by the issue-area of urban transportation. The BART case is only one of the five cases we shall be examining, and we shall want to reserve the bulk of the theoretical analysis for the overall pattern of political behavior observed in the five campaigns taken as a whole. Nevertheless, it is possible to make some preliminary observations. As of this point, there appears to be some support for both elitist and pluralist hypotheses. The dominant role in the creation of BART was clearly played by large corporations headquartered mostly in downtown San Francisco. The overriding goal was the promotion of central city development. BAC companies had planned for a system like BART for at least thirty years. I have also argued that the outcome of the BART campaign favored the interests of such businesses more than it favored other groups, such as taxpayers, minority populations, smaller business in areas outside San Francisco, or the majority of workday commuters. The involvement of the state government in passing the special legislation to allow the BART proposal to be put before voters appears to have been at the behest of the dominant San Francisco companies. Nor is it reasonable to see the companies that supported BART as constituting an effective countervailing force to automotive interests since BART was not designed to challenge the private automobile. The aims of the Bay Area Council companies were largely unopposed and seemingly carried the day.

On the other hand, pro-BART forces were not able to achieve all they may have desired. The plans for BART had to be cut back somewhat when two Bay Area counties (San Mateo and Marin) dropped out of the district. This defection was presumably due to the perception of elites and taxpayers in those counties that San Francisco would be the main beneficiary of BART, that the system was not of the best technical design, and that local taxes would go up. Moreover, although the BART bond issue did pass at the polls, the election was close and voters in a number of counties did reject the measure (even though it made no actual difference in the overall result of the district-wide election). The persuasive power of elites in San Francisco apparently was not without limits.

The case of BART does not therefore provide unequivocal

support for either the pluralist or elitist model. However, in light of the above considerations, an elitist interpretation would seem to be the better one. Elites were generally unified and they did win. The examination of the remaining four cases will provide more evidence and insights and will allow a fuller assessment of the political models.

The successful BART campaign was important far beyond California. It set an example that was to be tried by other cities across the United States, including Los Angeles, Washington, and Atlanta. During the late 1960s and early 1970s, business elites, transit planners, and urban officials began to talk in increasingly enthusiastic terms about their visions of sleek, automated, expensive, new urban transportation systems. It appeared, in the words of Institute for Rapid Transit President Ronan, that the United States was experiencing a "transit renaissance" that would mark a "new beginning" in urban transportation history. Los Angeles came up with one of the first and most ambitious of the post-BART plans. In what ways was the Los Angeles' plan similar to BART? What groups initiated and supported the plan? What were their goals? What can the Los Angeles case add to our understanding of the political forces and alignments that determined the direction and shape of the urban transit resurgence? These questions are taken up in the following chapter.

CHAPTER THREE

TRYING TO EMULATE BART:
THE LOS ANGELES CAMPAIGNS

> Rapid Transit may prove to be of considerable benefit in
> attracting new industries into the local area. It would be of
> particular value to firms of a "headquarters" nature which
> would locate in the Central area and require efficient trans-
> portation to suburban residential areas. The development
> of transit in Los Angeles would offset any competitive posi-
> tion San Francisco might have as a result of the inaugura-
> tion of BARTD.
> —Citizens Advisory Council on Public Transportation

The example of BART in Northern California was not lost on
elites in Southern California. There was concern in the Los Angeles region that the system might produce an advantage for San
Francisco in the competition for growth between the two largest
metropolitan areas in the state. There was a surge of interest in
building a similar system. Six years after the BART bond issue
was passed, Los Angeles made an attempt to develop a transit
system much like BART. Proposition A was presented to Los
Angeles County voters on November 5, 1968. The campaign for
that measure reveals, as in the BART case, heavy support for rail
transit by centrally located Los Angeles businesses. I shall argue
that here too the overriding goal of these large businesses was the
attainment of urban growth. Essentially the same pattern was to
be repeated in 1974, when a similar Proposition A was submitted
to Los Angeles' voters.

KING OF THE ROAD

Compared with the San Francisco Bay Area, Los Angeles is a
more dispersed urban area. Spread out over roughly a thirty-mile

radius around the downtown area are seventy-eight cities in Los Angeles County alone (Lamare, 1973:110). Los Angeles thus has no geographically determined "transportation corridors" and its central business district is not as compact or well-defined as that of San Francisco. For these reasons, private automobiles are usually thought to be the "natural" and inevitable means of transportation in Los Angeles. Yet, astoundingly enough, during the 1920s, 1930s, and most of the 1940s, the area had an extensive and effective rail transit system that played a very important role in the development of the region. Reaching maximum extent in 1926 with 1,164 miles of track, the "Big Red Cars" of the Pacific Electric Railway ran from Santa Monica to San Bernardino and from Balboa to San Fernando (Crump, 1962:163). The coming of the automobile to Southern California gradually reduced the interurban efficiency not only through direct competition for passengers, but through significantly increased transit times due to the burgeoning number of automobile rights-of-way across tracks. Cars were given priority over trains! According to Crump, "In the 1920's it was becoming increasingly obvious that the electric urbans would be doomed unless steps were taken to go over—or under—the automobile traffic" (Crump, 1962:147). General Motors et al. took over in 1944 when the system was sold to GM's National City Lines. The name was changed to Los Angeles Transit Lines, and conversion to buses began (Crump, 1962:94).

Thus, the region's electric transit system was being dismantled simultaneously with, or slightly before, the post-war burgeoning of private automobile ownership and early freeway construction. Today, the Los Angeles metropolitan area is criss-crossed with many miles of freeways and the pattern of land use has been largely determined by automobile transportation. Los Angeles County has the largest concentration of automobiles of any comparable area in the world, the automobile population having grown in the post-World War II period more rapidly than the human population. In 1967, a study reported that "there are currently more motor vehicles in . . . [Los Angeles] County than in any state in the Union with the exception of New York, Illinois, Ohio, Pennsylvania, and Texas."[1] This extreme dominance by the au-

[1] *Improving Public Transportation in Los Angeles: A Report to the Community*

tomobile and the dispersion of population in the Los Angeles Basin has made it difficult for transit advocates to generate a convincing case for creating a new public transportation system (particularly a rail system) in Los Angeles. Most authorities in the transit field maintain that relatively high population densities are required to justify a rail system (e.g., Meyer et al., 1965:364). Lack of sufficient density and devotion to a life style based on the private automobile (e.g., Lamare, 1973) have been used by transit critics (including the highway lobby) to argue against such rail systems in Los Angeles. The debate over the merits of rapid transit for Los Angeles has been going on for a long time: *Railway Age* recently reported that "Los Angeles is a Sargasso sea of rapid transit proposals; 19 plans have been proposed and abandoned since 1925" (Kizzia, 1974:30). This chapter will examine the two most recent proposals, proposals that are different from the earlier ones in a crucial way: they make it possible for the researcher to determine directly the nature of support and opposition to rapid transit in Los Angeles. These two proposals (unlike the former ones) were ballot propositions that entailed political campaigns. As a result, lists of contributors for and against these two measures are available in the files of the California Secretary of State.

BACKGROUND ON TRANSIT

As in San Francisco and most cities, the Los Angeles business community has long been active in transportation matters. In 1947, for example, the Los Angeles Chamber of Commerce was congratulating itself on its role in getting the California legislature to increase gasoline taxes and to expand the Los Angeles "freeway" (a new word then) system. Although the thrust of the group's efforts was obviously toward highways, it was remarked in passing by the chamber's Metropolitan Traffic and Transit Committee in a 1947 publication that "expressways alone will not solve Los Angeles' traffic problems without adequate off-street parking and mass transportation." What was meant by "mass transportation"

on Public Transportation, Citizens Advisory Council on Public Transportation, July 25, 1967, pp. 24-25 (hereafter referred to as *IPT*).

was not revealed, but this reference is perhaps to be taken with a grain of salt since at the time it was written National City Lines was being allowed to essentially dismantle the Pacific Electric Railway.

A later sign of more substantial business concern with the issue of public transportation came in 1967. At the initiation of the Los Angeles Chamber of Commerce, a Citizens Advisory Council on Public Transportation was organized in 1965. The council was composed overwhelmingly of businessmen (fifty out of sixty-four, or 78 percent) and included representatives of some of the largest businesses in Los Angeles (e.g., Southern Pacific, General Dynamics, Occidental Life Insurance, etc.; *Improving Public Transportation in Los Angeles*: VI-VII). During the next twenty months, the council looked into the question of rapid transit for Los Angeles. In 1967, the group presented its report, *Improving Public Transportation in Los Angeles* (*IPT*). The conclusion was that the county needed "a new rapid transit system" to "*supplement* the motor vehicle system [emphasis added]" (*IPT*:5). Los Angeles, the document observes, has an "excellent network of freeways," but the system is inadequate to handle peak hour traffic congestion (*IPT*:6). The major benefits to be derived from the construction of a rapid transit system are seen to be: greater mobility for the populace, increased land values, reduced traffic congestion, and improved tax base (due to "improved mobility and greater urban capacity").

The anticipated increase in property values is given particular emphasis. As in the BART case, the "Toronto" experience is referred to, although here the claims are more moderate: "Another significant beneficiary of the new system would be the property owner. The property owner in the vicinity of the stations would benefit directly. Based on actual experience in Toronto and emerging patterns in San Francisco, property values in the vicinity of the stations can be expected to increase as much as 100% or more as a result of proximity to transit" (*IPT*:11). It is maintained that property values would be "enhanced materially," particularly in "Downtown Los Angeles, Beverly Hills, mid-Wilshire, and Century City." "In some cases," the report dramatically states, "such as Downtown Los Angeles and mid-Wilshire, rapid transit may mean *the difference between sound economic growth and ultimate stagnation"* (emphasis added; *IPT*:94).

Centralization is also a dominant theme. It is pointed out that the "Central area [extending from near Santa Monica to downtown Los Angeles] is expected to continue to have the greatest population density and employment concentration of any area [in the region] by 1980. Since there will be a surplus of jobs over workers in the Central area, that area will continue to be a labor 'import' area, requiring commuting facilities" (*IPT*:20-21). This growth of centralized employment will be the result of construction in the area. It is noted that: "of total 'high-rise' construction between 1960 and 1965 approximately 42 percent was built in the Central area, primarily along the Wilshire 'corridor' between Santa Monica and Downtown Los Angeles. Over 40 new high-rise structures have been built in this corridor since 1960" (*IPT*:22). As in the San Francisco case, a high rise future is projected for the central area: "High rise construction activity . . . is expected to continue *a strong tendency toward centralization* particularly in Downtown Los Angeles and Century City" (emphasis added; *IPT*:24). Mass transit is seen as a means of making this projection become a reality.

In addition to the emphasis on rising land values and urban development, there is another similarity with the BART planning documents: it is clear that the new mass transit system will not challenge the dominance of the automobile. In the words of the report, "The major transportation facility serving these emerging growth trends at present and in the foreseeable future is the private motor vehicle 'system' " (*IPT*:24). The purpose of transit, the report states again and again, is to "supplement" the automobile. This is particularly necessary in the central area, where "the most severe peak hour congestion occurs on freeways leading to and from Downtown Los Angeles" (*IPT*:36).

The council proposes a rail system similar to BART. The system would run from West Los Angeles to El Monte, and from Van Nuys to Long Beach, with trunk connections in downtown Los Angeles and the mid-Wilshire area (*IPT*:80-89).

It is apparent, however, that the council was in favor of the market mechanism, not in favor of operating subsidies for the new system. The report states: "The Council believes that the full burden of these [maintenance and operating] costs should fall on the transit user. The Council believes that there is no intrinsic community 'good' to be served in keeping transit fares artificially low for social and political reasons" (*IPT*:97). Moreover, development costs of the system are to be met by the "community" through a "multi-burden taxation program" (e.g., property taxes, sales taxes, motor vehicle taxes, etc.) to be worked out by the state legislature (*IPT*:102).

This explicit rejection by the council of operating subsidies appears to be a disavowal of the findings two years before of the Watts Riot Commission. The riot commission had concluded that lack of adequate public transportation was an important source of social disadvantage and frustration for people in the Watts area. Recommendations were made by the commission for improved transit services and for public subsidization of transit (i.e., bus) lines.[2] This rejection by the transit planners of the subsidy principle may indicate the accuracy of a statement by Asa Call, the author of that part of the Riot Commission's report dealing with transit. Until his recent death, Call was one of the most prominent businessmen in Los Angeles. When I asked him about the impact of the report's transit recommendations on the Los Angeles business community, he responded, "They didn't pay much attention to it."

In sum, it is clear from this planning document, put together under the supervision of businessmen, that a principal benefit of the proposed transit system was its presumed ability to nurture the tendency toward centralized urban development. The system was seen as a way of raising land values and increasing the accessibility of large financial and administrative businesses in the central area in such a way as to encourage the centralized expansion of these functions. It is also clear that rapid transit was not seen as a challenge to the auto-highway system. Once again, there was not to be a zero-sum game between automobiles and public transit. The parallels to the BART case are obvious.

---

[2] *Violence in the City—An End or a Beginning?* Report by the Governor's Commission on the Los Angeles Riots, December 2, 1965, pp. 65-68.

THE CAMPAIGNS

The Los Angeles business community shared these attitudes of the planners. Key business leaders who involved themselves in the transit campaign expressed such ideas. Most importantly, the campaign contributions for the ballot measures came largely from big businesses in the central area of Los Angeles.

The first ballot measure with which Los Angeles voters were presented was being prepared by the Southern California Rapid Transit District (SCRTD) at the same time that the Citizens Advisory Council was producing its report on transit. The SCRTD proposal (Proposition A of November 1968, as it later was designated) was to construct a rail and feeder bus system for the Los Angeles area. It was to be more extensive and more expensive than BART. The bulk of the proposal was an eighty-nine-mile combination subway, surface, and elevated rail system. The rails were to be arranged in five corridors, running from Reseda to Long Beach, and from Westwood to El Monte. An additional line was to connect the Los Angeles Airport with downtown. Major cross-connections were to be located downtown and at mid-Wilshire, areas where the most growth was anticipated.

The SCRTD plan was quite similar to the Citizens Advisory Council proposal, but there was one important difference: while the council had proposed a "multi-burden taxation program," the SCRTD plan was to be financed by only one method: the imposition of a one-half cent sales tax in Los Angeles County—a tax that was to run for a period of forty-eight years. Total of cost of the system was to be $5 billion, or more than five times the planned cost of BART (*LAT*, Nov. 6, 1968:3).

It is not clear why the SCRTD decided to rely solely on a sales tax to support the new system. In San Francisco, the BART plan had originally utilized a property tax, although sales tax financing was added later. There may have been objections to a property tax by large property owners in Los Angeles, or from property owners whose buildings would not be near transit stations. The council had, in fact, evidenced sensitivity to the latter issue in their report. They had advocated a system of property taxation that would affect only such property holders who held property within hypothetical "Transit Benefit Districts" surrounding transit stops (*IPT*:99). One of the originators of the sales tax idea was both a director of the SCRTD and an executive of Southern California Edison Company (the electric utility). In an interview, he stated: "We really developed the idea that you couldn't finance it out of the property tax and so the only viable means of financing was a special levy on the sales tax to be dedicated to transportation in general so that the northern cow counties could—or the rural counties—could spend money on grade separation, bridges, and road improvement, and we could use it in this area for a balanced urban transportation system." Whatever the reason for choosing the sales tax, the result would be that everyone (including the poor and propertyless) in the district would pay, not just property holders near transit stations. Thus, the plan was even more economically regressive than a property tax.

The SCRTD unveiled its transit plan in May 1968, and it was placed on the November ballot. A Citizens Committee for Rapid Transit was organized to support the measure. There were close ties between the committee and the Citizens Advisory Council. The committee finance chairman, Earl Clark, president of Occidental Life Insurance Company, had been a member of the Citizens Advisory Council on Public Transportation. The general chairman of the group, Ernest J. Loebbecke, was also chairman and chief executive officer of Title Insurance and Trust Company, like Occidental located in downtown Los Angeles. Loebbecke acknowledges that the Los Angeles Chamber of Commerce was the "moving force" behind the creation of the committee. Loebbecke had been active as a fund-raiser (e.g., United Way founding president, American Red Cross, etc.) and is a well-known businessman in Los Angeles, having been western regional president of the United States Chamber of Commerce, and president of the California chamber. In addition, his connection with Title Insurance and Trust Company played a part in his selection to head the campaign for the transit issue. "We feel," Loebbecke told me, "as a downtown business that's here and are trying to anchor the central city, that . . . public transportation is an important thing." Like other businessmen, he sees a relation between lack of transit and the decay of downtown Los Angeles: "There's tremendous waste of valuable property, there's tremendous waste of time, there are tremendous wastes of resources by areas which have gone down hill and which can never be built up unless there's a public transportation system again.''

Loebbecke and Clark conducted a media campaign in an attempt to convince voters to approve Proposition A. As in the BART campaign, relief of traffic congestion was presented as the prime benefit of rapid transit. The ads also show clearly that transit was not to be an alternative to the auto, but an aid. The new system would take ''at least a half million cars off our roads,'' making more room for *automobile drivers*, and would ''return . . . our streets and freeways to a normal flow'' (*LAT*, Nov. 3, 1968:A-15). Transit, in other words, was portrayed as something for the ''other guy'' to ride. One business executive who was very active in the campaign for Proposition A, admitted to me that he himself probably would not use mass transit. Publicly, the Los Angeles voter was essentially being asked to pay to get some of the other people off the streets; privately, it was hoped that he or she would, in essence, pay for an ''urban redevelopment'' plan to promote growth in the central business district.

Loebbecke and Clark approached the Los Angeles business community and other groups for contributions. They were very successful. Analysis of campaign contribution lists on file with the county clerk of Los Angeles indicates that they collected $458,612.50. Of this, an overwhelming 85.6 percent ($392,635) came from business. The remaining 14.4 percent was contributed by labor unions and individuals.

Of the amount contributed by business, general industrial corporations—a broad category—were the largest contributors with 28.3 percent; followed by insurance companies (12.6 percent); oil companies (10.9 percent); and banks (6.4 percent). Not surprisingly, there is a strong tendency for business contributions to come from the central area of Los Angeles. That is where, by and large, the administrative and financial functions of big business are located. As can be seen from the following Postal Zip Code map (Figure 1) the indicated zip code zones are roughly definitive of the Citizens Advisory Council's ''Central area'' of Los Angeles. Almost two-thirds ($249,585 or 63.3 percent) of all business contributions came from firms that had headquarters in this area. Indeed, as the downtown area is approached, the pattern becomes even more concentrated: almost half (46.6 percent) of the money came from five central zip code zones (i.e., 90005, 90010, 90015, 90014, and 90017), with more than one-fourth (29.4 percent) coming from one small zone (90017) in the heart of downtown.

Campaign contributions for Proposition A of 1968, then, came overwhelmingly from business (85.6 percent) and exhibited a great tendency to come from the central area of the city (63.6 percent), roughly that area lying between downtown and Century City (i.e., the "Wilshire Corridor"). As in San Francisco, it was once again the large, centrally located businesses (e.g., Pacific Telephone and Telegraph Company, Westinghouse Electric Corporation, Travelers Insurance, Shell Oil, etc.) that indicated, through their contributions, major support for rapid transit development.

There was some opposition to Proposition A, but it was minimal. A small group of people formed Taxpayers Against Transit Measure A. They ran an ad or two in local newspapers stressing the great cost of the system, saying that benefits would not be sufficient to justify it. Subsidies needed to operate the system would mean new taxes and would primarily serve downtown commuters (*LAT*, Nov. 1, 1968: II-4). The chairman of the group was Mel Pierovich, a Los Angeles lawyer. Apparently, Pierovich himself was the main actor in the creation of the committee. He told me that he felt that public rail transportation in Los Angeles would be a waste of money, because of the commitment of people to "individual, private transportation." The system would be "an economic disaster" because no one would use it. Pierovich anticipated, not surprisingly, that his position would find support from elements of the highway lobby, notably the oil companies. He contacted the major oil companies and automobile dealers in Los Angeles. Interestingly enough, he got little support for his position, and none at all from the oil companies. Pierovich believes that the oil companies did not support his anti-Proposition A stand because they have office buildings downtown and expected property values there to increase. In his words, they are also "carrying water on both shoulders" (i.e., supporting both

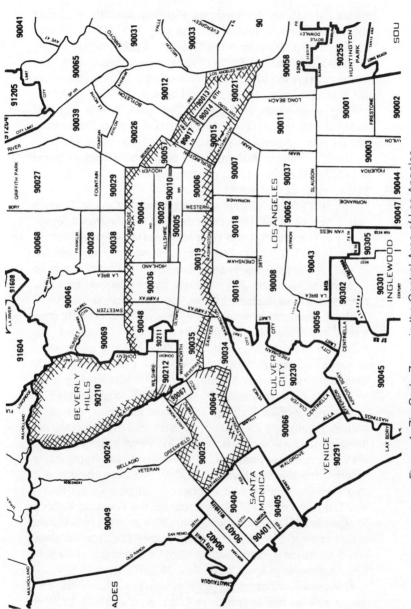

Figure 1. Zip Code Zones in the Central Area of Los Angeles.

transit and highway development). Pierovich was able, according to his campaign statement, to raise only $25,000, the money coming from a car dealer, a rental agency, a public relations firm, an individual, and one $7,500 "anonymous" contribution. The anonymous contribution, Pierovich conceded, actually came from the head of a large cement firm in Los Angeles.

Proposition A was put to a vote on November 5, 1968. It needed to secure a 60 percent favorable vote in order to pass. The measure fell far short of passage, getting only 44.7 percent (*LAT*, Nov. 7, 1968:3). Thus, with almost half a million dollars behind it and only $25,000 against it, the measure still failed to gain approval by Los Angeles area voters.

The SCRTD immediately announced that they would try again with a new proposal, saying that they felt that the reason for the failure of Proposition A was voter resistance to a sales tax increase (*LAT*, Nov. 7, 1968:3). This assessment was probably correct. In fact, it was to be six years before another proposal would be presented to the voters. In the interim, business support for a new rapid transit system seemed to become even stronger.

The feeling was growing among business leaders that mass transit was needed in order to make possible the continued centralization of business growth. The office building construction in the central area that the Citizens Advisory Council on Public Transportation had noted during the 1960s continued into the 1970s. For example, during the years 1971 through early 1975, fifty-four new office buildings (of at least six stories) with 18.9 million square feet of space were built in Los Angeles (i.e., downtown, mid-Wilshire, Beverly Hills, Westwood, Brentwood, West Los Angeles, Century City, Hollywood, the airport, Santa Monica, and the San Fernando Valley). This construction was overwhelmingly in the central area (i.e., all areas except Hollywood, the airport, Santa Monica, and the San Fernando Valley): 75.9 percent (41) of the buildings with 87.8 percent (16.6 million square feet) of the office space. Downtown Los Angeles alone was the location of more than one-third (35.5 percent) of the new Los Angeles office space (*LAT*, Jan. 26, 1975:1).

This centralized expansion of administrative office space presented at least one important problem. Starting about 1970, it became clear that construction was creating new space faster than it could be rented. Rapid transit was again seen as a solution. The Real Estate section of the *Los Angeles Times* noted that "growing vacancy rates in office buildings, some retail sales stagnation and poor hotel business [along Wilshire Boulevard] are . . . helping to develop rapid transit supporters." With vacancy rates at around 25 percent on Wilshire, office managers were reported to believe that rapid transit would be a "shot in the arm" (*LAT*, Nov. 19, 1972:G-1). The final article of the three-part series on the subject of Wilshire Boulevard was headed "Subway Could Boost Values: Wilshire Blvd. Line Seen As Spur to Growth." It concluded that *"the greatest single group of private property beneficiaries [of a new subway] will probably be downtown Los Angeles interests—*investors in office buildings, stores, and currently underutilized land" (emphasis added; *LAT*, Dec. 3, 1972:G-1).

There were important people in the business community who also believed that transit would benefit office buildings. "If it were more convenient [to get around] then you'd make it easier for people who own office buildings to rent them," I was informed by Neil Petree, the honorary chairman of Barker Associated Companies in Los Angeles. Petree is one of the most prominent business leaders in Los Angeles; he serves on the board of several large firms (e.g., Pacific Mutual Life Insurance Company, Investment Company of America, Pacific Lighting Company) and has been active in business and community affairs for a long time. In 1945 he was the chairman of a Los Angeles Chamber of Commerce committee that had a great deal to do with getting the California legislature to approve construction of the Los Angeles freeway system. After serving as president of the Automobile Club of Southern California, he was appointed to the Los Angeles City Planning Commission by Mayor Yorty in 1971 (*LAT*, July 14, 1971:1). He is currently a member of the Los Angeles "Committee of 25," an elite group of Los Angeles businessmen who meet to discuss—in Petree's words—what seems to be the "principal problem in the city" at the time (*LAT*, Dec. 3, 1972:1). Noting that "we don't like publicity," Petree acknowledges that transportation has often been a topic of concern for the Committee of 25. He is now also a director of the Central City Development,

Inc., a planning group financed jointly by business and the city. Petree points out that the earlier Central City Association (a private group of downtown businesses) could have done the job of re-developing the downtown area with private funds, but it would have cost a great deal of money. As Petree observed to me, the creation of Central City Development was an effective way to induce government support: "Politically it was a good thing to go to the city and be able to say we're creating a non-profit corporation of the following people and we'll put up the money if you'll put up the money." One of the redevelopment goals is to "get rid of Skid Row." It is also envisaged that an additional rapid transit system will be built in the downtown area (perhaps a "people mover" system) to mesh with a SCRTD system.

This official government support for business goals in urban development is also evidenced in the general development plan for the Los Angeles area. The city planning commission created, and the city council recently approved, the "Centers Concept." The plan calls essentially for the promotion of current trends in Los Angeles growth. The idea is to encourage high-density de-velopment in such designated "centers" as downtown, Wilshire Boulevard, and Century City. Proponents maintain that this is the least costly alternative and that by directing growth to centralized areas around the transit stations, low-density development will be preserved in other areas: "Each center would include high-rise office buildings, hotels, theaters, restaurants and government of-fices arranged in a quarter-mile-radius core with a *rapid transit station*" (emphasis added; *LAT*, May 1, 1974:27). It is clear that such a plan, involving centralized growth and rapid transit, should meet with widespread business approval. Said one prominent ex-ecutive to me: "I read it and thought it was a great idea."

Molotch (1975:443) states that the "political power of the local interest groups that make up the [urban] growth machine is trans-lated by city governments into policies appropriate to their needs." The business-government partnership in Los Angeles illustrates this. The "Center Concept," the goals of Central City Devel-opment, Inc., and the aims of rapid transit advocates all converge on the notion of centralized patterns of urban growth. In turn, these plans are supported by urban renewal projects in the downtown area of Los Angeles. Since 1959, for example, a massive and controversial urban renewal program has been managed by the city's Community Redevelopment Agency (CRA). The Bunker Hill project was called "one of the nation's largest removal efforts" by the *Los Angeles Times* (July 29, 1973:II-1). It has resulted in the displacement of thousands of low-income residents. The *Times* (which has investments in the area) points out: "The plan then—as now—was to transform the Bunker Hill slum into a neighborhood of new super-blocks, each with its own high-rise office, hotel or apartment complex" (*LAT*, July 7, 1973:II-1). High density development in the area is well underway. A number of large buildings have already been built, including Union Bank, Security Pacific National Bank, and the Los Angeles World Trade Center (*LAT*, July 29, 1972:II-1). Others are being built or planned. One developer said, "Downtown Los Angeles is destined to be one of the great downtowns of the world (*LAT*, Sept. 19, 1974:II-1)." A *Times* editorial said that these plans constitute "something of an urban renaissance for Los Angeles (*LAT*, Sept. 24, 1974:II-4)." Mayor Bradley said that it represented a "new faith in Los Angeles—a rebuilding from the center for the city to remain vital" (*LAT*, Sept. 19, 1974:II-1).

Mayor Bradley had been elected in 1972. During his campaign, he had emphasized the need for Los Angeles to "escape urban decay facing Eastern cities" through a program of controlled growth, and made a strong pledge to work to get a transportation system for the city (*LAT*, July 4, 1974:23). The next transit campaign, Proposition A of 1974, gave him the opportunity to fulfill that pledge.

The SCRTD presented its second rapid transit plan to the voters on November 5, 1974. Probably the major reason for the six-year interval between the two plans is to be found in the structure of the SCRTD itself. Public policy in Los Angeles supports two of the goals of centrally located businesses: rail transit and growth. However, the SCRTD is structured in such a way as to make the expression of these goals problematic.

The SCRTD was created in 1964 by the California legislature. Its goal was to operate buses throughout the seventy-eight-city metropolitan region, and the directors are appointed by public officials over the entire region. By itself, Los Angeles has only two of the eleven representatives on the board. The diversity of the board has made it difficult for agreement to be reached on transit proposals; the agency has not been aggressive in transit matters. Much of this rather conservative attitude is undoubtedly due to the influence of communities and interests outside the central area of Los Angeles. As in San Francisco, there has been some opposition to rapid transit development centered in these areas. Part of this opposition comes from the realization that outlying areas will not benefit as much as the central city. Speaking of Bradley's campaign for rapid transit, one city official noted the conflict the issue provoked: "The rapid transit thing was the biggest mistake of his life. Businessmen in the [San Fernando] valley were livid, saying, 'It doesn't do anything for us; it does everything for the downtown business community' " (*LAT*, Dec. 24, 1974:II-1). Even posh Beverly Hills has opposed rail transit development in the Wilshire corridor. A spokesman for the Beverly Hills City Council told a meeting of the SCRTD board that the principal beneficiaries of the route running through Beverly Hills would be Century City and downtown. Beverly Hills is interested in rolling back densities and limiting growth, and is not in favor of "great expansion" along the Wilshire corridor, he said (*LAT*, June 7, 1974:3). Conflicts with central city goals are expressed on the SCRTD board. A former director of the SCRTD representing Los Angeles, and a Los Angeles business executive, when asked about problems of the SCRTD, said with feeling: "You get a civic leader mayor type from an outlying community and he acts like he is only representing that area, and unless there's some benefit to him, he makes a long speech like a politician and he [breaks off]. . . . Many of the opinions, I have to say, are just emotional, they're uninformed, but they are taxpayers . . . and they're entitled to their day."

Not surprisingly, the SCRTD board has been much criticized by Los Angeles business leaders, media, and city and county officials. They see it as inefficient and not sufficiently responsive to the needs of Los Angeles. There have been numerous calls for "restructuring" the membership of the SCRTD.

The *Los Angeles Times* pointed out that the SCRTD had "emphasized buses and forgot rapid transit'' for several years after the defeat of Proposition A in 1968. Then, as a response to "political pressure,'' the SCRTD in 1973 had private consultants draw up another transit plan (*LAT*, July 22, 1973:1). Although the *Times* does not specify the source of this pressure, it is safe to assume that most if not all of it came from the Los Angeles business community. The new SCRTD plan became the basis for Proposition A of 1974.

Like the earlier Los Angeles plan, the new proposal was for a combination of rails (now called "guideways'') and bus service. Also added were "personal rapid transit'' (PRT) systems for downtown, the airport, Century City, and Long Beach. The guideway portion was to consist of surface, subway, and elevated lines, and was more extensive (145 miles) than the earlier proposal (89 miles). Total cost had nearly doubled, now expected to be from $8 to 10 billion. A major difference this time was that it was expected that the federal government, due to passage of certain legislation at the national level (Chapter Four), would pay up to 80 percent of construction costs. The local share was to be financed by a 1 cent sales tax (as in 1968). Routes would follow in the same general lines as in 1968, but would be longer. There would also be lines connecting with populous Orange County.

The group formed to campaign for Proposition A was called Citizens for Better Transportation. Its chairman was Mayor Bradley. Chairman of the Executive Committee was Thornton F. Bradshaw, president of Atlantic Richfield Company. ARCO is the owner of the largest office building in Los Angeles, the Atlantic Richfield Plaza, located in the heart of downtown (*LAT*, Jan. 26, 1975:1). Bradshaw was suggested to Bradley as a member of the campaign committee by the Los Angeles Chamber of Commerce. The chamber also put a number of people on the finance committee of the campaign organization, a committee made up of, in the words of a chamber official, "the movers and shakers of this community.'' The chamber also asked the president of Century City to establish a speakers' bureau to support Proposition A.

As in the BART campaign, the issue of urban growth was largely a "hidden agenda'' item. When an article by Bradshaw promoting transit appeared in the *Los Angeles Times*, no mention was made of the role of transit in the promotion of urban growth. Proposition A, if passed, would "turn back the tides of congestion, diminish unnecessary fuel consumption, and alleviate air pollution" (*LAT*, Oct. 27, 1974:IX-5). In fact, due to massive automobile ownership in the Los Angeles Basin, rapid transit "would not necessarily have a significant effect on air pollution" as had been recognized by the 1967 Citizens Advisory Council on Public Transportation study (*IPT*:49). Estimated smog improvement due to the creation of a Los Angeles rapid transit system varied from approximately 2 to 6 percent. As one city planner revealed to me: "I don't think it's going to clean the air a damn bit."

There was some media advertising against Proposition A. A group called United Organization of Taxpayers, Inc., placed one small ad in the newspaper. The main objection was the system's cost. It called the plan "obsolete" and said that it would serve only a small portion of Los Angeles commuters. The piece ended by noting: "It appears to us that the principal promoters of this system want to use billions of taxpayer dollars to 'save the downtown business section' " (*LAT*, Oct. 22, 1974:8).

The major anti-Proposition A advertisement occupied an entire page and was paid for by a group of mayors and chambers of commerce from cities and towns surrounding Los Angeles. The largest communities represented were Pasadena, Glendale, and Beverly Hills. Most were small (e.g., San Dimas, Rosemead). The ad called the measure "regressive and inflationary," and said that it was "for the benefit of major corporations along Wilshire Blvd. and downtown Los Angeles who will profit most by so-called rapid transit" (*LAT*, Nov. 4, 1974:27). As in the BART case, there were conflicts between business desires in the central city and outlying communities.

Campaign contributions for Proposition A indicate a pattern of support almost identical to that of 1968. More money ($562,827.16) was collected than in 1968 ($458,612.50) and a greater proportion (93.6 percent) was from business than before (85.6 percent). With ARCO as the leader ($48,135), oil companies were the largest contributors with 22.9 percent of total business contributions. Next came industrial firms (20.2 percent); construction, engineering, and architecture (20.1 percent); banks (8.9 percent); merchandising (5.5 percent), and insurance companies (4.9 percent). Generally, the pattern was the same as 1968, with oil companies (i.e., ARCO) giving more, and insurance companies giving less, than in the earlier campaign.

Again, there was the tendency for business contributions to come from the central area of the city. This time the figure was 60.5 percent as opposed to 63.6 percent in 1968. Exactly the same percentage (46.6) came from the same five central zip code zones (90005, 90010, 90015, 90014) as in 1968 (see Figure 1). Once more, the single zip code zone with the most contributions (21.9 percent in 1974; 29.4 percent in 1968) was the one (90017) in the center of downtown. Rapid transit support still came almost exclusively from business and most of that support was located in the central area of the immense region. There was no record of any contributions made against Proposition A. (In 1968, $25,000 was raised to oppose that transit measure).

Once more, in spite of the large sums of money spent to support the measure, Proposition A lost at the polls on November 5, 1974, getting 46.3 percent of the vote in Los Angeles County. (It required only 50 percent this time as opposed to the needed 60 percent in 1968.) In addition to voter resistance to the sales tax increase, Los Angeles transit supporters blamed a sixty-eight-day strike by SCRTD workers shortly before the election for the defeat of the proposal (*LAT*, Nov. 7, 1974:3). Once again, the SCRTD came under attack. The *Los Angeles Times* joined with others in renewed calls for a ''restructuring'' of the SCRTD (*LAT*, Nov. 7, 1974:II-6). Mayor Bradley said that the SCRTD board should be restructured to make it more ''responsive and accountable'' (*LAT*, Dec. 20, 1974:II-7).

Transit proponents also made it clear that they were not going to give up. The *Los Angeles Times* editorialized that the defeat was ''a serious setback.'' ''But,'' the paper asserted, ''we are convinced that mass rapid transit has to come, and is going to come, and we are certain that when it does come it will be even more expensive than it would be now'' (*LAT*, Nov. 7, 1974:II-6).

There were hints that attempts to get transit for Los Angeles might in the future be made in such a way as to circumvent the elective process. It was not clear just how this might be done. Musing over the defeat of Proposition A, one member of the Executive Committee of the Los Angeles Chamber of Commerce, observed to me: "I don't know whether we can ever do it by a vote or not. Public officials are going to have to bite the bullet maybe and—or maybe we can get enough grants. I've gone, the chamber's gone to Washington, and we've talked to secretary— I went back a couple of times and talked to secretary [of Transportation] Brinegar who had another idea of how it should be done." Brinegar preferred buses, not rails.

Conclusion

I have argued that the constellation of forces behind the proposed mass transit systems in Los Angeles were essentially the same as those that produced BART in San Francisco: the desire by large businesses, mostly those in the central areas of the city, to use new and very expensive rail or "fixed guideway" systems as a tool to shape urban growth. Such technologies are thought of chiefly as cogs in the urban growth machine. Unlike the case in San Francisco, political efforts to create a transit system in Los Angeles have not yet been successful. There are indications that future attempts will be made.

In both the San Francisco and the Los Angeles cases there was no opposition to public transit campaigns by members of the highway lobby. In fact, there was some support by oil companies (particularly ARCO) for the Los Angeles plans. These transit systems were designed to supplement automobile transportation, not replace it. There was no reason for highway lobby opposition. Moreover, in accordance with the pluralist conception of cross-cutting allegiances, most oil companies maintain their corporate headquarters downtown and like other firms wish to protect and enhance their central city interests through both highway and supplementary rail transit systems. Thus, we have not yet observed political activity by the highway lobby in any of these campaigns.

However, there was a transit campaign in which the lobby

became heavily involved and also showed the nature of its constituency. Shortly after the first Proposition A campaign in Los Angeles in 1968, Proposition 18 appeared on the California statewide ballot in 1970. Proposition 18 proposed to divert some of the monies in the state's highway trust fund to other transportation uses (including transit systems such as BART). It was to encounter intense opposition by California highway-oil-automobile interests. They put up a great deal of money to successfully defeat the plan. Yet a similar plan (Proposition 5) that appeared on the ballot in California just four years later got no highway lobby opposition. In fact, it received substantial business support and was passed. What were these two campaigns about and how were they related to San Francisco and Los Angeles transit plans? Most crucially, how does one understand the strange shift in political behavior by the highway lobby between the 1970 and 1974 campaigns? These campaigns add considerably to our insights into urban transportation politics and help us to see the special relevance of the class-dialectical model of political power. The Proposition 18 and Proposition 5 campaigns are analyzed in the following chapter.

CHAPTER FOUR

THE CALIFORNIA HIGHWAY TRUST FUND: THE LOBBY SHOWS ITS HAND

You know, California after World War II with the development of the automobile and the growth of population—that highway trust fund in California was the greatest slot machine ever invented.
—California business executive

The last two chapters have demonstrated the identity and goals of the organized groups that support rapid transit development in San Francisco and Los Angeles. They have argued that these consist mainly of large, centrally located businesses of an administrative and financial nature whose essential goals are economic development and preservation of property values and other investments in central city areas.

There was in these three campaigns no discoverable opposition by the fabled highway lobby. This raises several important questions. Does the highway lobby really exist? If so, what is its position on rapid transit? If there are conflicts between the lobby and transit interests, how are they handled? What other political goals does the highway lobby have? What organizational and political tactics does it employ? How can we find evidence as to the composition of the lobby membership?

The Proposition 18 and Proposition 5 elections both occurred in the period between the two Los Angeles transit campaigns (of 1968 and 1974) discussed in the previous chapter. In contrast to the other elections, they were state-wide rather than local campaigns. Both of them were not proposals to build transit systems, but to divert some of the California highway trust fund monies to public transportation purposes. In other words, they attempted to redistribute some money from highways to public transit. The more controversial and instructive of the two campaigns came first and will be examined first.

BACKGROUND

California's highway trust fund was established in 1938 with the passage of Article XXVI of the California constitution. California thus became one of the first states to "earmark" highway revenues exclusively for purposes of highway construction and maintenance. Business interests had strongly advocated the trust fund concept, and California's reputedly powerful highway lobby is reported to have over the years successfully defended the fund against diversion to other uses. Public attention began to be focused on the lobby with the publication of an article in 1968. The piece, entitled "The Freeway Establishment," appeared in the magazine *Cry California* in the spring of that year (Simmons, 1968). Simmons, the Sacramento bureau chief of a Los Angeles television station, began by noting the effective power of the group: "An informal but extremely powerful alliance of special-interest groups, fattened by the massive California highway program, is effectively preventing the development of alternatives which can prove easier, cheaper, faster, safer, and more comfortable" (Simmons, 1968:31). He goes on to identify those interests as the trucking industry, the auto clubs (AAA), the petroleum industry, heavy-equipment manufacturers, auto manufacturers and dealers, concrete producers, general contractors, the lumber industry, rock and aggregate producers, and the California Division of Highways. According to Simmons the groups "rally behind the prestigious banner of the California State Chamber of Commerce and in the Legislature they work very closely with the pervasively influential Senate Transportation Committee Chairman Randolph Collier, Democrat of Yreka. The most active and effective lobbyists of the group—those representing the truckers, auto clubs, and petroleum interests—are known affectionately in the Capitol corridors as Randy's Rat Pack" (Simmons, 1968:31).

In addition to the lobbyists representing the truckers, auto clubs, and oil companies, Simmons writes that the California Division of Highways' lobby is "one of the most potent in Sacramento" (Simmons, 1968:34). He notes that up until that time the lobby had been "wholly successful" in defending the state highway trust fund, although a "few voices in the legislature, and increasing numbers outside of government" were beginning to insist that "some alternative be considered" (Simmons, 1968:31).

The success of the highway lobby has been attested to by a former consultant to the State Assembly Transportation Committee. In an interview, he maintained that only in the last few years have opponents of the highway program dared to challenge the lobby. Previously, attacks on the fund were considered doomed to failure. As Bachrach and Baratz (1962:949) point out, "to the extent that a person or group—consciously or unconsciously—creates or reinforces barriers to the public airing of policy conflicts, that person or group has power." If the consultant's assessment is correct, the highway lobby has traditionally exercised this kind of suppressive power. What are we to make then of the growing number of dissident voices mentioned by Simmons? What interests might they represent, and does their outspokenness represent a decline in the ability of the highway lobby to suppress such issues?

It is reasonable to suppose that the business groups that support rapid transit development (such as those in San Francisco and Los Angeles) would be interested in raising the issue of the highway trust fund as a possible source of transit funding. That would make the job of building new systems easier since new taxes are often resisted by voters. Were these pro-transit interests the forces that got Proposition 18 on the ballot?

By the late 1960s San Francisco's BART was in financial difficulty. The San Francisco business community had played a role in getting the legislature to impose a sales tax to aid BART, but it was not enough. In January 1970, the California Constitution Revision Commission voted to recommend the broadening of Article XXVI (the basis for the highway trust fund) to include other modes of transportation. BART's financial situation probably influenced the vote of the commission. During the legislative session that followed, according to Assemblyman John Foran, four bills were considered that would have allowed the use of highway funds

for mass transit. Of those bills, one was passed by the legislature
and submitted to the electorate.

PROPOSITION 18

Senate Constitutional Amendment 18 became Proposition 18 on
the November 1970 ballot. The measure would have allowed the
legislature to use an unspecified amount of the revenue derived
from the California motor vehicle fuel tax and license fees (highway fund monies as of that time) for purposes of "control of
environmental pollution caused by motor vehicles." More importantly, the proposition would have given voters in local areas
the option of using up to 25 percent of the above revenues collected
in their city or county for mass transit purposes. Proposition 18
was thus a rather mild measure: local voters could elect to continue
using all local funds for streets and roads, or could use a maximum
of one-fourth of those funds for mass transit.

Since it was a constitutional amendment, Proposition 18 needed
a two-thirds vote in both houses of the California legislature, but
did not require the signature of the governor. It barely passed,
receiving the minimum number of votes necessary in the assembly, and only one vote to spare in the senate. The amendment's
passage caught both opponents and proponents by surprise. The
author of the bill, Senator James Mills, observed in a letter that
"it is surprising that Proposition 18 made it on the ballot at all."
He maintains that intense opposition was encountered from the
highway lobby from the outset. After a difficult passage through
the assembly Transportation Committee, it was first rejected by
the assembly. Proponents then succeeded in gaining reconsider-
ation. Mills writes:

> Finally on August 19 [the last day of the legislative session]
> it came to a vote. That afternoon, after a number of tallies
> it seemed it would not pass. I left the Assembly chambers
> myself, thinking the bill had died.
> But it did pass. Partly, I suspect in spite of the treatment
> given John Foran in the Senate [Foran was the author of

ACA 38, killed by the Senate Transportation Committee]
and because the Assemblymen who co-sponsored Foran's
ACA 38 realized that if SCA 18 failed in the Assembly there
would be no ecology bill on the bill.

Perhaps some members of the assembly voted for SCA 18
because they felt that it was going to fail anyway, but that a
symbolic yes vote on an "ecology bill" would be politic. Alternatively, perhaps the dominance of highway forces was slipping
within the legislature and pro-transit interests were beginning to
assert themselves. The vote on Proposition 18 may thus have
been, from a pluralist perspective, the first significant expression
of countervailing power on this issue. There is some circumstantial
evidence to support this interpretation.

Prior to consideration by the full legislature, SCA 18 had been
approved by the senate Transportation Committee, chaired for
more than twenty years by Senator Randolph Collier of Yreka,
known as the "Father of the Freeways," and generally considered
to be a personification of the highway lobby. However, it was
clear that by 1970 the lobby's dominance of Collier's committee
was not all that it might have been. SCA 18 did pass, and ACA
38 came close. It has been suggested that the 1966 reapportion-
ment of the California legislature that weakened the strength of
rural areas aided the passage of Proposition 18 (*Washington Post*,
Mar. 7, 1971:3). Moreover, all but one of the legislators who
introduced rapid transit bills in 1970 were from the Bay Area:
ACA-38, Foran (D, San Francisco); SCA-18, Mills (D, San Diego);
SCA-5, Marks (R, San Francisco); SCA-13, Petris (D, Oakland).
Obviously, the Bay Area Rapid Transit system could greatly benefit by legislation of this nature. Money from the highway fund
could be made available to help retire BART's several hundred
million dollar bond issue, for example.

There was also growing popular opposition (including areas
outside of the Bay Area) to highway building. That highway
interests felt the need as early as 1964 to defend the state's road
program is implied by the establishment in that year of a "public
education" association known as Californians for Modern Highways. Its president was Senator Collier; other officers represented

the spectrum of highway interests (Simmons, 1968:36). Said the press representative of the association regarding critics of a proposed highway of that time: "We're out to get rid of the goddamn posey pluckers" (Simmons, 1968:37). Californians for Modern Highways later passed out of existence, and its place was taken by the Freeway Support Committee of the state Chamber of Commerce, which will be discussed presently.

Until Proposition 18 slipped through the legislature, the California highway fund had not been an electoral issue since 1939 when it was created. Was this an example of countervailing power? If so, what was its nature and source? Upon the surprise passage of Proposition 18, opponents and proponents had only eleven weeks to prepare for the coming electoral conflict.

In spite of the reasonable assumption that business interests supporting urban transit development would be in favor of Proposition 18, the campaign for that measure (in contrast with the other three measures I have discussed) was not organized by business. It was organized by civic and environmental groups. Proponents of Proposition 18 formed an organization called Californians Against Smog with a $10,000 contribution from the Tuberculosis and Respiratory Diseases Association of California (TARDAC). In addition to TARDAC, the Sierra Club and the League of Women Voters were represented on the organization's board of directors. Californians Against Smog operated out of the Oakland and Los Angeles offices of TARDAC and attempted to raise money for Proposition 18. The main driving forces behind the organization of the campaign were the Sierra Club and TARDAC. The Coalition for Clean Air, representing various environmental groups in Southern California, provided volunteer labor.

Also allied with pro-18 groups was the Citizen's Transportation Committee in Los Angeles. According to Dr. Jule Lamm, the committee's vice chairman, the group had been organized in 1965 by homeowners in the Beverly Hills area who were opposed to construction of the Beverly Hills Freeway. The organization had been a strong supporter of Proposition A in 1968 and as a result had developed connections with the pro-transit business community.

At the beginning, pro-18 forces were optimistic and believed they would succeed rather handily. Due to lack of time, it was felt that the Citizens Transportation Committee (CTC), with its existing ties to business, would be most likely to bring in substantial contributions. In hopeful tones, a CTC spokesman told Proposition 18 campaign workers: "You are a real army. Your foot soldiers should get the message to the grassroots. We don't have your numbers, but . . . Pat Brown [former governor of California] and our people from Century City and Tishman can talk to the business community. CTC raised $400,000 in '68. . . . You only need $200,000 this time. 18's a good issue. That's all it'll take" (Nevins, 1971:35).

In this case, what business involvement there was, was against Proposition 18. Opponents of Proposition 18 established a group they called Californians Against the Street and Road Tax Trap. Campaign offices were opened in Sacramento and Los Angeles. The interests represented by this group were not revealed, nor were the affiliations of the group's officials. After the election, it was reported by the *Los Angeles Times* (Dec. 27, 1970:F-1) that the chairman was a retired general manager of the California State Chamber of Commerce, and that the treasurer was a "part-time membership consultant" to the chamber.

The state Chamber of Commerce, an original endorser of Article XXVI in 1938 (*Santa Barbara News Press*, Nov. 2, 1938), was reported early in 1970 to be "preparing a grass roots campaign to defeat the ballot measure in November" should the lobbying effort fail to halt the proposed amendment (Proposition 18) in the legislature (*California Journal*, 1970a:10). "Throughout the 1970 legislative sessions, the State Chamber of Commerce attacked gas tax diversion bills in mailings to all local chambers, county boards of supervisors and every city councilman in the state" (*LAT*, Jan. 27, 1970:F-1).

The chamber's promotion of highways has been a long one. It plays a quasigovernmental role in the setting of priorities for the construction of highways. As a chamber spokesman explained before the Assembly Transportation Committee on March 19, 1970: "For 41 years the California State Chamber of Commerce has conducted these meetings through local business organizations, and representatives of city and county governments, to receive each county's recommendations [for highway construction]." The chamber then makes its presentation to the state Highway Commission. That such proposals by business are usually rubber-stamped by the commission is indicated by a quote from a chamber official: "We usually have about 90 percent of our program adopted. One year it was as high as 97 percent" (Simmons, 1968:37). There is also doubt as to how much the chamber is swayed by desires of local communities. Simmons notes that residents of the San Joaquin Valley "have for years sought top priority for improvements on U.S. 99, connecting the principal valley cities. But instead, the state chamber's top priority recommendation has been the [new] Westside Freeway (Interstate 5)." Says a chamber spokesman: "Most of the time our function [at meetings] is to explain to the local people why they cannot change the priority already established [by the Division of Highways]" (Simmons, 1968:37-38).

The chamber's activities are not limited to the setting of priorities for highway construction. As mentioned previously, the functions of the earlier Californians for Modern Highways have been assumed by the chamber. On October 21, 1966, the chamber created the California Freeway Support Committee (FSC) to "coordinate California Highways, support interest, and foster an *educational program*" (emphasis in original) designed to "re-establish, in the minds of the general public and of state and local legislative bodies . . . an awareness of the urgent need for the orderly development of highway facilities required to meet the growing demands for the movement of persons and goods as generated by a vigorous and expanding economy." Another goal, as stated in a state Chamber of Commerce information sheet, was to "prevent a diversion of highway user taxes for purposes other than highways and to prevent the imposition of additional taxes upon the motor vehicle owner for nonhighway purposes." The FSC's first president told me that the purpose of the group was to "resell" the freeway system to those people who had become "disenchanted" with it. Also, he believed that "part of the opposition [to highways] came from vested interests . . . General Electric and people like that who would gain from building rapid transit systems of one kind or another."

The state Chamber of Commerce's opposition to Proposition 18 was therefore consistent with its traditional political role in highway matters. This opposition is also not surprising in view of the representation of highway interests on the chamber's board of directors, a matter which will be discussed later.

The interests of the chamber and other highway groups were strikingly revealed in the Proposition 18 campaign. The contest has been called "a classic in campaign controversy" (Nevins, 1971:35). It was a campaign filled with voluminous rhetoric, denunciations, protest, law suits, charges of misrepresentation and perfidy, and disillusionment for supporters of 18.

The campaign rhetoric went like this. Proponents of Proposition 18 argued that building more highways cannot solve traffic problems since new roads are overrun by autos as soon as they open, and that funds produced by the automobile should logically be used to control air pollution—also produced by the automobile. Citing studies that were said to show that "up to 87 percent of the travel on State highways terminates within the county of origin," they maintained that the state road system was basically a local transportation system. It followed that local voters should be able to determine the kind of local system of transport they desired. Present "earmarking" of highway funds, they argued, leads to inflexibility and inequality of funding state projects. Under Proposition 18, benefits would also accrue to rural residents, it was said, because they would be able to use their 25 percent of highway revenues for the construction and maintenance of local roads, if they so voted. Federal matching funds for rapid transit would become available, easing the present burden of property taxes to pay for such transit. The availability of rapid transit facilities would help reduce traffic congestion on the freeways and would decrease air pollution.

Opponents of Proposition 18 countered that the "freeway master plan, adopted by the legislature in 1959, is only about 36 percent developed to freeway standards and the remainder of that system may never be finished if highway gasoline tax money is used to finance rapid transit." Rapid transit, they said, is very expensive and will not be able to compete successfully with automobile transportation. Moreover, "It is unfair and economically unsound to impose a tax burden upon one form of transportation to finance another." The building of highways, they continued, is a very complex and long range process: "The very nature of this type of program demands a predictable, steady, and assured source of revenue, making a special purpose fund and tax source highly desirable." Noting that some highway funds were already available for the support of the State Air Resources Board and air pollution research,[1] they said that it was not necessary to amend the California Constitution for this purpose. Finally, opponents argued that by the time rapid transit systems could be built, "much will have been accomplished through engine and fuel modifications in the elimination of automobile air pollution."[2]

Early in the campaign, various organizations took public stands as being for or against Proposition 18. Supporters included the Tuberculosis and Respiratory Diseases Association of California, the Sierra Club, League of Women Voters, California Medical Association, Planning and Conservation League, American Association of University Women, League of California Cities, California Association of Life Underwriters, Coalition for Clean Air, Stamp Out Smog, and Californians Against Smog.

Virtually all businesses that announced a position were opposed. Declared opponents of Proposition 18 included the Automobile Club of Southern California, California State Automobile Association, the Teamster's Union, California Trucking Association, California State Chamber of Commerce, County Supervisors Association of California, Atlantic Richfield Company, E. R. DuPont de Nemours & Company, Ethyl Corporation, Gulf Oil Corporation, Humble Oil & Refining Company, Mobil Oil Corporation, Phillips Petroleum Company, Standard Oil of California, Union Oil Company of California, California Taxpayers'

[1] The State Air Resources Board is funded from motor vehicle registration, weight fees, and drivers' license fees. During fiscal year 1970-71, the board and the Department of Justice together received a total of $4,848,465. That same year the California Highway Commission released $1,000,000 for "air pollution control." Both of these figures combined are less than 7/10 of one percent of that year's increment to the highway fund in California (based on budget figures from the California Division of Highways).

[2] Arguments for and against Proposition 18 are summaries of material contained in the Town Hall of California's "Ballot Measures Report" of November 3, 1970.

Association, California State Employees Association, California Farm Bureau, California Real Estate Association, and the Property Owner's Tax Association of California (*Sacramento Bee*, Oct. 11, 1970:A-7: *LAT*, Oct. 30, 1970:II-2).

Perhaps the only organizations in the above list whose interests are not obvious are the two tax associations, the California State Employees Association, and the County Supervisors Association. One of the directors of the California Taxpayers' Association was also a director of the California State Automobile Association. The president of the Property Owner's Tax Association was Claiborn A. Saint, a director of the Automobile Club of Southern California.[3] The stand taken by the California State Employees Association was probably the result of pressure from state employees in highway-related fields, such as the engineers in the Division of Highways. It has been estimated, for example, that during fiscal 1971-72, the state of California had 32,800 highway-related employees (18,000 in the Department of Public Works—including the Division of Highways; 8,200 in the California Highway Patrol; and 6,600 in the Department of Motor Vehicles) compared to 21 in air transportation, and none in public transportation.[4]

Opponents of Proposition 18 hired Milton Kramer to run their media campaign, a man described by one newspaper as a "rotund, 52-year-old political consultant from suburban Los Angeles, who had waged a successful campaign a few months before against a ballot proposition that would have shifted education costs to the state" (*Washington Post*, Mar. 7, 1971).

During the second week in October, Kramer reported to me that he put up around 700 billboards across the state which said only "More taxes? No No. 18" (*Sacramento Bee*, Oct. 20, 1970: A-6). The billboards were placed so as to achieve a hypothetical "100 percent showing," that is, every person in the state should theoretically have seen such a billboard at least once before elec-

[3] Information concerning Saint was obtained from a publication of the Property Owners' Tax Association of California called "Tax Facts." *The Auto Club News Pictorial* of October 1970 lists Saint as a director of the Automobile Club.

[4] From a statement by a legislative analyst before the Assembly Transportation Committee on November 16, 1971.

tion time (except in those few counties, such as Santa Barbara, that ban billboards). Opponents argued that these advertisements were justified since the state highway system was already behind schedule, revenues were inadequate to meet the need for highways, and that any diversion of monies from the highway trust fund would have to be compensated for by an increase in taxes. A political advertisement which appeared in newspapers four days before the election recommended a vote against 18. The ad, by the Property Owners' Tax Association of California, warned: "Approval of Proposition 18 would bring a sharp increase in gasoline taxes. For this you have the word of State Senator Randolph Collier, for 20 years the chairman of the Senate Transportation Committee, a foremost authority on highway traffic and a leader in the opposition to Proposition 18" (*LAT*, Oct. 30, 1970: IV-25).

Proponents of 18 strongly denied the charge that the amendment would raise taxes, pointing out that only a diversion of money from the highway fund was involved.

With the appearance of the billboards, campaign rhetoric became more heated. All of the major newspapers in the state, with the exception of the *Oakland Tribune* and the *San Diego Union* (*California Journal*, 1970b:308), supported Proposition 18.[5] Editorials in the *Los Angeles Times* and the *Sacramento Bee* castigated the opposition campaign and the highway lobby. In endorsing 18, the *Bee* accused that: "This modest step is too much for the highway lobby, an aggregation of oil companies, cement firms, automobile clubs, truckers, contractors, and others with vested interests in restricting the use of gasoline tax revenue for highway purposes" (*Sacramento Bee*, Oct. 19, 1970:A-18).

The *Los Angeles Times* called the opposition campaign by "powerful special interests" one of "deliberate confusion and misinformation" designed to deceive the voters (*LAT*, Oct. 14, 1970:II-6). The *Times* was becoming a more vigorous supporter of rapid transit in Los Angeles than had been true a few years

---

[5] It is not surprising that the *Tribune* was opposed to Proposition 18; its publisher, William Knowland, was a leader in the 1938 campaign for Article XXVI during his tenure in the California Assembly (*Washington Post*, Mar. 7, 1971). Both the *Tribune* and *Union* are known to be conservative newspapers.

earlier. In 1968, the newspaper had "reluctantly" recommended a "no" vote on Proposition A, citing the inflexibility of a rail system and problems with SCRTD mismanagement (*LAT*, Sept. 27, 1968:6, 6). However, by the time of the next transit vote in 1974, the *Times* was an ardent proponent of rapid transit, calling such a system "mandatory" for Los Angeles (*LAT*, Nov. 7, 1974: II-6).

The nature of the opposition media campaign was only one impediment that Proposition 18 supporters had to overcome. It became increasingly apparent during the month of October that their initial optimism was not justified. Organizations and individuals that proponents had counted on for support let them down.

Edgar Kaiser, head of Kaiser Industries (and a major proponent of BART), had agreed to head the campaign for 18 in Northern California, but later withdrew, supposedly when Californians Against Smog could not find a prominent businessman to lead the Southern California campaign. Two bankers who had been active on behalf of Proposition A in 1968 were asked to lead the Southern California drive. Both Louis Lundborg, Bank of America chairman, and John Vaughn, vice-chairman of Crocker-Citizens National Bank, saying they were too busy, declined the offers. As the *Los Angeles Times* was to point out after the election, Otto Miller, chairman of Standard Oil of California, was on the board of directors of Crocker-Citizens, and the Bank of America board included the head of Getty Oil, George Getty (*LAT*, Dec. 27, 1970:F-1). Standard and Getty both made large contributions against Proposition 18.

The *Times* also recounted another difficulty for Proposition 18 proponents: "Century City, the massive Los Angeles office and real estate development of Aluminum Co. of America (Alcoa), donated an office for Proposition 18. But Robert Hatfield, Century City president, never issued a public endorsement that had been prepared for him by the campaign staff" (*LAT*, Dec. 27, 1970: F-1).

This failure occurred in spite of Alcoa's presumed interest in rapid transit development (BART was expected to use a total of 2 million pounds of Alcoa aluminum, according to the firm's 1970 Annual Report), and in spite of Century City's (100 percent Alcoa-owned) strong support of rapid transit development in Los Angeles. In addition, Century City President Hatfield was a member of the chief Proposition 18 fund-raising group, the Citizens' Transportation Committee, at the time of the campaign.

Why did Century City not support 18? The office complex's seeming ambivalence with regard to Proposition 18 may be accounted for by its relationship with other businesses, particularly those that opposed the measure. An article in the *Times* reported: "It's been pointed out . . . that two major Century City tenants are oil companies—Humble Oil and Refining Co., and Gulf Oil Corp. Millions of shares of stock in Pittsburg-based Gulf Oil are controlled by the Mellon family companies, which have three seats on the Gulf board. The family also controls Mellon National Bank, which has made extensive loans to Alcoa. . . . In addition, the Mellons have big blocks of Alcoa stock" (*LAT*, Dec. 27, 1970:F-1). Humble and Gulf are by no means the only Century City tenants who might have been opposed to Proposition 18.[6]

In an interview, a Century City executive took pains to deny that the Mellons had anything to do with decisions concerning Proposition 18. While that may be true, it is also true that Alcoa, the owner of Century City, does a great deal of business with highway interests. For example, the company produces highway products such as bridge rail systems, median rails, and Interstate highway signs and supports (Moody's, 1971).[7] Many automotive components are made of aluminum: General Motor's 1970 Vega used ninety-eight pounds of Alcoa aluminum per automobile (Alcoa Annual Report, 1970). Therefore, companies like Alcoa might understandably be reluctant to risk the loss of such business by supporting a political issue anathematized by auto interests.

Large corporations do not operate independently from other large corporations. Their market and political power is such that

---

[6] Among Century City tenants: Jade Oil & Gas, American Energy Corp., Lacal Oil, National Oil Marketers, Superior Oil, General Motors, Thomson Oil, Witco Chemical, Equitex Petroleum, Havenstrite Oil, Indonesian Development, Occidental Petroleum Land and Development Corp., Pennzoil United, Presidio Oil Funds, and Venezam Oil. This information came from a personal inspection at Century City.

[7] Unless otherwise indicated, "Moody's" refers to *Moody's Industrial Manual*.

they must take each other into account in their actions. They often
do business with each other, and there is the need to avoid of-
fending powerful segments of the business community by taking
an unpopular political stance. This is a crucial—and largely overlooked—source of social control and conformity among business
leaders. These pressures for consensus are clearly spelled-out in
a statement by a prominent San Francisco banker. When I asked
him why San Francisco companies that had supported BART did
not give money for Proposition 18, he confided: "Standard Oil
and the other oil companies are extremely important customers
and they have a lot of clout in many ways, and I think a lot of
people are unhappy about being in opposition. You take a banker,
and Standard Oil, Union Oil, Shell, you name it, Mobil, Atlantic-
Richfield are good customers and if they say 'we're opposed to
this,' it's awfully hard for the banker to say, 'Well, we're in favor
of it.' "

The opposition to Proposition 18 by the powerful highway lobby
companies apparently influenced the actions of non-lobby companies in the campaign. The Citizens' Transportation Committee
had difficulty in obtaining both endorsements by business interests
and donations. Part of the proponents' initial optimism resulted
from pledges of support from businesses that had been made
earlier. These pledges were later withdrawn. According to Dr.
Jule Lamm, vice-chairman of the Citizens' Transportation Committee, and a fund-raiser for Proposition 18: "Merchants in the
commercial areas of Westwood, Wilshire Boulevard and Century
City, who would benefit from mass transit and who had given
willingly in 1968, were now unavailable" (*Washington Post*, Mar.
7, 1971). William Roberts, air and water conservation coordinator
for the Tuberculosis and Respiratory Diseases Association of California, and a member of the Northern California Steering Committee for Proposition 18, complained of the problems created by
the links and cohesion among the business community, bringing
up the possibility that interlocking boards of directors may have
also played a role: "The most frustrating thing was the difficulty
in obtaining financing and leadership. The buddy system balked
us everywhere we turned. People said they would check with their
associates before making a contribution. Their associates were

often business friends in oil companies. I think the interlocking boards of directors killed us in trying to get money" (*LAT*, Dec. 27, 1970:F-1).

In an ironic phrase, Leo Simon, a leader of the Proposition 18 campaign in Southern California, has termed this process "interlocking corporate good will." Another 18 unidentified supporter reportedly used stronger language: "The opposition was able to mount a fearful campaign by intimidation. They scared businessmen off. Companies said they were afraid to become a target area" (*Washington Post*, Mar. 7, 1971). In an interview, the Century City executive agreed, saying businesses did not want to "antagonize" their fellow businessmen by supporting the amendment. Money sources for the measure virtually dried up. A leading Proposition 18 organizer explains: "Three weeks before election day, the Citizens Transportation Committee press aide told the Californians Against Smog, 'We've all but given up hope of raising money for radio, television, or even billboards.' They advised Citizens [sic] Against Smog to go it alone. CAS launched a pitiful nickel-dime effort, and held their breath for the one major hope, endorsement from the Los Angeles Chamber of Commerce, to break down the big money barrier" (Nevins, 1971:35).

It had looked as though Proposition 18 would get the endorsement of the Los Angeles Chamber of Commerce, but about the same time that pledges from business began to be withdrawn, opposition in that organization forced a delay. Even though the chamber did finally support 18, proponents contend that the endorsement was half-hearted and came too late to aid their cause.

In San Francisco, the Chamber of Commerce, a major BART supporter, went on record as against Proposition 18. San Francisco Mayor Joseph Alioto expressed dismay over the action, saying: "I am appalled at the position of the Chamber of Commerce on an issue which would give San Francisco between $72 million and 90 million to aid the Municipal Railway and fight pollution" (*San Francisco Chronicle*, Oct. 30, 1970:14). Phillip Berry, president of the Sierra Club, charged that Standard Oil of California "induced" the San Francisco Chamber to oppose the measure. Berry charged that the position of the group was "formulated in a closed door session in which oil industry and highway lobby pressure overrode the public interest.'' Although the assistant general manager of the chamber denied Berry's accusation, he did concede that Charles Wood, a Standard Oil official and chamber member, was present and did take part in the debate (*San Francisco Chronicle*, Oct. 22, 1970:11). Berry later noted in a letter to me: ''Interestingly, Standard never denied the part it took in causing the Chamber to take the position it did.''

Proponents of Proposition 18 also saw opposition voiced against their amendment in indirect ways. The Freeway Support Committee (FSC) of the state chamber sponsored a six-page supplement that appeared in the *Los Angeles Times* one week before the election. Although the $14,000 supplement did not mention Proposition 18, thus qualifying for the lower ''educational'' rate rather than the ''political'' rate (*LAT*, Dec. 27, 1970:F-1), the supplement eulogized the state highway system in pictures and text, and provided a card for registering reader approval (*LAT*, Oct. 27, 1970). The chairman of the FSC was at that time Neil Petree, also president of the Automobile Club of Southern California. Automobile clubs were well represented on the FSC. In addition to Petree, the thirteen members included A. O. Beckman, also a director of the Automobile Club of Southern California; Arthur H. Breed, Jr., a director of both the California State Automobile Association and the American Automobile Association; Charles F. Bullotte, Jr., chairman of the Board of the California State Automobile Association; Asa V. Call, director of the Automobile Club of Southern California; and Harry D. Holt, past president of the AAA and director of the California State Automobile Association.[8]

A few months prior to the Proposition 18 campaign, Petree had told the state chamber's annual meeting that ''The purpose of this committee is quite simple: to encourage the early completion of California's planned freeway and expressway system and to pre-

[8] From: *Auto Club News Pictorial* (October, 1970); a list of the Freeway Support Committee members from the state Chamber of Commerce; an interview with *Los Angeles Times* reporter, Robert Rosenblatt (Sept. 14, 1971); *Poor's Register of Corporations, Directors, and Executives* (1970) and *Motorland* (magazine of the California State Automobile Association).

vent the diversion of highway user funds to non-highway purposes" (*LAT*, Dec. 27, 1970:F-1).

The auto club was of course opposed to Proposition 18, as was
the California State Automobile Association (both affiliates of the
American Automobile Association). The magazines of these two
organizations were another source of opposition to the measure.
With a combined membership of approximately two and a half
million, the clubs' publications may have significantly influenced
the final vote. For instance, in October, the Automobile Club of
Southern California published an editorial and three other articles
which strongly condemned Proposition 18.[9]

It is probably fair to say that most auto club members are
concerned only with the road and travel services that such associations offer, services that are generally of a high order. Member
apathy is conducive to oligarchical control. Ralph Nader and other
critics have charged that the American Automobile Association
is not adequately meeting member needs and has extensive ties
with the highway lobby (*LAT*, Sept. 21, 1973:3). Local auto clubs
are also big business. Many sell tires, batteries, and automobile
insurance. The California State Automobile Association, for example, has reported that it wrote more than $120 million worth
of insurance in 1970.[10]

Petree maintains that the auto club's "vigorous opposition" to
Proposition 18 was "entirely consistent with its Articles of Incorporation which charge it with the obligation of 'promoting just
and uniform highway or other legislation in any way pertaining
to motor vehicles or the ownership or use thereof.' "[11] In this
light, the following incident is instructive.

On January 17, 1968—about eighteen months before the Proposition 18 campaign began—the Technical Advisory Committee
of the Division of Highways held a meeting in Sacramento. The
unannounced gathering was infiltrated by two newspaper report-

---

[9] "Proposition 18 should be defeated." *Auto Club News Pictorial*, 62 (October,
1970:3).

[10] "Inter-Insurance Bureau report for 1970," California State Automobile Association. *Motorland* 92 (May/June, 1971:46).

[11] "Preserving natural surroundings: a club tradition," *Auto Club News Pictorial*, Annual Report (April 1971:2).

ers. The purpose of the meeting was to discuss a report to be submitted to the legislature that intended to prove the need for an increase in the California gasoline tax for financing highways. The highway lobby has long opposed an increase in the gasoline tax for non-highway purposes (*LAT*, Dec. 27, 1970:F-1). At the meeting, the journalists report, several committee members spoke of the need for an impartial-looking report which would not be challengeable. The executive vice president of the Automobile Club of Southern California reportedly spoke of the political value of mobilizing the club's membership on the issue: "We'll get a million of our members in Southern California interested in this and it won't be 'ours.' We would just raise up all the ivory tower thinkers, and they'd be on television and just pull the rug out from under us within 30 minutes" (*Sacramento Bee*, Apr. 13, 1969:H-4).

The Technical Advisory Committee had two external consultants: the Automobile Safety Foundation, a group identified as a member of the national highway lobby by Kelley (1971:45-50); and Price Waterhouse & Company. The impartiality of the eventual committee report was further impugned by the conclusion by Price Waterhouse that the fiscal findings of the report were based "on various assumptions and estimates rather than accomplished facts." Price Waterhouse wrote: "In these circumstances and also in compliance with the rules and regulations of the California State Board of Accountancy, we do not express an independent accountant's opinion of the projections" (*Sacramento Bee*, Apr. 13, 1969:H-4).

Supporters of Proposition 18 were severely hampered by their lack of campaign money. Campaign organizer Leo Simon told me that endorsements by Sugar Ray Robinson, Carol Burnett, and Jack Lemmon were taped, but the shortage of funds precluded more than a few media broadcasts of the ten-, thirty-, and sixty-second "spots." After the Citizens Transportation Committee gave up the fight to raise money, two full-time staff members hired by the proponents of 18 had to be let go for lack of money. During the final month before the election, the campaign ran on the efforts of some two thousand to four thousand volunteers (*LAT*, Dec. 27, 1970:F-1). Six days before the election, Write For Your

Life, an environmental group, picketed the Los Angeles office of the Automobile Club of Southern California over the club's opposition to Proposition 18 (*LAT*, Oct. 29, 1970:3).

In contrast, opponents of 18 were well-financed and well-organized. The expenditures by both sides for their media campaigns have been estimated as reported in Table 3.

Proponents of 18 maintain that the final blow to Proposition 18's chances was delivered by opponents during the last days of the campaign. The head of the Anti-18 media campaign, Milton Kramer, acknowledges that anti-18 forces waged a media "blitz" via television for the last seven days, newspapers for the last five days, and radio for the last five days. The central theme was that Proposition 18 would increase taxes. It was suggested that dreaded toll booths would appear on freeways if money was diverted from highways. An editorial in the *Sacramento Bee*, one of the most liberal newspapers in California, (Oct. 31, 1970:A-14) thundered: "If the highway lobby were only trying to sell mouthwash, the FTC would not allow it to get away with such misrepresentations."

The opposition campaign was successful. On November 3 the amendment was defeated by a vote of 2.7 million (45.9 percent) to 3.2 million (54.1 percent). Proposition 18 passed in only eight of the fifty-eight California counties, all but one of which (Santa Barbara) are located in Northern California, primarily around the Bay Area, the area most affected by BART's financial troubles. The counties approving 18 were Marin, Monterey, San Francisco, San Mateo, Santa Barbara, Santa Clara, Santa Cruz, and Yolo.

Table 3. Estimated Media Expenditures in Proposition 18 Campaign

	Opponents	Proponents
Billboards	$123,000	—
Television	60,000	$1,400
Newspaper	17,000	1,456
Radio	15,000	2,401

SOURCE: *LAT*, Dec. 27, 1970:F-1.

The pro-18 vote was heaviest in San Francisco (64.8 percent) and Marin (60.2 percent) counties.[12]

Exactly who were the campaign supporters and opponents of Proposition 18? The campaign contribution reports filed with the secretary of state provide valuable data. Contrary to the situation in other transit campaigns, the anti-18 forces received heavy criticism in the press. Therefore, some opponents of 18 may have been reluctant to have their contributions recorded. However, it is safe to assume that if contributors are listed, they did contribute. Contributions are more likely to be understated than overstated. With this caveat in mind, we shall treat the Proposition 18 contribution lists as indices of the nature of the forces against the amendment.

According to these reports, opponents spend about fifteen times as much as proponents ($333,455.69 versus $22,721.81). Total contributions against and for 18 were $348,830.00 and $17,714.20 respectively. The big money was overwhelmingly on the side of the opposition. Also, it was almost entirely (98.6 percent) business money in opposition (i.e., from the highway lobby). Those organizations that contributed $1,000 or more are reported in Table 4.

By contrast, supporters of the amendment received only three contributions of more than $1,000. They were from two companies with mass transit interests, Kaiser Industries ($2,500) and Rohr Corporation ($2,000), and from the Citizens Transportation Committee ($3,345.98), the CTC money representing that group's working capital (*LAT*, Dec. 27, 1970:F-1).

Opposition money came primarily from large contributions, while money for 18 came from small donations: the median contribution for the anti-18 campaign was $500; the median contribution for the pro-18 campaign was $5. More than three-fourths (75.1 percent) of the opposition money came from oil companies. Other anti-18 interests were (in order of contribution): automobile clubs and their insurance bureaus (12.9 percent); highway equipment, construction companies (7.9 percent); trucking and taxi

[12] California Secretary of State, "Statement of vote," State of California General Election, November 3, 1970.

Table 4. Contributions of $1,000 or More Against Proposition 18

Contributor	Contributions
1. Standard Oil of California	$75,000
2. Shell Oil Company	50,000
3. Mobil Oil	30,000
4. Automobile Club of Southern California	22,000
5. Gulf Oil	20,000
6. Texaco	20,000
7. Union Oil Company of California	20,000
8. Sully Miller Company	15,000
9. Phillips Oil	15,000
10. Humble Oil and Refining Company	12,000
11. California State Automobile Association	11,000
12. Interinsurance Bureau, Los Angeles	10,000
13. California Trucking Association	5,000
14. San Diego Rock Products	5,000
15. Douglas Oil	5,000
16. Standard Oil of Indiana	5,000
17. Getty Oil Company	5,000
18. So. California Rock Product Association	2,500
19. International Union of Operating Engineers, San Francisco	2,500
20. Sun Oil	2,000
21. Custom Farm Service	2,000
22. Interinsurance Bureau, San Francisco	2,000
23. International Union of Operating Engineers, Los Angeles	1,000
24. Highway—Heavy Chapter EGCA	1,000
25. Boise Cascade Corp.	1,000
26. California Asphalt	1,000
27. Marathon Oil	1,000
28. Pacific Motor Trucking Company	1,000

companies (1.8 percent); labor unions representing highway construction employees (1.4 percent); forest products and land companies (0.5 percent); tire and rubber companies (0.3 percent); and individuals (0.1 percent). Thus, the contributors matched closely the members of the California highway lobby described earlier by Simmons (1968:31).

The full involvement of oil companies in the campaign was not immediately apparent. Engler (1961:366) points out that political contributions by oil companies are often concealed through "cash giving, misleading listings, padded expense accounts, and dummy bonuses for executives, with the understanding that the money is to go for politics. Institutional advertising, 'educational' and association activities are often essentially political, as are the quiet loan of corporate facilities and personnel.'' Some or all of these activities undoubtedly occurred during the Proposition 18 campaign. There were, at least, several attempts at concealment.

The opposition's contribution report, filed about three weeks after the election, listed four ''anonymous'' donations totalling $95,000. Secretary of State Elect Edmund G. Brown, Jr., pressured the anti-18 committee to disclose the identities of these contributors. Over the next several weeks, and with extreme reluctance on the part of campaign officials and donors, it was revealed that the contributions had come from Mobil Oil ($30,000), Gulf Oil ($20,000) and Standard Oil ($45,000). Standard Oil was thus the largest single donor with a total of $75,000.

Oil companies played the predominant part in opposing Proposition 18 not only in terms of money, but also in terms of organization. Harry Morrison, general manager of the Western Oil and Gas Association (WOGA), and the ex-public relations officer for Shell Oil, Carl Totten, worked with Kramer on the opposition media campaign. Totten was selected for this job by the public relations committee of WOGA.

All of the major, integrated oil companies in California belong to WOGA. WOGA did not take a public stand against Proposition 18, but Morrison told me that it is WOGA's policy—in line with the American Petroleum Institute's position—to oppose any diversion of gas tax funds. That precedent might, in his words, open the door to uses such as education and welfare. When I asked why oil companies such as Sun Oil (with headquarters in Philadelphia and no service stations in California) and Standard of Indiana saw fit to donate money to oppose 18, Morrison responded that the oil industry saw the campaign as a very important one. The issue had symbolic value. If diversion could happen in California, it could, in Morrison's words, ''happen anywhere.'' A spokesman for an oil company that requested anonymity agreed with Morrison's interpretation: he called the issue a ''bellwether nationally'' as far as oil companies were concerned.

Even so, one major oil company doing business in California,

Atlantic-Richfield, did not contribute money to the opposition campaign. ARCO is not listed on the contribution lists although the company was reported early in the campaign to be opposed to Proposition 18 (*Sacramento Bee*, Oct. 11, 1970:A-7). This opposition to 18 was confirmed after the election by a company spokesman. Respondents in interviews have described ARCO, and particularly its president, Thornton F. Bradshaw, as a "maverick" in the oil industry. In the late 1960s, ARCO had advocated an opening of the highway trust fund for transit studies. "That was probably the most unpopular thing we have ever done. At that time, the trust fund was sacrosanct," writes Bradshaw.[13] Late in 1973, ARCO became the first major oil company to call for an end of the controversial oil depletion allowance (provided, significantly, that oil companies be allowed to raise prices to make up the difference). The oil companies' tarnished public image was one motivation. Said Bradshaw of the move: "We have got to get some credibility with the public, or else the public might decide it doesn't need the private oil industry anymore" (*LAT*, Dec. 25, 1973:III-9). Thus the quest for legitimacy played a role in ARCO's actions.

ARCO had joined with other oil companies in 1968 to donate some money ($10,000) for Proposition A. After the Proposition 18 campaign, the company in 1972 moved its national headquarters from Philadelphia to Los Angeles, establishing the Atlantic-Richfield Plaza in the heart of downtown. Bradshaw had been working to get a rapid transit system for Philadelphia while the company was located there, and these policies were continued in Los Angeles. He played a central organizing role in both the Los Angeles transit campaign of 1974 and in the Proposition 5 campaign (to be discussed next). ARCO donated a great deal of money in both of those campaigns (a total of almost $150,000). Although the company did not go along with the other oil companies and donate money against Proposition 18, it did not donate money for Proposition 18 either. Apparently the company was ambivalent toward 18, and stayed neutral.

A Western Oil and Gas Association official acknowledged in

---

[13] Bradshaw, quoted in *Mass Transit* 1 (October 1974:26).

a letter that "there were some differences of opinion among our member companies" concerning the anti-18 campaign. "Not all companies wanted to go along," said another oil industry executive who declined to be identified. They felt the "press would give them a bad time." He said that the campaign was a "money versus motherhood" issue. The *Los Angeles Times* quotes one source in the oil industry as saying: "Some of us were reluctant about the bad image we would get by opposing Proposition 18 and we wanted to stay neutral. But [Otto] Miller [chairman of the board of Standard Oil of California] and [Fred] Hartley [head of Union Oil] reminded us persuasively of all the joint ventures in exploration where we work with their companies" (*LAT*, Dec. 27, 1970:F-1). One WOGA executive, when asked about the role of Miller and Hartley, did concede that they are "influential" in oil circles. Another oil company executive volunteered privately to me that the decision to oppose Proposition 18 was probably made by "ten or twelve key oil industry executives." An organizer for Proposition 18 used stronger words. He said he felt that Standard Oil and Bank of America "run San Francisco." However accurate such appraisals may be, it is clear that the dissent over tactics among oil companies did not become a public issue, and all the major companies but one did contribute money to oppose 18. Whatever the private misgivings that may have existed, they did not seem to affect much the public behavior of these companies.

The general pattern of business contributions observed in the previous three campaigns was reversed in the case of Proposition 18. Before, virtually all business money was for measures favoring transit systems. Proposition 18 could have aided the transit systems whose development had been supported by numerous large corporations in both San Francisco and Los Angeles. Yet, with the exception of modest contributions (totalling only $5,000) from Rohr and Kaiser, virtually none of these companies interested in transit gave money for Proposition 18. Business (i.e., highway lobby) money was all on the other side. Pluralist expectations are confirmed in one sense. Civic groups did use their influence and personnel to work for Proposition 18, and a few companies gave some money. However, these pro-18 groups did not control the crucial campaign resource of money. Pluralist expectations are not confirmed in that business interests already demonstrating their support of new mass transportation systems (as in the BART and Los Angeles' cases) did not provide their endorsements nor their contributions, both of which were eagerly sought and which may have had great impact on the election results. Here, countervailing power was largely ineffective. On the surface, this appears to be a curious failure of consistency and self-interest by transit-minded firms.

The next, and final, transit campaign (Proposition 5 of 1974) to be examined will add to our understanding of this seeming inconsistency. At first, the story will grow more complex. For Proposition 5 elicited a pattern of support that was a radical reversal of the earlier pattern for Proposition 18—even though the actual proposals were very similar.

Before examining the Proposition 5 campaign, we should briefly look at events at the national level that were related to the political struggles in California.

The National Scene

During the 1970-74 period, important transportation events were occurring at the national level. The Federal Highway Trust Fund was coming under attack. In early 1972, Secretary of Transportation John Volpe—himself a former road contractor (Mowbray, 1971:428)—announced that urban areas should be allowed to use their shares of the Federal Highway Trust Fund to buy buses and to build commuter rail systems (*New York Times*, Oct. 24, 1972).

Three months later, the federal government sponsored the ambitious Transpo '72 in Washington. As Rothschild observes: "Government officials described Transpo as the largest industrial exhibition in the history of the world, bringing together the finest 'hardware and concepts' of the booming transportation industry, and the 'products, equipment, techniques, and concepts that can solve today's transportation crisis' " (Rothschild, 1972:27). Transpo's message seemed to be that expensive, high-performance technology would solve urban transit woes. Numerous defense (especially aerospace) contractors were participants in the exhibition. Also in attendance were the "big three" auto makers, now calling themselves "total transportation" companies. Ford and General Motors exhibited their own experimental mass transit systems, and Henry Ford II proclaimed that a "limited portion" of the Federal Highway Trust Fund should be used for research into "new transportation concepts" (Rothschild, 1972:27). GM later made a similar announcement. With defense contractors and even auto makers joining to promote the new transit systems, it seemed that a rapid transit renaissance had indeed begun.

Shortly after Transpo '72, Volpe was made ambassador to Italy and was replaced as secretary of transportation by a former senior vice president of Union Oil (Union had been a major opponent of Proposition 18), Claude S. Brinegar (*LAT*, Dec. 8, 1972:1). Advocates of opening the highway fund were fearful of a damaging setback with the departure of Volpe. However, Brinegar soon made it clear that the Nixon administration supported diversion of highway monies for transit (*LAT*, Feb. 8, 1973:1). Nixon himself affirmed his approval of such a policy less than a month later (*LAT*, Mar. 5, 1973:1). Within a few months, the largest oil company in the world, Exxon, pledged support for the elimination of the highway fund, as such, through the "creation of transportation trust funds rather than the existing highway trust funds, with monies from these funds being used for the travel systems—including mass transit—that state and local governments choose to install as best meeting their needs."[14]

During the time that these numerous signs of support for opening the fund were being made, a struggle was going on in the United States Congress over the issue. A coalition made up of voluntary associations (such as the Highway Action Coalition), the Nixon administration, and transit interests, was battling the highway lobby over diversion of the Federal Highway Trust Fund. Addressing the Institute for Rapid Transit (made up of the transit industry) in mid-1973, IRT president Ronan declared, "Although our efforts to secure capital grant assistance for all forms of transit from the Highway Trust Fund have not succeeded to date, we

[14] Highway Action Coalition, "The Concrete Opposition," August 1973.

intend to continue to press this aspect of our legislative program and are confident of ultimate success."[15] After approximately a two-year struggle, marked with several defeats for proponents of opening the fund, a compromise measure was agreed to. Countervailing power at the national level seemed to be developing. The Federal Aid Highway Act of 1973 made federal money available for either transit or highways, depending on the desires of cities and state governments. It was to run for only three fiscal years (1974, 1975, and 1976) and would make about $1 billion available from the highway fund for these purposes over this period. Most transit advocates felt that this was not a very large amount, especially since the figure represented only about 5 percent of the total highway fund that would be available over the three years. The other 95 percent ($19 billion) would still go for highways. In addition, the total trust fund money available for transit would fall light-years short of the amount transit advocates say is needed (e.g., even one city's costs for a rail system like BART could not be met). Moreover, there was no indication that the money would be spent on rails at all. Brinegar and other administration officials were strong advocates of buses and had been discouraging cities such as Los Angeles from building rail systems (*LAT*, May 17, 1974:II-1).

Highway interests, of course, also support the use of buses. Buses run on streets and highways and burn gasoline. Large sales of buses would be quite profitable to General Motors, since that company has a near monopoly on domestic bus production, accounting directly for 75 percent of production. In addition, the firm controls virtually all the remaining 25 percent, since the two other bus manufacturers, Flexible Company and Motor Coach Industries, are dependent on GM for engines and parts (Snell, 1974:26).

PROPOSITION 5

Even though only a small crack had been opened in the Federal Highway Trust Fund, the passage of the 1973 Federal Aid High-

[15] IRT Annual Conference Digest, 1973, p. 4.

way Act had a certain symbolic value for California transportation politics. The possibility that federal matching funds would be available for transit was used by proponents in arguing for the approval of Proposition A in 1974, and backers of the Proposition 18-like Proposition 5 said that the opening of the Federal Highway Trust Fund indicated that the time had come for California to follow suit.

California Senator James Mills, who had been the author of Proposition 18 in 1970, introduced a new bill in the California legislature in early 1973, later to be known as Proposition 5 of 1974. Like Proposition 18, it allowed local areas the option (upon a vote) of using some of the state highway trust fund for mass transit. However, the measure was milder than Proposition 18: instead of an initial 25 percent, the maximum amount that could be diverted was to be 5 percent the first year, increasing by increments of 5 percent annually, until a maximum of 25 percent was reached in the 1978-79 fiscal year. As in the case of Proposition 18, the money could be used for capital outlays only, not for operating subsidies of transit systems. Unlike Proposition 18, Proposition 5 specifically forbade the use of the fund monies to cover maintenance and operating costs of transit systems. The funds had to be used for new "hardware," not for subsidies to existing systems (or to new ones). I was told by one strong business supporter of Proposition 5: "Our theory [position] was that we would support the Proposition 5 if there were controls as to where they used it. We didn't want the highway trust fund to be the supplement to the fare box."

From the time that Mills' bill was introduced in the legislature, it began to look as if the Proposition 5 campaign was going to be strikingly different from the Proposition 18 campaign. Support by the administration of Governor Reagan was obtained after Mills introduced that provision that placed limits (i.e., 5 percent the first year, up to a maximum of 25 percent, instead of 25 percent initially) on the amount of highway money that could be diverted. After that agreement, it was reported that the bill had "no visible opposition from the powerful oil industry lobby." Although the Southern California Automobile Club and the California Chamber of Commerce sent representatives to lobby against the plan, without the oil companies (who had three years before given three-fourths of the anti-18 money) the opposition lacked potency (*LAT*, Aug. 22, 1973:24). Mills' bill passed through the legislature handily and was placed on the June 4, 1974 California ballot as Proposition 5.

The vote on Proposition 5 was to precede the vote on Proposition A in Los Angeles by five months. The campaigns for the two issues were organized by essentially the same people. Virtually all of the Proposition 5 campaign committee (Californians for Better Transportation) were later on the Proposition A committee (Citizens for Better Transportation). Mayor Bradley was chairman of the Proposition A campaign, and also Southern California chairman for the Proposition 5 campaign. Bradshaw of ARCO was Executive Committee chairman in both campaigns and played the leading roles in both. Other large businesses represented on the Proposition 5 committee were Bank of America, United California Bank, Crocker National Bank, Occidental Life Insurance Company, Northrop Corporation, Century City, and Dart Industries. These businesses are mostly located in the Los Angeles area. Thus, it appeared that Proposition 5 would have substantial business support, especially in Southern California. By this time, it was also clear that the oil companies would not oppose the measure. The *Los Angeles Times* noted that "Most of the major [oil] companies have indicated neutrality" (*LAT*, May 7, 1974:II-6).

The remainder of the campaign confirmed these early impressions. There was little opposition to Proposition 5. According to the regional representative of the National Highway Users' Federation (a national-level highway lobby organization) the group was officially against it, but was not active in the campaign. The Automobile Club of Southern California did run an editorial against Proposition 5 in the club's magazine,[16] but did not engage in much activity beyond that. On June 4, 1974, the ballot measure passed by a wide margin in the state, getting 60.3 percent of the vote (*LAT*, June 6, 1974:23).

Further and stronger confirmation of this pattern of lack of lobby

[16] *Auto Club News Pictorial*, 43 (June 1974:3-4).

opposition comes from the campaign contribution list. Only $1,700.29 was put up against Proposition 5, all of it from the Automobile Club of Southern California. On the other side $203,215 was contributed for the measure, with 99.4 percent coming from business. ARCO was the indisputable leader of the pro-5 contributors. The company gave almost half ($100,252) of the total collected for Proposition 5. No other oil company gave any money for the measure. Fifteen percent of the money came from insurance companies, 6.5 percent from other industries, and 5 percent from banks. The remainder came from financial, merchandising, aerospace, construction, and utility companies.

The pattern of support for Proposition 5 was in essence the reverse of that for Proposition 18. This time, virtually all of the business money was for the measure, with an oil company as the leader, and no oil companies gave money against Proposition 5.

How does one explain this dramatic reversal between the Proposition 18 and Proposition 5 campaigns? Did the member firms of the highway lobby switch their political behavior for strategic reasons? If so, why? Or was the growing power of the transit interests sufficient to crush political opposition to highway fund diversion? Was this an example of countervailing power in operation, or are there other possible explanations of this phenomenon? Most importantly, which of the three sets of hypotheses derived from the elite, pluralist, and dialectic models is best supported by these case studies? In order to answer these questions it will be necessary to peel away another layer of the onion and go to a deeper level of analysis. The next chapter will address these central analytical and theoretical issues.

CHAPTER FIVE

WHAT THESE CAMPAIGNS TELL US ABOUT POLITICAL POWER: THE PLURALIST AND ELITIST INTERPRETATIONS

We have now examined the five most important transportation-related elections that occurred in the most populous state in the country between 1962 and 1974, a period at the beginning of what has been called the rapid transit renaissance. (The reader again is referred to Table 2 in Chapter One for a summary of these ballot measures.) These events were of importance not only to the state of California and its major cities, but also to the nation, for they both reflected a new politics of transportation at the national level and helped to shape that new politics. In addition to providing substantive insights into the nature and dynamics of this new turn in metropolitan transportation politics, these campaigns, taken as an integrated whole, give us an excellent means of testing the explanatory capabilities of the pluralist, elitist, and dialectic models of political power. An empirical evaluation of these models is the main goal of this work.

We are now in a position to begin to evaluate the three sets of hypotheses presented in Chapter One. To the casual glance, it appears that the transit campaigns so far examined present no clear pattern. Businesses that supported BART and a similar system for Los Angeles did not support Proposition 18, a measure that would have aided urban transit development. The highway lobby did not oppose transit development. The highway lobby did not oppose transit systems in San Francisco and Los Angeles, but did oppose Proposition 18. Yet when the similar Proposition 5 was put before voters a few years later, there was no opposition by highway forces and considerable support from companies that had been silent during the Proposition 18 campaign. How does one understand this complex and shifting pattern? Is there a pattern? I shall argue that there is. In the initial analyses, we have seen the first layer or so of the onion—during the continuing evaluation we shall see the deeper layers as overarching patterns are discovered and as additional empirical materials are brought into the analysis.

PLURALIST MODEL

The first task is to see how well the pluralist model appears to be able to handle the series of political events we have observed. For convenience, let us recall the pluralist hypotheses as presented in Chapter One:

> *Pluralist hypotheses:* If the pluralist model is correct, the study of an important political issue should reveal (1) the active involvement of numerous interest groups, (2) divergent goals and interests among the groups, (3) a vigorous, competitive relationship among the groups, (4) interests and alliances that shift over time, and (5) political outcomes that consistently favor no particular group more than others.

It was noted earlier that although the case of BART and the two Los Angeles transportation campaigns seem to offer only limited support for pluralist hypotheses, the overall pattern of the five campaigns in the issue-area might offer stronger support.

Pluralists might attack the problem from one of two distinct but related perspectives. Nontraditional pluralists, such as Lowi (1969), might argue that the pattern of the campaigns is essentially the chaotic reflection of a fragmented political system. As such, it is the result of a clash of narrow interest groups not able to agree upon nor to formulate a consistent, general policy on urban transit matters. In short, there is no real pattern revealed here. For reasons that will soon become evident, I shall maintain that this interpretation is fundamentally incorrect. More conventional pluralists would likely put forth an explanation such as the following.

At the most simple level, these campaigns do appear to provide partial support for the pluralist model. It could be argued that there was active involvement of several groups in these campaigns, groups with divergent interests that engaged in competition to affect public policy. For instance, the pattern of financial support exhibited in the five transit campaigns shows there are two relatively distinct interest groups (i.e., the highway lobby and the downtown transit interests) within the business world that compete to influence public transportation policy. Thus Table 2 shows that the transit interests supported the BART campaign, the two Los Angeles transit campaigns (Proposition A of 1968 and Proposition A of 1974), and the most recent successful attempt to divert money from the highway trust fund to mass transit (Proposition 5 of 1974). The hand of the opposing highway interests was revealed in the intense campaign waged against the earlier unsuccessful try to divert trust fund monies (Proposition 18 of 1970). That interests and alliances have shifted over the course of the campaigns is indicated by the change in patterns of support between the Proposition 18 and Proposition 5 campaigns. The highway lobby opposed the earlier measure, but did not oppose the later, similar Proposition 5. Moreover, while Proposition 18 received no support from downtown business, Proposition 5 got a great deal of support from these interests. It might be reasoned, therefore, that the successful passage of legislation (Proposition 5) to free some highway money for development of urban mass transit is a reflection of the growing power of nonhighway interests to countervail (see Galbraith, 1956) against the highway lobby and to force compromises.

Pluralists would further contend that these nonhighway interests include not only the business interests directly involved in producing modern mass transit equipment, but also elected officials in both the state and national legislatures who favored opening the highway funds, voluntary organizations (such as the Highway Action Coalition) that worked for such legislation, and local voters who played a role by approving BART and Proposition 5, and in rejecting Proposition 18 and the two transit proposals in Los Angeles, thereby going against the big money three out of five times. Thus, it would be asserted that political outcomes have moved away from almost exclusively favoring highway interests, demonstrating that political power is pluralistic rather than concentrated or, in the pluralist phrase, "monolithic."

This argument has its merits in that it does paint a fairly accurate picture of some aspects of the political events we have seen. However, these aspects make up only part of the whole story. The pluralist research paradigm tells researchers that political power can be studied in a rather direct manner by using techniques (e.g., the decisional method) that do not probe very far beneath the surface of overt, individual and group behavior (see Lukes, 1974). The deeper layers of the onion are not penetrated. The possibility, for example, of suppression of status quo challenging political issues (Bachrach and Baratz, 1962) is not considered. Consequently, the decisional techniques typically used in pluralist research would not have discovered such suppression as that of the air pollution issue which occurred in Gary, Indiana (Crenson, 1971).

In addition to missing the possibility of issue suppression, pluralist methods of research tend to underestimate seriously the extent to which local elites are linked to one another and to powerful elites at the national level. Regarding the latter point, Domhoff (1978) has reanalyzed the New Haven case, attempting to show that Dahl's methods did not dig sufficiently deep into the political and social life of that city. In particular, Domhoff argues that Dahl's methods did not allow him to uncover the extent to which social cohesion and policy consensus among elites in New Haven and between these elites and national elites shaped in crucial ways the political events in that city. Likewise, I shall argue that this underestimation of elite unity and interconnectedness is inherent in the decisional method, and that this important defect in the pluralist approach leads such researchers to make unwarranted conclusions about the distribution of power.

So far, this present analysis has relied largely on pluralist methods of research. Now it is necessary to go beyond those methods. Specifically, it is necessary to address the issue that the pluralist approach has overlooked: the question as to the degree to which business elites are divided or unified. The elitist model and its methods of research represent a useful initial step in that direction.

ELITIST MODEL

It is appropriate to recall the elitist hypotheses:

Elitist hypotheses. If the power elitist model is correct, the study of an important political issue should reveal (1) a high degree of elite involvement, (2) general convergence of interest among elites, (3) elite unity and dominance on the issue, (4) stability of political allegiances, and (5) outcomes that tend to favor elite interests.

The evidence shows that there was a high degree of business elite involvement and dominance in the campaigns herein studied. Rather than consisting of a pluralistic range of voluntary associations, the groups directly involved in organizing and financing the campaigns—with the exception of the supporters of Proposition 18 (i.e., state legislators, the Tuberculosis and Respiratory Diseases Association, the League of Women Voters)—were overwhelmingly made up of business elites. At the simplest level, this would tend to support the elitist model. However, elitists would go on to maintain that these elites would be relatively unified in their goals and policy preferences, while pluralists might concede elite involvement but would look for contending elites divided by divergent interests. In other words, do we have a unified elite or divided, "plural" elites?

An important issue in the evaluation of the elitist model is the extent to which elite interests converged on these issues (as the elite model would predict) or were divergent (which pluralist theory would predict). Here, the pattern is not as clear-cut as a simple competitive model would indicate. Interests are not the same as behavior. While there undoubtedly were some differences in interests (i.e., downtown businesses that desired new urban transit versus suburban firms wanting additional circumferential highway development) the firms involved exhibited largely noncompetitive behavior. For example, in each of the five campaigns, business contributions fall into an essentially noncompetitive pattern: the money is virtually all on one side or the other of the issue (see Table 2). In spite of whatever conflicts of interest among the firms there may have been, there was no direct competition in terms of campaign money. This is especially clear in the case of the dramatic shift between Proposition 18 and Proposition 5. All business money was against Proposition 18 in 1970. Four years later, all business money was for the similar Proposition 5. This change was not, however, the result of individual companies switching sides. Those businesses that opposed Proposition 18 dropped out of sight in the Proposition 5 campaign, while the supporters of Proposition 5 did not give for Proposition 18. Of the fifty-two firms that had contributed against Proposition 18, only one (i.e., the Automobile Club of Southern California) gave against Proposition 5; of fifty-six companies that supported Proposition 5, only two (i.e., Rohr and Kaiser, with trivial contributions) had given for Proposition 18. Thus there was a virtually complete reversal of business support for this policy (diversion of highway funds) and a 97.2 percent (105 of 108) turnover in the firms involved. Such a thoroughgoing change would appear unlikely to be caused by each company making a totally independent decision on this policy question.

Elitists might see this pattern as reflecting elite political coordination and unity. Clearly, this noncompetitive pattern does not fit the conventional pluralist model. However, some pluralists might attempt to counter by arguing that this pattern is merely a result of the understandable desire by companies to avoid overt (and costly) conflict. Lowi (1969:295), for example, has observed: "Competition tends to last only until each group learns the goals of the few other groups. Each adjusts to the others. Real confrontation leads to a net loss for all rather than gain for any. Rather than countervailing power there will more than likely be accommodating power."

It is often in the interests of large businesses to avoid competition with each other, as in the case of the oligopolistic automobile industry (Snell, 1974; Rothschild, 1973). To such industries, lack of competition means operating under external conditions that are more predictable and that allow higher levels of profit.

Moreover, in an interdependent economy of mammoth economic units, many firms must do business with each other (see Averitt, 1968). This mutual dependence can operate as a source of social control, preventing deviance beyond certain boundaries.

Here we can recall the comments of the San Francisco banker (Chapter Four) who noted how difficult it is for a bank to oppose a "good customer" such as a large oil company.

In order to resolve the issue of whether this noncompetitive pattern is indicative of positive elite coordination (elite model) or merely conflict avoidance (a variant of the pluralist model) it is once again necessary to dig deeper.

Conflict avoidance is an essentially passive strategy that requires little or no intra-elite communication or negotiation. On the other hand, elite coordination would require not only communication networks but also some means of settling differences and working out at least minimal joint plans of action. It is quite clear in the cases under investigation that communication and shared understanding did exist among the potential competitors. Almost without exception, business leaders speak of the "business community." As the former head of the Automobile Club of Southern California, current chairman of a conglomerate, and member of the exclusive Los Angeles Committee of 25, told me: "I'm sure the business community is not the only group of people who consult with each other. . . . It's a natural thing. So you kind of talk to the people you know and say, 'What do you think about this?' "

This "natural" process of communication, common to many self-identified groups in society, is especially consequential within the business community. As Schattschneider (1935:287) reminds us: "Businessmen collectively constitute the most class-conscious group in American society. As a class they are the most highly organized, more easily mobilized, have more facilities for communication, are more like-minded, and are more accustomed to stand together in defense of their privileges than any other group."

All of the things mentioned by Schattschneider—class-consciousness, organization, communication, like-mindedness, and unity of action—are present in these case studies. Like-mindedness was commented upon by one executive I interviewed: "I would say . . . business thinking, without being in collusion or anything like that, generally is on one side or the other of something because they are thinking along the same lines and they get the same information." Like-mindedness is very important politically, for it means that business people will often know how others are thinking, so that common purpose may sometimes result without the need for explicit, issue-by-issue communication, discussion, and decision making. As Bachrach and Baratz (1962) have argued, such shared attitudes and predispositions are not observable as overt decisions, but nevertheless may have profound political consequences.

The desire for unity of action as noted by Schattschneider was reflected in a statement one former business trade association executive made to me. He observed: "And of course there's this thing that they want to get along as a community of businessmen and they don't want to go off in different directions."

A recent study by Moore (1979) has demonstrated the extent of elite communication and discussion networks in the United States. Using data from the American Leadership Study which are based on interviews with 545 leaders of major economic, political, and social institutions, Moore's most significant finding for present purposes was that almost one-third of these leaders made up one enormous clique. Members of that clique discussed a broad spectrum of issues, resided in various parts of the country, and were generally quite heterogeneous in terms of institutional affiliations.

Similarly, at the more local level addressed by this present study, extensive and effective friendship and communication networks apparently do exist. Businessmen know and talk to one another. In conducting interviews with these people, one quickly gains the impression that there is widespread acquaintance and communication among the leaders of California (and perhaps national) big business. They tend to know not only the names and corporate connections of other business leaders, but will often mention that the person in question is an "old friend" or that they have worked together before in some business or civic organization. Often, political figures also are included. For example, two central people in the California highway lobby are a California state senator and another businessman who was a charter member of the Freeway Support Committee of the California State Chamber of Commerce. Yet, the first general manager of BART (and former head of an oil trade association) says both of these men are his old friends. Ben Wilson (a pseudonym) another friend of the above FSC charter member (who describes Wilson as "one of the most powerful men in the state") received a telephone call from a former presidential advisor while the author was interviewing Wilson. Later, Wilson placed a telephone call to the president of an automobile club and the two discussed the previous night's meeting of the Committee of 25. Wilson also mentioned to me that former President Nixon had telephoned him a few days previously. An interview with a San Francisco banker and business consultant was conducted at the Merchant's Exchange Club in San Francisco. It was quite apparent that the banker was widely known to other members of the business club.

Many other such impressionistic bits of data could be cited, but little purpose would be served. The extent of this friendship and communications network is an empirical question, but there can be no doubt of its existence. This network would appear to be an important resource in business attempts to achieve unity and coordination.

Schattschneider's observation concerning the highly organized nature of the business community is amply supported in these case studies. Business organizations that include more than one type of industry, such as the Bay Area Council, the Committee of 25, and the Chamber of Commerce, provide important forums for business negotiation and coordination. A prominent executive's words, recorded during an interview, describe the functions of such forums. When asked how business solves its problems, he said:

> The Bay Area Council represents the Bay Area as a . . . business community and they probably work out the answers to these community problems. In the case of the California State Chamber of Commerce, representing business on a statewide basis, their board of directors, on the basis of staff recommendations, will adopt policy concerning legislation in Sacramento and ballot measures and—these men sitting around a table, here you get the presidents of Standard Oil, and the Southern Pacific, Southern California Edison Com-

pany, and so on. So . . . based on my experience that's how
community problems or statewide problems are handled.

The Bay Area Council is regionally based, but some important
business organizations are nationally oriented. For example,
G. William Domhoff has shown that such business policy-creating
groups as the Business Council, the Committee for Economic
Development, the Conference Board, and the Advertising Council
are made up of the representatives of the largest corporations from
all over the country (Domhoff, 1975:179).

Indeed, in the transportation campaigns business organizations
played an important role. It was in such organizations that, in
spite of initial differences of opinion among firms, extensive and
rather effective attempts were made to overcome these diverse
points of view and to achieve unity. As one leading businessman
who had been very active in the campaigns told me: "Between
Proposition 18 and 5 we fought the thing out in the halls of the
legislature and in the chambers of commerce and the community
organizations, in SCAG [Southern California Associated Govern-
ments] and all the rest of the places. . . . That's one of the reasons
we belong to organizations like that." He also pointed out the
central role of organizations such as Chamber of Commerce in
business conflict resolution and consensus creation. Concerning
the issue of Proposition 18 and Proposition 5, he said:

> Some of the people that opposed Proposition 18 also opposed
> Proposition 5. We couldn't get them to support it. I got into
> great arguments with some of my friends. In fact, I was
> president of the chamber the year of Proposition 5. And I
> had the president of an oil company and the president of a
> railroad company opposing me on the fight, but I won the
> fight before the directors of the chamber for our position.
> And when we won the fight both of those guys supported
> us. . . . When the thing was over with and sixty guys had
> voted, and there was only—I don't know—five or six votes
> on their side, they weren't going to fight the trend.

This statement implies that conflicts within the business community over the use of a small portion of the California highway

trust fund for rapid transit development were essentially resolved within the business community between Proposition 18 and Proposition 5. This could account for the lack of conflict in the public political arena: intrabusiness resolution obviates public resolution, posing obvious problems for pluralist decisional methods. The solution of this political conflict reflects the general tendency of the business community to seek consensus. As a former bank executive pointed out in an interview, the pressure for consensus is strong. He used the analogy of the business community as a club: "Well, if you belong to a club and the membership is up for a vote—if it's a secret ballot of course you don't know, but if there's any leakage that indicates that someone is opposed to someone, then you find that an awful lot of people follow the lead."

This club analogy is particularly appropriate in that, as Domhoff (1970; 1974) has shown, clubs and policy organizations are also important in providing places for ironing out differences, discussing policies, and generating social solidarity among elites. In addition to socializing, business is also accomplished in clubs. When I was interviewing the general manager of a trade association, an aid to the manager came in to the office and informed him that a certain business meeting was scheduled for that evening. The aid asked for and was given permission to use the manager's name in requesting a room for the meeting at the highly exclusive Jonathon Club in Los Angeles. In another case, the Los Angeles Club was the site of a dinner at which Bradshaw of ARCO and Mayor Bradley urged the business community to support Los Angeles' Proposition A in 1974. A retired business executive, formerly a staff member of the California State Chamber of Commerce, and ex-head of the Western Oil and Gas Association, was asked about the role of face-to-face relationships in working out problems in the business community. He said:

> Well, up on Nob Hill there's the Pacific Union Club. It's the most exclusive club in San Francisco and it's just across from the Fairmont and the Mark Hopkins [hotels]. All right, the leaders of San Francisco business go up there for lunch and maybe they have a big round table with twelve guys

around the table, guys alone, otherwise they come in sometimes and they bring in guests, and they know each other on
a first name basis and they [breaks off]. . . . So they work
together, partly on the basis of personal friendship, partly
on the basis of devotion to the community, and I think they
want to protect their own reputations as being cooperative.

At the national level, the top corporations in the land are linked
through social clubs and business organizations. Domhoff (1975)
has done a study of the extent of the connections between large
businesses and these clubs and organizations. Of the 797 corporations (500 industrials, 50 banks, 50 insurance companies, 50
transportation companies, 50 utilities, 50 retailers, and 47 conglomerates) listed in *Fortune* in 1969, a total of 84.4 percent (673)
of them had at least one member of their board of directors who
was also a member of one of four business policy organizations
(Business Council, Committee for Economic Development, Council on Foreign Relations, National Association of Manufacturers)
or one of the top eleven business social clubs (e.g., Links Club,
Pacific Union, Chicago Club, etc.). When one looks at the top
25 corporations in each category, the links are even more impressive: 25 of 25 industrials, 25 of 25 banks, 23 of 25 insurance
companies, 24 of 25 transportation firms, 24 of 25 utilities, 19
of 25 retailers, and 18 of 25 conglomerates have connections to
at least one of these fifteen exclusive business and social organizations (Domhoff, 1975:179). These organizational links provide
many opportunities for the creation of social solidarity and consensus, for the resolution of political differences, and for coordination to be attempted.

The potential for coordination can become a reality, as was
revealed in an event that happened in California during the period
covered by this study. The People's Lobby, a California public
interest group, succeeded in gathering enough signatures to qualify
an initiative for the June 1972 California ballot. The complex
measure (Proposition 9 of 1972) was oriented toward environmental reform. Its provisions included the phasing out of leaded
gasoline, closer monitoring of polluting industries, the banning
of offshore oil drilling, a five-year moratorium on new nuclear

power plant construction, and the banning of persistent chlorinated hydrocarbons such as DDT. Thus, it was reasonable to expect strong opposition from heavy industry, especially oil and utility companies.

Molotch and Lester (1974) point out the usefulness of studying accidents and scandals as a means of learning about political processes. In the Proposition 9 case, the scandal grew out of a memorandum from the office of the chairman of Standard Oil of California that was copied and given to the sponsors of Proposition 9 (the People's Lobby) by an employee of Standard. People's Lobby made the memo public and its contents were reported by the press. The memo was to the chairman of the board of Standard Oil from a San Francisco lawyer and Sacramento oil lobbyist; the subject was the up-coming campaign over Proposition 9. The lobbyist suggested that a "citizens' committee" should be formed to "front" for the anti-9 forces rather than allow the function to be performed by the California Chamber of Commerce, the California Manufacturers' Association, or the governor of California. The written comments on the memo (presumably those of the chairman of Standard) indicate approval of the plan. The document also suggests that a public relations firm (a firm well-known to Californians as often being in the employ of conservative politicians and political· groups) be retained to manage the campaign. Attached to the memo was a preliminary campaign plan drawn up by that firm. Among other things it says: "In short, the campaign against the People's Lobby initiative must not be spearheaded *publicly* by business and industry. *It should be publicly launched by responsible conservationists, by academicians, labor spokesmen, leaders of the Democratic party,* and joined at the appropriate time in the appropriate fashion by business, industry, agriculture, and the Republican party leadership" (emphasis in original). The plan also made clear who would actually be running the campaign—the oil and utility companies of the state: "The involvement of the principal oil companies and the principal utilities . . . *is not a public involvement.* Rather, in a non-publicized sense, it is a means of directing the campaign under the aegis of a *public* citizens committee as outlined. In the doing, total control of the public campaign strategy and direction is maintained" (emphasis in the original). This "total control" would be achieved by "a small steering committee which would not become public, composed of the delegated spokesmen for the principal utilities and oil companies." As a front, it would be necessary to create a "public citizens' committee" that would be "expanded obviously right up to election day." The public structure was needed in order to avoid "a big business versus people's issue which can only be self-defeating."

The important thing about this memo is not that it reveals a Machiavellian attitude toward the political process. What is important is that the whole tone of the document takes for granted that total control by big business of a public campaign is entirely possible and does not consider problematic the concurrence of other oil and utility companies, business and industry, the California Chamber of Commerce, the California Manufacturers Association, or even the governor. The company appears entirely confident that it can control the campaign and that other interested parties will go along with the plan. Such hubris does not arise from the give-and-take of pluralistic politics but from the experiences of business elites who are accustomed to playing decisive political roles in these matters. Furthermore, the plan envisaged in the memo was more than idle talk: it appears that it became a reality and did guide the actual unfolding of the campaign.[1]

[1] The public relations firm mentioned in the memo was hired to manage the anti-9 campaign, and a group called Californians Against the Pollution Initiative was formed to oppose the measure. Another part of the original plan was to conduct "intensive opinion research . . . to test public attitudes on all relevant matters and to test the public validity of arguments to be set forth in the course of the campaign." The apparent fruit of that effort was a strident "scare" campaign that was designed to play on voter fears and insecurities. Garishly colored pamphlets were printed that described a host of supposed horrors that would befall the populace should Proposition 9 become law. For example:

> You will not be able to provide yourself and your family with the necessities of life—because most trains, ships, and trucks that bring food and goods of all kinds to your local community will be unable to operate in California for two or more years. . . . You can lose your job, in any of a wide array of industries. . . . You can expect to bring home wormy fruit and insect-laden vegetables from the grocery store. . . . Your very life will be endangered.

Anti-9 campaign contributions totaled almost $1.5 million, with heavy industry

Another strong indication of political coordination by business elites emerges from data relating to the transit campaigns. The pattern of contributions against Proposition 18 and for Proposition 5 provides evidence of a high degree of organization and coordination, suggesting some sort of assessment system based on the value of assets or on sales volume. Table 5 shows the relationship between the amount of gasoline sold by the largest companies in California (including two that did not donate) and the size of their contributions against Proposition 18. It is doubtful that such a strong relationship, in which nearly 90 percent of the variance is accounted for, would hold in campaigns which are truly spontaneous and uncoordinated (and where each does not know the amounts given by others).

An even stronger relationship, a nearly perfect one, is found in the case of bank contributions for Proposition 5. Table 6 shows the total assets of the largest eight banks in the state (all of whom gave) and the amounts contributed. In this case, bank assets entirely account for size of contribution. And even though each

Table 5. Oil Company Contributions against Proposition 18 by Amount of Gasoline Sold in California

Company	Gas Sold (1969)* (x)	Contribution (y)
1. Standard of Calif.	1,642 million gallons	$75,000
2. Shell	1,497 million gallons	50,000
3. Union	876 million gallons	20,000
4. ARCO	824 million gallons	—
5. Mobil	810 million gallons	30,000
6. Texaco	689 million gallons	20,000
7. Phillips	415 million gallons	15,000
8. Gulf	410 million gallons	20,000
9. Humble	320 million gallons	20,000
10. Signal	242 million gallons	—
11. Douglas	192 million gallons	5,000

$r^2 = .76$
$r^2 = .89$ when ARCO and Signal are deleted.

*SOURCE: 1969 gasoline sales figures from California Board of Equalization.

(especially oil, chemical, and utilities) predominating. On June 6, 1972, the measure failed by a wide margin (65 to 35 percent) (*LAT*, June 6, 1972:22).

Table 6. Bank Contributions for Proposition 5 by Total Assets

Bank	Assets* (x)	Contribution (y)
1. Bank of America (SF)	$49.0 billion	$4,210
2. Security Pacific (LA)	13.4 billion	1,610
3. Wells Fargo (SF)	11.6 billion	1,280
4. Crocker National (SF)	9.5 billion	1,070
5. United California (LA)	9.0 billion	920
6. Union Bank (LA)	4.8 billion	410
7. Bank of California (SF)	3.0 billion	290
8. First Western (LA)	1.4 billion	210
		$10,000

$r^2 = .98$

* SOURCE: Bank assets from the Los Angeles *Times* (5/12/74) annual roster of California businesses.

contribution is for an unusual amount (e.g., $1,070), the total for the largest banks is an even $10,000, suggesting that an overall quota was set for this group with smaller banks assessed on a proportionate basis.

How are these supposedly competitive corporations able to achieve such unity of political action and such a high degree of hierarchically ordered coordination? Through what organizational structure is this done? A comment by a former general manager of the oil industry trade association, the Western Oil and Gas Association, provides a clue. When asked how disagreements within the business community might be handled, he responded:

> Well, I think that matters not having to do with individual companies, but with broad [business] community interest . . . would be worked out through trade associations. The Western Oil and Gas Association represents the oil industry of the Pacific coast states. Community problems like regulation of the transportation of gasoline . . . or problems relating to taxation or to the gasoline tax . . . [are] discussed at meetings of the board of directors of the Western Oil and Gas Association.

If trade associations play such roles, it is logical to suppose that they might also have a hand in the formulation and carrying out of political strategies, such as the assignment and coordination of contributions. Later interviews confirmed this hypothesis. In the case of the oil companies, the Western Oil and Gas Association (WOGA) was the agent for coordination. The general manager of WOGA calculated the "fair share" of oil contributions based on "gallonage" of gasoline sold in California. He then told the companies what amounts would be appropriate, "if they were going to give." This prorating of contributions by WOGA has been going on at least since the 1940s, according to a former WOGA general manager.

The analogous function was performed for the banks by their clearinghouse (formally organized to settle accounts between banks, as by exchanging checks drawn on other member banks, etc.). An executive of Wells Fargo Bank told me that it has long been a practice for the banks' clearinghouse to decide how much to give on an issue, with the banks then contributing "in relation to their size."

Here again we have evidence of the effective political coordination that may be attained through the organizational structures available to the business community. Pluralist theory gives us no reason to expect that such things would happen, and thus pluralist methods of research often overlook them. A peeling away of the surface of the onion by elitist research methods may reveal elite integration nearer the core.

This chapter will conclude with the examination of one final means of business community integration and coordination that is also largely neglected by political researchers. That means of coordination is the corporate interlocking directorate. Persons who sit simultaneously on the boards of directors of several companies would appear to be in an excellent position to serve as agents of communication and possibly of coordination and control among corporations. To the extent that such links characterize the corporate world, they could provide an important source of systemic integration and political coherence.

Yet, in spite of the theoretical potential and practical relevance of studying interlocking directorates, until very recently little work has been done in this area, especially by sociologists. There are probably two main reasons for this general pattern of neglect. The first concerns the issue of the assumed locus of corporate control, and the second has to do with the availability of methods or techniques of analysis.

The biggest hindrance to systematic analysis of interlocking directorates has been the conventional assumption that boards of directors play a slight role in corporate affairs since corporations are generally held to be controlled by top managers rather than by directors. The managerial control thesis posits a separation between ownership and control of modern corporations, with management able to choose members for the board of directors effectively through use of stock proxies. Control of the corporation, then, lies with the bureaucratic managers rather than with ownership as represented by the directors.

If one accepts the thesis of managerial control, therefore, the study of interlocking directorates does not appear to be of great moment. According to this view, management uses the board of directors for "advice, criticism, prestige, and, to a minor extent, for business contacts" (Sonquist and Koenig, 1975:197). Thus whatever might be said of interlocks in terms of the distribution of business expertise or prestige, or in terms of communication patterns among businesses, little or nothing would be ascertainable regarding corporate control and power relationships. Since many (if not most) sociologists subscribe to the managerial control view, it is not surprising that few have studied interlocking directorates. However, a study by Zeitlin (1974) challenges this dominant point of view. After an extensive review of problems of method and measurement in numerous studies dealing with the issue of corporate control, Zeitlin concludes that the question of managerial versus owner control (via the board of directors) is not yet settled and that "the empirical question is quite open" (Zeitlin, 1974:1073).

The study of interlocking directorates is important, especially so if the directors themselves exercise significant corporate control. In addition to whatever these patterns of interlocks may reveal about sociometric relationships among the corporate elite, they may also provide crucial insights into corporate power and politics. In the present study, although none was specifically questioned about interlocks, some interview respondents did volunteer that they felt that interlocking directorates made a practical difference in the campaigns studied. For instance, as reported in Chapter Four, William Roberts, a member of the Northern California steering committee for Proposition 18, believes that interlocks among companies made it difficult to raise money for the measure. The same feeling has been voiced by Ray King, Proposition 18's campaign director and chief fund raiser. The *Los Angeles Times*, in attempting to account for the failure of Century City (i.e., Alcoa) to give money for Proposition 18, pointed out that the powerful Mellon family has "three seats on the Gulf Oil board" in addition to having ownership of large amounts of Alcoa stock. A Los Angeles Area Chamber of Commerce official noted in an interview that some downtown Los Angeles companies may have failed to support 18 because they are "automobile-oriented, or their board may be automobile-oriented." These statements suggest that those involved in political campaigns hold the opinion that boards of directors are influential in determining a firm's political policies, and that interlocking directorates may function to promote political coherence among structurally linked companies.

Another reason for the relative paucity of studies of interlocking directorates relates to the lack of adequate techniques of analysis. Interlocking directorates are characteristic features of the corporate world and the pattern of relationships is extremely complex. For example, Figure 2 shows the links, as of about 1970, among the Freeway Support Committee of the California State Chamber of Commerce and a number of large California corporations. This intricate network was discovered by first identifying all firms and other organizations in California that shared at least one director with the Freeway Support Committee (FSC) of the California State Chamber of Commerce. Thus, as the diagram indicates, the FSC shares two directors with the Automobile Club of Southern California, two directors with United California Bank, and two directors with the California State Automobile Association. Additionally, a number of other organizations and businesses, such as Pacific Mutual Life, Standard Oil of California, North American Rockwell, and Union Oil, are linked to the FSC by single interlocks. The next step involved the determination of all of the

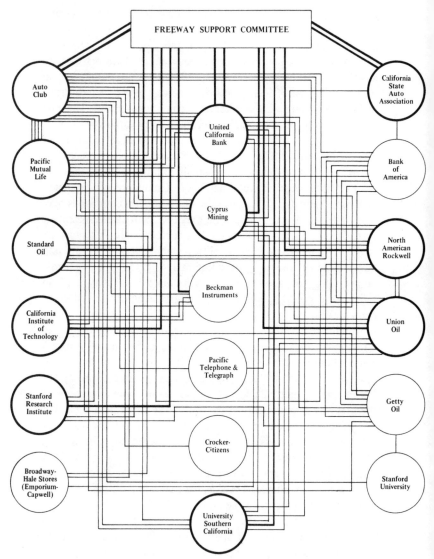

Figure 2. Freeway Support Committee Interlocks.

interlocks among the FSC-related organizations uncovered in the first step. Thus, it was discovered that some companies, such as North American Rockwell and Union Oil, are not only each linked to the FSC, but are also interlocked with each other. The second step also brought in companies (e.g., Bank of America) that are not linked to the FSC, but that are linked to a number of the FSC-related organizations (e.g., the Auto Club, Standard Oil, Pacific Mutual Life). In addition to the interlocks shown, many of these companies are interlocked with other firms not represented in the diagram. The complexity and the extensiveness of the ties between the organizations in this limited sample shows that the FSC is "well-connected" with the California business community. This may help to explain the power of the highway lobby and also the reluctance of business to support rapid transit development. Is there a different pattern of interlocks for firms that support the development of rapid transit as compared with the pattern for highway interests? Can interlocking directorate analysis shed any light on the remarkable distribution of campaign contributions observed in the five transit issues we have examined?

Sonquist and Koenig (1975) describe the recent development of statistical methods, computational algorithms, and computer programs designed to analyze intricate patterns of interlocking directorates. Basically, this analysis involves isolating and identifying "cliques" of companies, much as is done in traditional sociometric analysis of friendship networks.

Since the remainder of this chapter will be concerned with the relevance of the analysis of interlocking directorates for the study of corporate political power, it is necessary to describe in some detail the analytical techniques required. The approach outlined by Sonquist and Koenig (1975) is based on that branch of mathematics called graph theory. A set of points and a set of lines between these points is a "graph." Points represent corporations and lines represent connections between two corporations. Since in this case we are interested in interlocking directorates, a line between two firms stands for a shared member of their board of directors.

Of much significance is the question of what pattern of interconnection among a group of corporations will be defined as constituting a closely linked knot or "clique" of corporations. One wishes to define a clique in such a way that a high proportion of the pairs of corporations in the group are connected by a line (i.e., the pairs are "adjacent"), and so that connections among clique members are much more numerous than are connections between members and nonmembers. Sonquist and Koenig describe the algorithm used to calculate the "N-clique":

> 1. From the original graph of linked pairs of firms draw a new graph which has a line between each pair of points that are connected by a "path" of length N or less in the original graph. (A "path" is a line or series of lines connecting any two points). The rationale of this first step is very simply to treat paths of two or more lines between two points as if they were a single direct line. . . .
> 2. Find the "maximal complete subgraph" of this new graph and select out the points in this subgraph (A "maximal complete subgraph" is a subset of the total graph which has every pair of its points directly connected ("adjacent").
> 3. Connect the points selected in Step 2 with the lines from the *original* graph connecting them. These are the "cliques" within the graph. (emphasis in the original; Sonquist and Koenig, 1975:202)

This definition of a clique has the advantage of permitting connections of pairs of firms through intermediate "third" firms that may themselves be outside the clique. A disadvantage is that the diameter of such a clique (the length of the longest direct path between a pair of corporations in the clique), may be greater than N. To avoid this, the N-clique is restricted to cliques of diameter N, with larger diameters not being treated as cliques. As defined, a single point (a corporation) can be in more than one clique. This raises the problem of overlap between cliques. How many common members can two cliques have before we may be justified in treating the two cliques as one large clique? Sonquist and Koenig have dealt with this problem by merging cliques to form ones of larger diameter whenever the degree of overlap reached an arbitrary proportion of the members present in the smaller of both cliques (in this case, the overlap criterion was 0.33).

The data base analyzed was compiled from the *Fortune 500* list for 1969 by Professor Michael Schwartz of the State University of New York, Stony Brook. Boards of director memberships for these companies were obtained from annual reports or from *Standard and Poor's Register of Corporations, Directors, and Executives*. Information was compiled for 797 corporations in the United States (including the 500 largest industrials, 50 largest banks, 50 largest insurance companies, 50 largest retailers, 50 largest transportation firms, 50 largest utilities, and 47 conglomerates and other miscellaneous firms), 8,623 individuals, and 11,290 directorships (Sonquist and Koenig, 1975:203).

Sonquist and Koenig note an important technical problem that arose: "Preliminary investigation of the data suggested that the level of connectedness in the total group of 797 corporations was so high that defining a link between corporations as one or more overlapping board members would result in the algorithm being used exceeding available computing capabilities by several orders of magnitude" (Sonquist and Koenig, 1975:204). In order to avoid this problem, it was decided to use the criterion of two or more shared board members as defining a link. It should be noted that this constituted a very stringent requirement that would isolate tightly connected cliques of interlocked firms, but would considerably understate the overall level of integration within the corporate world.

Analysis of the data proceeded as follows. Only those corporations that were linked to at least one other by two or more directors in common were selected for further analysis; others were left out of the analysis. This step yielded a group of 401 corporations. Next, all maximal complete subgraphs among these corporations were calculated (step 2 of the algorithm). Those maximal complete subgraphs that were trivial in size (i.e., made up of only two companies), or were tree-shaped, were discarded. The remaining subgraphs were then merged to form larger subgraphs. Two subgraphs were merged if their membership differed by only one corporation. In the next step, additional merging was done. In this step, two subgraphs were merged whenever membership overlap exceeded a fixed proportion (i.e., 0.33) of the number of points in the smaller of the two groups. However, this final merging was also contingent on the level of "completeness" (the ratio of the count of lines joining points within the proposed new merged subgraph to the count of all such lines possible in the subgraph) that would result. If the level of completeness would be greater than would be expected on the basis of random probability, then the two subgraphs were merged and treated as one clique. If not, the subgraphs were left separate. Sonquist and Koenig describe the findings as follows: "The analysis yielded thirty-two cliques of corporations ranging in size from three to fifteen members. The bulk of the cliques comprising the central groups contained six or fewer corporations. About one-third of the clique groups contained three members and another third contained four or five. The completeness levels of the 32 cliques ranged from about 25% of the possible lines in a clique to 100%. Almost one-third were 100% complete; that is, every corporation had two or more interlocking directorates with every other corporation in that central clique" (Sonquist and Koenig, 1975:205).

In addition to the central clique members, most cliques had peripheral or "satellite" members who had one or two connections with the central clique. Cliques were generally comprised of corporations with headquarters in the same region of the country, although some cliques contained members from widely scattered parts of the country. Clique number 4 (as numbered by Sonquist and Koenig) is perhaps representative of cliques with a strong regional base, while clique number 16 is somewhat more dispersed. All of the central members in clique number 4 are located in the Northeast, but clique number 16 contains central members from the Southwest, the West, and the Northeast (Table 7).

Of greatest interest to our present concerns are the five cliques that are predominantly based in California (Table 8).

Many of the companies in the five California cliques were active in the political campaigns examined in this work. A logical question to ask at this point is is there any relationship between the structure of interlocks and the observed pattern of political activity? For instance, is the structure of interlocks isomorphic with interest group structures?

If it is meaningful (as pluralists might contend) to speak of competing interest groups in the area of transportation politics,

Table 7. Examples of Corporate Cliques

Clique Number	Corporation Name	Type of Membership	SMSA Location
4	Pennwalt	Central Member	Philadelphia
	Prudential	"	Newark
	Public Service	"	Newark
	Bethlehem Steel	One Connection	Easton, PA.
	Englehard Miner	"	N.Y.
	First Pennsy.	"	Philadelphia
	R. H. Macy	"	N.Y.
	National Biscuit	"	N.Y.
	Providence Mutual	"	Philadelphia
16	Braniff	Central Member	Dallas
	1st National Bank	"	Dallas
	LTV	"	Dallas
	Norton Simon	"	Los Angeles
	Pepsico	"	N.Y.
	Southwest Life	"	Dallas
	Burlington Northern	One Connection	Minneapolis
	Keebler	"	Chicago
	May Co.	"	St. Louis
	Republic Nat'l Bank	"	Dallas

SOURCE: Sonquist and Koenig, 1975:221 and 224.

then the Proposition 18 and Proposition 5 campaigns should provide the clearest example: the two measures were very similar, both proposing diversion of highway trust fund monies to develop transit systems, yet the first met strong business opposition and the second received a great deal of corporate support. Moreover, the opponents of 18 and the proponents of 5 were almost entirely separate groups of firms. It might be argued that although these two groups did not confront one another within a single campaign, they did compete over the two campaigns as a whole. If these are competing interest groups, what reflection of this competition is contained in the pattern of interlocks within and between these two groups? The simplest assumption would be that each group is tightly interlocked internally, but that few, if any, interlocks exist between the two groups. Interlocks would then match apparent political alignments.

Table 8. California-based Corporate Cliques

Clique Number	Corporation Name	Type of Membership	SMSA Location
2	Times Mirror	Central Member	Los Angeles
	Union America	"	Los Angeles
	Western Airlines	"	Los Angeles
	MGM	One Connection	N.Y.
	TRW	"	Cleveland
6	Lockheed Aircraft	Central Member	Los Angeles
	N. American Rockwell	"	Los Angeles
	Pacific Mutual Life	"	Los Angeles
	Security Pacific Nat'l	"	Los Angeles
	Southern Calif. Edison	"	Los Angeles
	Western Bancorp.	"	Los Angeles
	Union Oil	Two Connections	Los Angeles
	Rockwell Mfg.	One Connection	Pittsburgh
	Safeway	"	San Francisco
	Southern Pacific	"	San Francisco
	Wells Fargo	"	San Francisco
28	Caterpillar	Central Member	Peoria
	Crocker Nat'l	"	San Francisco
	Del Monte	"	San Francisco
	Fibreboard	"	San Francisco
	Pacific Gas & Elec.	"	San Francisco
	Wells Fargo	"	San Francisco
	1st Chicago City	One Connection	Chicago
	FMC	"	San Jose
	Greyhound	"	Chicago
	Hewlitt-Packard	"	San Jose
	Pacific Lighting	"	Los Angeles
	Pacific Mutual	"	Los Angeles
	Safeway	"	San Francisco
	Southern Pacific	"	San Francisco
29	Bank of America	Central Member	San Francisco
	Broadway-Hale	"	Los Angeles
	Di Giorgio	"	San Francisco
	Union	"	Los Angeles
	Bekins	One Connection	Los Angeles
	Dillingham	"	Honolulu
	Foremost-McKesson	"	San Francisco
	Getty Oil	"	Los Angeles
	N. American Rockwell	"	Los Angeles
	Pacific Lighting	"	Los Angeles

Table 8. *(Cont.)*

Clique Number	Corporation Name	Type of Membership	SMSA Location
	Sears	"	Chicago
	Western Bancorp.	"	Los Angeles
30	Bank of America	Central Member	San Francisco
	Bekins	"	Los Angeles
	Foremost-McKesson	"	San Francisco
	Pacific Lighting	"	Los Angeles
	Broadway-Hale	One Connection	Los Angeles
	Caterpillar	"	Peoria
	Di Giorgio	"	San Francisco
	Dillingham	"	Honolulu
	Getty Oil	"	Los Angeles
	Sears	"	Chicago
	Union Oil	"	Los Angeles

SOURCE: Sonquist and Koenig, 1975:221-228.

Analysis shows that this hypothesis is not well supported: while there are differences between the pattern of interlocks within each group, the overall pattern is more complex and problematic than this simple model of interest groups would suggest.

Before the following analysis is done, it is necessary to divide the Proposition 18 opponents and Proposition 5 supporters into two groups: those firms in each group that are large enough to be listed in the *Fortune* data, and those smaller firms that are not listed. The first thing to be noted is that the Proposition 5 companies are listed more frequently. Of the fifty-six firms that gave money for Proposition 5, 50 percent (28) are in the *Fortune* list; while for the Proposition 18 opponents the figure is only 33 percent (17 of 52). Thus, the Proposition 5 group has a greater proportion of major corporations.

Tables 6 and 7 use only those Proposition 5 and Proposition 18 firms that are listed in the *Fortune* data on 797 United States corporations. Information on interlocks among the smaller, non-*Fortune* companies, is not available. In reading the following analysis, therefore, the reader should keep in mind that we do not have a complete picture of all the interlocks, only those among major firms in each group. Nevertheless, that is sufficient for the limited analysis undertaken here.

Tables 9 and 10 show the clique memberships for each *Fortune* company that gave money against Proposition 18 or for Proposition 5. Type of membership is specified along with the main regional location of the clique. Cliques are referred to in terms of the arbitrary numbers assigned by Sonquist and Koenig.

From these tables it is clear that, first of all, opponents of Proposition 18 and supporters of Proposition 5 did not simply constitute two big cliques. There are sixteen different cliques represented among firms that opposed Proposition 18 and 10 different cliques represented among proponents of Proposition 5. Also, there is a great deal of overlap in clique membership between opponents of 18 and supporters of 5: 60 percent (6 of 10) of those

Table 9. Clique Membership of Opponents of Proposition 18

	Type of Membership		
Company	Central	2 connections	1 connection
1. Boise Cascade			19 (Midwest)
2. Douglas Oil	14 (East)		9 (East), 19 (Midwest)
3. Firestone Tire			
4. Getty Oil			29 & 30 (West)
5. Goodyear Tire			10 (Midwest), 24 (East)
6. Gulf Oil	31 (East)		
7. Marathon Oil			10 & 22 (Midwest)
8. Mobil Oil	13 (East)		26 (East)
9. Pac. Motor Truck.			6 & 28 (West)
10. Phillips Oil			
11. Shell Oil			
12. Standard Oil (Ca.)			
13. Standard Oil (Ind.)	17 (Midwest)	18 (Midwest)	
14. Standard Oil (N.J.)			13 & 27 (East)
15. Sun Oil			
16. Texaco			26 (East)
17. Union Oil	29 (West)	6 (West)	30 (West)

Table 10. Clique Membership of Supporters of Proposition 5

	Type of Membership		
Company	Central	2 connections	1 connection
1. Atlantic-Richfield	5 (East)		
2. Bank of California			
3. Bank of America	29 & 30 (West)		
4. Bekins	30 (West)		29 (West)
5. Broadway-Hale	29 (West)		30 (West)
6. Alcoa (Century City)	31 (East)		
7. Coca-Cola			
8. Crocker Nat'l Bank	28 (West)		
9. Dart Industries			
10. Fluor Corp.			
11. General Telephone	24 (East)		
12. Levi Strauss			
13. Litton Industries			
14. MCA			
15. May Co.			16 (Southwest)
16. Norris Industries			
17. Occidental Life			
18. Pacific G & E	28 (West)		
19. Security Pac. N.B.	6 (West)		
20. So. Cal. Edison	6 (West)		
21. Stauffer Chemical			
22. Union Bank	2 (West)		
23. United Air Lines			
24. United Cal. Bank	6 (West)		29 (West)
25. Wells Fargo	28 (West)		6 (West)
26. Rohr Corp.			
27. Kaiser Industries	11 (West)		
28. Kaiser Steel	11 (West)		

cliques represented by Proposition 5 supporters are also represented among anti-Proposition 18 companies, while 38 perent (6 of 16) of anti-Proposition 18 cliques are represented among Proposition 5 supporters. These data tend to argue against the hypothesis of two separate, tightly interlocked, competing interest groups.

There are interesting differences between the two groups, however. The pattern of clique membership by anti-Proposition 18 companies is more diffuse than in the case of Proposition 5 firms. Not only is a greater range of cliques represented by Proposition 18 opponents (16 versus 10), but average clique membership is larger among anti-Proposition 18 companies: 1.35 clique memberships per firm versus 0.75 for Proposition 5. Cliques represented by Proposition 18 opponents are also more geographically dispersed, coming almost equally from the East (9 cliques), West (7 cliques), and Midwest (7 cliques). On the other hand, Proposition 5 cliques were centered primarily in the West (17 cliques) with few from the East (3 cliques), one from the Southwest, and none from the Midwest.

Probably the most striking difference between the Proposition 18 and Proposition 5 firms is in terms of type of clique membership. Although the Proposition 18 group maintains more average clique memberships per firm (1.35 versus 0.75), those memberships are of a more peripheral nature: of all Proposition 18 clique memberships, only 22 percent (5 of 23) are central memberships, compared with 76 percent (16 of 21) for Proposition 5 companies. Thus, Proposition 18 companies are loosely connected to a wide variety of cliques across the country, while firms that supported Proposition 5 tend to be central members of California-based cliques. Not only are Proposition 5 proponents generally large firms with central memberships in California-based cliques, they also are typically headquartered in the state. Seventy-eight percent (21 of 27) of Proposition 5 companies are headquartered in California (mostly Southern California), while only 20 percent (3 of 15) of Proposition 18 companies are headquartered in the state. (The reader is cautioned, however, that this includes only those companies listed in *Fortune*. Smaller firms are not included in this analysis.) Proposition 5 supporters, then, probably have a stronger interest in local metropolitan and statewide politics affecting the immediate environments in which they are headquartered, while the more geographically dispersed, diffusely linked Proposition 18 firms (mostly oil companies) are possibly somewhat more attuned to less localized common interests (such as protecting the various state and national highway trust funds) and to those issues (like Proposition 18) which carry symbolic significance for national politics. If highway fund diversion could happen in California, it could, in the words of WOGA's general manager, "happen anywhere." In addition to not wanting to see the California trust fund tapped, the highway lobby did not want to see an undesirable precedent established for other states and the national level.

What more does the pattern of clique memberships tell us about the structural relations among the proponents and opponents of these issues and about the relation between the two groups? First of all, it demonstrates that there is no simple isomorphic relation between interest group composition and clique memberships (at least on this issue). Yet it would appear that the intriguing differences discovered between the two groups in terms of clique relationships may have some political implications. For example, if it is true that interlocks can play some role in providing a means of integration and coordination among the members of a group of firms, then there is reason to believe that supporters of Proposition 5 would be favored in this regard over anti-Proposition 18 firms. For one thing, the cliques in which the former are members are fewer in number and are geographically concentrated in the West (i.e., primarily in San Francisco and Los Angeles). Lines of communication and coordination could therefore be more simple and direct. It is also possible that coordination via cliques of linked companies is more effective when the firms involved are central members of cliques rather than marginal associates. More than three-fourths of the clique memberships in the Proposition 5 group are central, as compared with less than one-fourth in the case of the Proposition 18 firms. Moreover, it is logical to suppose that the most direct and effective coordination among companies may occur when they are all members of the same clique. The larger the number of companies in a single clique, the more effective that clique should become. The anti-Proposition 18 group contains seven instances in which two companies are members of the same clique. However, in the Proposition 5 group, there are two instances in which four companies are members of a single clique, two instances in which three companies are members of the same clique, and one instance of two companies in a single clique. These larger-sized clusters of firms within a clique, coupled with the other aforementioned advantages of central memberships and geographical concentration, may mean that interlocks were more politically useful to proponents of Proposition 5 than they were to Proposition 18 opponents.

That interlocking patterns do mean something, that they actually do affect the behavior of linked corporations, is strongly suggested in a recent study by Ratcliff (1979). In an examination of commercial banks' mortgage lending practices, he has demonstrated that banks that are heavily interlocked with other corporations tend to make less mortgage money available to the local area. Ratcliff explains this phenomenon by arguing that interlocks ensure that corporations will have top priority for the banks' available assets. Lending to corporations means that less money is available to the local residential mortgage market. Thus, interlocks function, in this case, to drain capital out of local communities and into the coffers of large, multinational corporations. Ratcliff has shown then that interlocks have an economic function which has political implications. The availability of residential mortgage money, or lack of it, has a great deal to do with which areas of the city grow or decline, the dynamics of property values, and the lives of community residents.

The intriguing patterns of interlocks discovered in the Proposition 18 and Proposition 5 cases may have analogous functions. For example, the companies that supported Proposition 5 are largely "local" companies in that they are more likely than Proposition 18 opponents to be based in California. One may speculate that such local companies are more sensitive to the issues of legitimacy and the general political climate in the region. They are more likely to be concerned about the potential of local insurrectionary movements, class cleavages, middle-class disillusionment, as well as the material conditions (e.g., transportation, city growth, and so on) under which regional business must operate. From this perspective, Proposition 5 can perhaps be seen as a way of attempting to bolster legitimacy of electoral politics, to improve the material conditions of business in marginal ways, and to allow a group of companies to lead the way in expressing a new business consensus. More will be said on these points in the final chapter.

Before we proceed, there is one final path concerning the meaning of interlocks that is worth pursuing. It was argued earlier that an analysis based on interest groups alone is of questionable utility in the understanding of these transportation issues. Similarly, it may be a waste of time to search for interest groups in the structure of interlocking directorates. Perhaps another approach to interlocks is required. It may be, for example, that interlocks do serve to integrate the business community, but in ways more general than would be expected on the basis of traditional interest group analysis.

Sociometric methods of analyzing patterns of interlocking directorates are based on the idea that discrete knots, or cliques, of linked companies should be isolated from the overall network of interlocks, the goal being, as Sonquist and Koenig (1975:204) put it, to provide "a kind of 'neutral density' filter sufficient to detect contrast in varying degrees of connectedness, while screening out more sparsely connected segments." In other words, this method ensures that attention will be focused on only those unusually dense portions of the network; that is, where anomalous conditions exist. It could be argued that this method produces results much like those that would be experienced by an explorer who has a topographic map of a geographical area that contains as features only the tops of the tallest peaks in the area. Such a map would not be of much use in enabling the explorer to understand the general lay of the land. Perhaps by looking too closely at the most prominent features of the network of interlocks (i.e., the cliques), we lose sight of more important general features and forget the significance of the pattern as a whole. Since clique analysis abstracts from the whole network of interlocks a series of separate units to be studied, it may be argued that this method is most useful (if at all) at the level of the model of discrete, competing interest groups, and that if one wants to map out politics at higher levels, one needs to use a different mode of analysis.

If there is merit to these considerations, then it should be noted that the clique analysis carried out by Sonquist and Koenig, which was used here to shed light on transit politics, may be subject to an additional limitation. It was earlier noted that due to technical restrictions, an extremely stringent criterion was used to define a "link" between two corporations: the companies had to have two or more directors in common. This double-interlock requirement meant that two companies that shared only one director were treated as if no connection at all existed between them. This resulted in the loss of much potentially useful data.

If it is important to look at the more general features of the pattern of interlocks, one can begin by changing the criterion defining a link. This criterion is rather arbitrary since there is no way of determining at this point whether a one-director link is in some sense less "important" than a two-director link. The use of the one-director criterion also permits a refinement of the analytical categories, since it distinguishes between companies that have a link between them (i.e., at least one shared director) and companies that are not linked (i.e., have no common members of their boards of directors). If interlocks have any significance, one would expect that this distinction (between link and no-link) would be crucial—probably more crucial than the distinction between single-linked and double-linked companies.

The author undertook an analysis of interlocks using the new criterion of one or more shared directors as defining a link between companies. Except for this change, the methods of analysis were identical to those described earlier. The technical problem of insufficient computer capabilities for an analysis of single-director interlocks among the 797 corporations in the United States was solved by selecting a subsample from the original data base. Since this study is primarily concerned with California political campaigns that mainly involved California-based corporations, only those firms headquartered in the state were selected for analysis. This stipulation resulted in a sample of 67 California-based corporations.

One disadvantage of looking only at California corporations is that the overall level of connections in the sample of companies is understated in two ways. First, California firms have a great many links to firms that are based outside of the state. California corporations are not insular in terms of ties with other large corporations across the country, and these links may have very important economic and political implications for both the national and California business communities. Secondly, by neglecting non-California corporations, the level of connectedness within California is probably understated. This is true since companies outside the state may indirectly serve to link two or more California companies that are interlocked with the outside firm. If these outside companies were included, the result might well be the discovery of more extensive cliques containing both California and non-California corporations.

In spite of these limitations, this method has the paramount advantage of removing the technical restraint, and making analysis of single-director interlocking cliques feasible. More importantly, it allows a more complete, yet geographically restricted, picture to be drawn of the network of interlocks among large corporations. It can be argued that it presents a more meaningful way to assess the general level of structural links and opportunities for communication and coordination among corporations in the United States.

The analysis of interlocks among the California companies produced a striking finding: the single resulting "clique" contained forty-eight central members, with an additional three companies having two connections, and six others with one connection to the central clique. In other words, the entire clique contained fifty-seven out of sixty-seven (or 85.1 percent) California-based corporations in the data set! This must be counted as a truly impressive example of corporate interconnectedness.

It should also be noted that this analysis was based on direct connection between pairs of corporations. That is, no provision was made for the possibility that two corporations may be indirectly linked through an intermediate third firm. This can be thought of in terms of the number of "steps" it would take for communication to get from one firm to another. For example, if companies A and B share a director, then there is only one step separating the two corporations: communication (via the shared director) can go directly from firm A to firm B. It is also reasonable to consider that companies may be linked by less direct means. If A and B do not share a director, they may still be linked in a two-step link through a third company (C). If A and B are both interlocked with C via one-director links, A is removed from B by two communication steps: A to C, and C to B. In sociometric analysis of friendship networks, the situation is analogous to two people who are not friends with each other, but who have a friend in common. Such an indirect link may still serve as a communication channel.

Another analysis of the California data was undertaken using the two step criterion (each step involving one or more shared directors) as constituting a link between companies. Thus, if A shared a director with C, and C shared another director with B, then A and B were defined as linked. Using this definition of indirect links, we see the resulting California clique contained fifty-six central members, with one corporation having two connections, and two corporations having one connection. In other words, 88 percent of the California corporations were within two steps of each other. Even this impressive figure probably represents a considerable understatement since the elimination of non-California corporations from the sample is likely to be particularly detrimental to discovering two step links among California corporations.

What of the larger group of corporations at the national level? A recent study by Mariolis (1975) analyzed the 797 American corporations in the Schwartz data base. It was found that interlocks are quite prevalent among these companies, with 92 percent of the firms having at least one interlock, 85 percent having at least two, and 10.5 percent having 25 or more interlocks. For all corporations in the United States, the median number of interlocks is 8 (Mariolis, 1975:430). As one would expect because of the large number of corporations involved (a total of 797 in the national sample, as compared with only 67 in the California subsample), the degree of integration on the national level is less than that which exists among California firms. Our previously mentioned study shows that 88 percent of the California corporations are within two steps of each other. Even so, in the Mariolis national sample, approximately 83 percent are within four steps of each other. As Mariolis observes: "Another indication of the commonplaceness and potential importance of corporate interlocks is that of 736 corporations with at least one interlock, 722 form a single, discrete, cluster. That is, starting with any one of the 722 boards of directors, it is possible to trace a link through overlapping board memberships between that one corporation and every single one of the 721 others'' (Mariolis, 1975:432-3).

This extensive network of interlocks at both the regional and national level implies a capability for communication and control of the business community in the United States that students of politics cannot afford to ignore. Sonquist and Koenig put the matter well:

> Perhaps the most significant fact about the clique-satellite structure of the coteries of top corporations and their inter-relations with one another, aside from their density, is their regional base. This lends face validity to a structure adduced entirely on mathematical grounds. It suggests strongly that these are real, cohesive, face-to-face groups [of individuals] that interact with one another outside of the board room. Yet, it also suggests strongly that though cliques have regional bases, the level of interaction of the total system is high. In other words, face-to-face contacts are by no means limited to regional levels. . . . The inescapable conclusion is that the upper echelon of the system of corporations is linked at a systemic level, to a higher degree possibly than ever was envisioned by earlier theorists. (Sonquist and Koenig, 1975:215-216)

Interlocks, therefore, are pervasive features of the corporate economy. It may not be possible to understand them simply in terms of their presumed ability to knit the members of interest groups together. However, they would seem to provide the corporate community with a wide-reaching and effective means of information-exchange, person-to-person contact, socialization for elites, ideological and cultural diffusion, and, quite possibly a degree of economic and political coordination. In conjunction with the cohesion provided by social clubs, trade associations, and the mere process of doing business together, a strong foundation for intrabusiness coordination exists.

CONCLUSION

This chapter has examined the ability of the pluralist and elitist hypotheses to account for the particular manner in which the five transit campaigns unfolded. It has concluded that, although the pluralist model does describe accurately certain features of the politics in these campaigns, it fails to probe beneath the surface of events and thus tends to overestimate the openness and fluidity of the modern political system in the United States. A great deal of additional understanding, however, can be gained by analyzing these political events from the elitist perspective. It was argued that the five campaigns provide evidence not only of the avoidance of political competition, but also of the resolution of potential conflicts within the business community, and of a substantial degree of political cohesion and coordination of action. Thus, the elitist hypotheses appear to be better supported than are the pluralist hypotheses. Specifically, in terms of the elitist hypotheses, we have seen extensive involvement and dominance by business elites in these five campaigns. Business elites played integral roles in planning the transit systems, organizing the campaigns, and contributing the election money. The only significant involvement by citizens' voluntary associations was on the advocacy (and unsuccessful) side of Proposition 18. In spite of potentially disruptive differences of opinion among business elites, there was no direct confrontation during the campaigns, conflicts apparently having been effectively resolved internally and a degree of mutual accommodation and cooperation achieved. We have also seen some strong evidence of tight control of campaign contributions and strategies by business elites. It has been argued that business can achieve integration and coordination of this sort through participation in business organizations, clubs, friendship networks, trade associations, and interlocking directorates.

What then of the final elite hypothesis, that outcomes tend to favor elite interests? Here the evidence is not as clear as in the preceding instances, suggesting that reality is more complex than the elitist hypothesis implies. True, the successful campaign to build BART was clearly in the interests of San Francisco Bay Area business elites who wanted to stimulate the local growth machine and defend central city property values. The same is true of the motives of business elites in the Los Angeles area who supported the two campaigns there aimed at creating a BART-like transit system, although here their efforts have not yet been rewarded with electoral approval. Thus, we had an elite victory in San Francisco, but no apparent victory for elites in Los Angeles. Also, what of the outcome of the strange Proposition 18 and Proposition 5 case? Whose interests were served by this radical shift in patterns of electoral support and political strategies? It would appear that the California highway lobby, which had vigorously campaigned against Proposition 18 in 1970, had been persuaded by 1974 not to oppose Proposition 5. We know that a new coalition of large businesses arose to support Proposition 5 and the contemporary and related Proposition A of that same year. The highway lobby did not publicly oppose the efforts of this new coalition, probably because the major conflicts had been worked out in the private organizations of the business community. But, other than the highly valued ideal of business community unity, what did the earlier opponents of highway fund diversion have to gain from this new political stance that was not opposed to some diversion? As pointed out previously, pluralists would say that the highway lobby had come to realize that it was time for a change in political tactics: the bad publicity that anti-Proposition 18 forces had received in 1970, coupled with the growing political clout of the rapid transit interests, forced a compromise and led to a neutral position by the lobby during the Proposition 5 campaign. From this perspective, the outcome of the latter election was a victory not for elites, but for the moderating, balancing effects of pluralistic politics.

On the point of outcomes, there would seem to be merit in both the pluralist and elitist interpretations. It looks as if some compromise and accommodation did take place, but it came about in the private councils of business in such a manner as to exact a high degree of behavioral coordination among elites who participated. The desire for business unity served to mute political challenge effectively in the public campaigns.

I shall argue that although the bulk of the evidence at this juncture generally favors the elitist model over the pluralist, important elements of the whole picture are still missing. Still more is to be gained by removing another layer of our analytical onion and examining the class-dialectic approach to the problem. We shall discover that the class-dialectic approach will not so much directly dispute the claims of the pluralist and elitist models as it will synthesize them and place them in a broader and more meaningful context. So far—as is common in both elitist and pluralist analysis—we have treated these five case studies as if they were essentially isolable, well-bounded events that can be extracted and studied apart from the larger historical and institutional contexts in which they are imbedded and through which their full significance must be appraised. At the extreme, to focus merely on proximate behavior of individuals and groups without seeking to discover how this behavior articulates with institutional imperatives in the larger society is analogous to trying to understand the behavior of people in a classroom setting without knowing that grading systems, ability testing programs, academic diplomas, social status indicators, and educational requirements for jobs exist. Both the environmental and institutional contexts within which classroom behavior takes place and the personal histories of the students in question are vital to an adequate understanding of why otherwise peculiar-seeming behavior is performed. In the same way, we cannot understand the political events here without appreciating the broader historical and institutional view.

Mankoff (1972:84) has pointed out that much pluralist analysis is "incredibly ahistorical, as if power struggles were conducted on Robinson Crusoe's island." Unfortunately, a similar charge is often made regarding elitist research. To the extent to which history is involved, it is usually in reference only to the most recent and obviously related events, the whole shaping and sifting influence of more long-run and general trends being largely overlooked. Analogously, Lukes (1974) has criticized both the pluralist and elitist schools for paying too much attention to proximate, directly observable behavior and ignoring the important role of social institutions in shaping political processes. We have, says Lukes, a too individualistic and behavioral conception of power. We need to take account of the fact that "decisions are choices consciously and intentionally made by individuals between alternatives, whereas the bias of the [political] system can be mobilised, recreated and reinforced in ways that are neither consciously chosen nor the intended result of particular individuals' choices. . . . Moreover, the bias of the system is not sustained simply by a series of individually chosen acts, but also, most importantly, by its socially structured and culturally patterned behavior of groups, and *practices of institutions*, which may indeed be manifested by *individuals' inaction*" (emphasis added; Lukes, 1974:21-2).

It is this important transindividual, institutional, and historical context of political action, *inter alia*, to which the class-dialectical model sensitizes us. The final chapter illustates how a more complete understanding of urban transportation politics follows from the inclusion of pertinent historical and institutional factors as analytical components. A political act, any political act, has meaning only to the extent that it is understood as an inseparable part of a specific unfolding historical process and as an event situated within a particular web of social institutions. It is not the act itself, but its context, that imparts meaning. Chapter Six will demonstrate how much more consistent and intelligible this historical slice of urban transportation politics becomes once we perceive the larger framework within which these events took place and by which they were shaped.

THE DIALECTICAL POLITICS OF TRANSIT

The pluralist and elitist models—particularly the latter—have added something to our understanding of these political events. Yet, I shall argue that it is the class-dialectical hypotheses that are the most fully supported by the data and that provide the keys for the most comprehensive and integrated explanation. The other models have illuminated parts of the picture; the dialectical model will now show us the larger panorama.

This panorama includes, as is clear from the class-dialectic hypotheses, the historical-institutional framework which bounds these phenomena. The main elements of this framework include the socioeconomic structure (which we can refer to in a convenient shorthand as corporate capitalism) and the politics of social class which arises within this structure. It is within this context that transportation issues in general—and these transit campaigns in particular—have their being and meaning. At last we come to the core of the onion.

Any large-scale, industrialized society requires some means of transporting goods and people and overcoming the "friction of space." In this the United States is no different. But, beyond this, the particular form of capitalist development in the United States has placed its own unique stamp upon how transportation is conceived, how it is produced, and what ends it is expected to serve. Transportation plays a dominant role in the political economy of the United States since it is intimately related to the accumulation process. Its primary role has been to promote the accumulation process, both for the capitalist class as a whole and for specific segments of that class, that is, those segments that profit directly from the production of transportation facilities and equipment.

Transportation in the United States then must be comprehended in light of (1) the logic and contradictions of capitalist development, and (2) the pervasive influence of the politics of class. It is the goal of this concluding chapter to show how capitalism and class shape transportation history and politics in the United States, and to indicate how these two elements of the class-dialectic model permit a fuller understanding of the California transportation events than does either the pluralist or the elitist model. First, we shall focus on the issue of class, reviewing some recent work that sheds light on the nature of the capitalist class in the United States and its segments. Next, we shall show how transportation has been influenced by general development in the economy and how certain problems and contradictions in transportation development and policy mirror corresponding contradictions in the political economy of capitalism. Finally, we shall demonstrate that these larger institutional processes and historical events allow us to grasp the fuller meaning of the empirical cases under study. In so doing, the analysis set forth in the preceding chapters will be reinterpreted in a new context.

Capitalist Society as Class-Based Society

The operation of our institutions, particularly the economic system, brings into existence dominant social classes of a particular nature and then nurtures those classes and class interests. In turn, those institutions are subjected to the imprint of actions by the dominant class. There is, therefore, a reciprocal relation between social institutions and dominant social classes, with both forces influencing and shaping the form and behavior of the other.

There is a vast literature on social class. It is not the intention here to review that literature nor to try to prove that classes exist. Rather, we shall consider how a class analysis (particularly a Marxian class analysis) can greatly contribute to our comprehension of the political events under study here. For this reason, only selected reference to the extensive work that has been done on class in America will be made.

Recently, an instructive and unique attempt has been made by

Wright and Perrone (1977) to demonstrate the empirical usefulness of Marxian class categories. Pointing out that "quantitative investigations of the causes and consequences of inequality have almost totally ignored Marxian categories" (1977:32), they set out to show that these categories can be successfully operationalized and that they do account for important observed differences in the structure and dynamics of American society. Noting that Marxist analysis of the class structure of capitalist society has traditionally centered on three criteria (i.e., ownership of the means of production, purchase of others' labor power, and sale of one's own labor power), the authors define their class categories in these terms: "The three criteria generate the three basic class categories of capitalist society: *capitalists* own their own means of production, purchase the labor power of others and do not sell their own labor power; *workers* do not own their own means of production and therefore cannot purchase the labor power of others, but do sell their own labor power to capitalists; and the *petty bourgeoisie* do not sell their own labor power, nor (except perhaps in a very limited way) purchase the labor power of others, but do own their own means of production" (emphasis in the original; Wright and Perrone, 1977:33).

Arguing that this tripartite classification is not sufficient for comprehending classes in present-day capitalism, they add a fourth category, that of managers, that is, those who are intermediate between workers and capitalists in that they do not own the means of production, do not formally purchase the labor power of others, but do control or supervise the labor of others and do sell their own labor power. Table 11 presents the four classes.

Having defined the relevant class categories, the authors demonstrate the usefulness of these categorizations in accounting for social inequalities in capitalist societies. Focusing on the relationships among class position, income, education, occupational status, age, sex, and race, they find that: "The differences between classes in levels of income and in the relationship between education and income are substantial, and these differences do not disappear when we control for variables such as occupational status, age, job tenure, sex, or race. Furthermore, in terms of explained variance in income, class position is at least as powerful

Table 11. Expanded Marxist Criteria for Class

	Ownership of the Means of Production	Purchase of the Labor Power of Others	Control of the Labor Power of Others	Sale of One's Own Labor Power
Capitalists	Yes	Yes	Yes	No
Managers	No	No	Yes	Yes
Workers	No	No	No	Yes
Petty Bourgeoisie	Yes	No	No	No

SOURCE: Wright and Perrone, 1977:34.

an explanatory variable as occupational status'' (Wright and Perrone, 1977:50).

Most traditional researchers have used some variation of socioeconomic status (usually income, education, and occupation) instead of class. However, the work of Wright and Perrone suggests that it does make good theoretical and empirical sense to analyze society in the United States in terms of its class structure.

From a somewhat different perspective, G. William Domhoff has produced a great deal of research (Domhoff, 1967, 1970, 1974, 1978, 1979) aimed at demonstrating that there is a ruling class in America. This he defines as the politically active segment of the social upper class together with its hired ''high-level managers and officials in corporations, law firms, foundations and associations controlled by members of the upper class.'' This coalition Domhoff terms the ''power elite'' (Domhoff, 1970:106), although he does not mean the same thing by the term as does C. Wright Mills. In Domhoff's words: ''The power elite has its roots in and serves the interests of the social upper class [the true power elite model of Mills is not a class analysis]. It is the operating arm of the upper class. It functions to maintain and manage a socioeconomic system which is organized in such a way that it yields an amazing proportion of its wealth to a minuscule upper class of big businessmen and their descendents'' (Domhoff, 1970:106-107).

According to Domhoff, the upper class not only controls the major corporations of the land, but also dominates the governmental structure. He argues that "members of the upper class sit in pivotal government offices, define most major policy issues, shape the policy proposals on issues raised outside their circles, and mold the rules of government" (Domhoff, 1970:105-106).

Moreover, he presents evidence (from data on in-group interaction, intermarriage, elite school attendance, winter and summer resort residence, and friendship and acquaintance patterns) that reveals a high degree of upper-class cohesion, in addition to evidence (from the perceptions of psychotherapists) of class consciousness by members of the upper class (Domhoff, 1970:75-97).

A number of points Domhoff makes are particularly noteworthy for our purposes. First, according to his criteria of ruling class membership, the people who were active in the five transportation campaigns studied herein (i.e., the directors and managers of major California and national corporations) are members of this governing class. Secondly, Domhoff argues that this class is politically dominant, class conscious, and socially cohesive. The evidence of political coordination we have discovered in the five campaigns is perhaps a product of class organization, rather than simply interest-group or elite organization. Indeed, in the analysis of interlocking directorates we saw that the patterns of interlocks do indicate a high degree of interconnectedness among corporate directors in general, but do not seem to lend support for a simple interest-group hypothesis. Are corporate interlocks—along with elite clubs and exclusive resorts and such—one expression of the general cohesion of a governing capitalist class, rather than merely an expression of narrow, specialized, and local interest groups?

Insufficient research on interlocks has yet been done to permit a clear answer to this question, but some preliminary studies do seem to point in this direction. Koenig, Gogel, and Sonquist (1973) have shown that there is a relationship between upper-class standing and holding multiple corporate directorships. People who sit on four or more corporate boards are almost four times as likely to be members of exclusive social clubs (an upper-class indicator) as are directors who sit on only one board (Koenig, Gogel, and Sonquist, 1973:10). Useem (1979) has extended this kind of analysis to demonstrate that the number of boards upon which a director sits is positively related to the person's membership in a wide range of nonbusiness and business institutions, such as nonprofit private organizations (e.g., cultural, scientific, educational, charitable), governmental advisory boards, and major business associations (e.g., Council on Foreign Relations, Committee for Economic Development, Business Council). The pattern of interlocks among corporations may be one way in which the general interests of the whole capitalist class are organized via the broad institutional, governmental, and corporate affiliations of active members of the upper class in the United States.

It is possible, then, that corporate interlocks may serve an integrating function for the upper class. This is not to say, however, that the active, governing portion of the upper class is entirely homogeneous, unified, and of identical values and political ideology. Zeitlin, Neuman, and Ratcliff (1976) have argued that in the case of Chile, for example, distinct "class segments" exist within the ruling capitalist class. Class segments arise as a result of a portion of the dominant class having "a relatively distinct location in the social process of production and, consequently, its own specific political economic requirements and concrete interests which may be contradictory to those of other class segments with which, nonetheless, it shares essentially the same relationship to ownership of productive property" (Zeitlin, Neuman and Ratcliff, 1976:1009). This distinct placement in the production process means that "a class segment has the inherent potential for developing a specific variant of 'intraclass consciousness' and common action in relation to other segments of the class" (1976:1009). The authors analyze the differential pattern of political activity in Chile by two such class segments, the landed and nonlanded executives and principal owners of capital in the largest corporations in the country. Results indicate that there is a different characteristic pattern of political participation for each of the two class segments, with the landed capitalists being significantly more likely to hold national political office. In fact, they are twice as likely to have held office as their nonlanded counterparts, and three times as likely to have held multiple political offices (Zeitlin, Neuman, and Ratcliff, 1976:1017). The authors explain this difference in formal participation in terms of the historically specific place of large estates, or *fundos*, in the system of production, the role of the estates in the social domination of the Chilean peasantry, and also in terms of the traditional political power of large landowners, and the need by landed capitalists to shape state policy actively to serve their somewhat more specific interests (1976:1025).

The value to us of this work on Chile is that it demonstrates, in the authors' words, "the heuristic utility, if not general explanatory value, of investigating the political relevance of intraclass social differentiation in the capitalist class" (1976:1025). It suggests that the capitalist class is not composed of identical positions in the process of production, precisely coinciding mutual interests, nor lock-step political goals and strategies. Intraclass differences may sometimes produce cross-cutting pressures and conflicts. In the case of Chile, conflicts among capitalists have revolved around a number of historical issues: "The problems of free trade versus protection, the free mobility of wage labor, the prices of foodstuffs and therefore, the wage bill for industry, the prices of industrial crops grown on the estates, ground-rent as a deduction from profits, etc., have figured at different times as the source of rivalry among them" (1976:1025).

These intraclass rivalries within the capitalist class must not be overstated nor confused with the pluralist idea of competing interest groups (see Whitt, 1979b). The class-dialectic analysis is a class analysis. It maintains that one can comprehend politics in a capitalist society only by acknowledging the impact of social classes, by understanding how classes derive from the fundamental structure of the economy, and by understanding the enormous extent to which political institutions and processes are reflective of class interests and class struggles. To say that there are intraclass conflicts between segments of the capitalist class is not the same as saying, as pluralists might, that the business community is so riven with cross-cutting allegiances and competing interests as to render meaningless any notion of common class interests or unity of action. On the contrary, it can be argued that capitalists have a great number of common interests and are held together as a class by a relation to the means of production which, at its foundation, is the same for all individual capitalists.

It is within this context of overall common class interests that the concept of class segments must be understood.

The conception offered is of a capitalist class that is Janus-faced. It is united in fundamental interests, but modulated by a segmentation of lesser interests at the more local and specific level. This can be seen clearly in the development of transportation policy in the United States. Oil companies and other members of the highway lobby have traditionally derived enormous benefit from the operation and expansion of the oil-auto-highway complex. Many of the lobby's interests have been transformed into specific governmental policies at the federal and state levels, as in the case of the ear-marked highway trust funds. The lobby has engaged in direct efforts to control and eliminate alternative forms of public transportation (Snell, 1974). Historically, the development and expansion of the automobile-highway system of transportation was a boon to the highway lobby and, indeed, for a time at least, to American capitalism as a whole. In the words of Baran and Sweezy (1966:219-20), the introduction, mass production, and intensive promotion of the private automobile produced ''a radical alteration of economic geography with attendant internal migrations and the building of whole new communities; each [i.e., the steam engine, the railroad, and the automobile] required or made possible the production of many new goods and services; each directly or indirectly enlarged the market for a whole range of industrial products.'' Clearly, these developments were very profitable for much of American industry and they especially provided a base for many large personal fortunes (Carnegie in steel, Ford in autos, Rockefeller in oil, etc.) and the growth of privileges in auto-related segments of the dominant capitalist class. The oil, automotive, and steel industries prospered and became central to the United States economy. Automobile historian James Flink (1975:140-41) highlights the dominant economic role of the automobile, a position maintained during the last half century:

> During the 1920's automobility became the backbone of a new consumer-goods-oriented society and economy that has persisted into the present. By the mid-1920's automobile

manufacturing ranked first in value of product and third in value of exports among American industries. . . . The automobile industry was the lifeblood of the petroleum industry, and the biggest consumer of many other industrial products, including plate glass, rubber, and lacquers. The technologies of these ancillary industries, particularly steel and petroleum, were revolutionized by the new demands of motorcar manufacturing. The construction of streets and highways was the second largest item of governmental expenditure during the 1920's. The motorcar was responsible for a suburban real estate boom and for the rise of many new small businesses, such as service stations and tourist accommodations.

Likewise, historian Thomas Cochran (1957:44) concludes that the tremendous amount of capital investment associated with the automobile was "probably the major factor in the boom of the 1920's, and hence in the glorification of American business."

Automobiles thus provided a powerful base for a large segment of the dominant class in America. But automobiles are not by any means the sole basis of capitalist prosperity. Moreover, in recent years the vitality of the auto-related areas of the economy has begun to dim. Flink (1975:233) heralds "the death knells of the automobile culture." Rothschild (1973) argues that the United States auto industry is now in a state of stagnation and decline, much as was true of the British rail industry of the nineteenth century. The contradictions and huge social costs of automobile production and use have become manifest. The decline of this and related industries, the energy crisis, the loss of viability of central cities (particularly in the Northeast), the challenge of foreign competition, and the demands of people for better public transportation have all forced a readjustment and response by the dominant class. The former "solution" of vast industrial expansion, healthy profits, and increased class privilege that attended the rise of the private automobile has revealed other contradictions. No solution lasts forever. The content of class actions had to change as conditions changed. The automobile revolution had, precisely as Flink (1975:190) puts it, "sown the seeds of its own destruction."

Automobiles and freeways spurred decentralization of the traditional city. New areas were opened up for development, and urban residents and economic activity could flee to the suburbs. The outward movement of the more affluent residents and the selective exodus of the more potentially mobile segments of business (particularly retailing and light industry) fundamentally changed the character of metropolitan regions and presented urban elites with both new possibilities and new problems. At first, the possibilities outweighed the problems. As inherent contradictions grew however, the problems began to outweigh the possibilities. As noted in Chapter One, Friedland (1976) argues that both the corporate class and the organized (unionized) working class were affected by these changes. The major thesis of his work "concerns the attempts of national corporations and labor unions to manage the contradictions of urban growth" (Friedland, 1976:1). From the standpoint of corporations, "the decline of the central city's economy and its changing ecological structure affects the profitability of all corporate investments, as well as the viability of the central city as a coordinating center for major corporations and financial intermediaries" (Friedland, 1976:1). For labor unions, "changes in the economic structure of the central city, particularly industrial decentralization and relocation, affect the level of unionized employment in the central city and the viability of all union wage and organizing strategies" (Friedland, 1976:1). In addition to these economic threats, there are also political threats: The changing class composition of the central city, the inflow of poor and non-white residents and the outflow of wealthier and whiter families, gives rise to political organization and challenge to corporate and union political dominance" (Friedland, 1976:2).

According to Friedland, corporations and labor unions have moved to contain the political threat and pacify the urban poor and minorities by the implementation of various policies such as welfare expansion, poverty programs, Model Cities programs, neighborhood city halls, and urban manpower projects. To combat economic decline, they have created policies designed to generate new capital investment in the central city. These include metropolitan area planning, urban renewal programs—and new urban transportation systems.

This work has focused on transportation issues. Contrary to what might be expected on the basis of Friedland's analysis, little or no involvement by labor unions was discovered in these campaigns. Possibly unions in California did not consider these issues of sufficient concern for their interests. Alternatively, lack of involvement may reflect lack of union strength: nationwide, only about 20 percent of the workforce is unionized, and most of this is in the Northeast and Midwest (Rifkin and Barber, 1978; Stephens, 1980). On the other hand, corporate involvement in these campaigns was overwhelming. Urban-oriented segments of the corporate class have clearly supported the construction of new BART-like transportation systems in the hopes of resolving these urban crises. That these expensive systems do not work very well in this regard is now being realized. Another series of intraclass conflicts and systemic contradictions awaits. As Chambliss (1979) argues, the "solution" of one contradiction leads to the emergence of others.

The case of transportation in the United States illustrates extremely well the essential elements of the class-dialectical model of political power; that is, it is a case of capitalist, class-based politics in the ever-changing, dialectic of history. Transportation, as presently constituted in the United States, is one important base of class power, yet the contradictions it contains are such as to vividly demonstrate the dialectical nature of capitalist development.

Before we look more closely at the five transit campaigns from the standpoint of the class-dialectic hypotheses, we must survey briefly the history of automotive development in the United States. We shall examine this history in relation to changes in the economy, the rise of auto-related contradictions and social costs, and the response of urban-based segments of the dominant class. The goal in recounting this history is to sharpen our understanding of the California transportation campaigns by putting them in their proper national and historical context. These are crucial points usually neglected by the pluralist and elitist perspectives.

At the end of this chapter we shall return to the class-dialectic hypotheses to determine how well they explain the data from the California transit campaigns. The point to be made here is that we cannot really understand the significance and meaning of the California campaigns without the historical background that follows. This requires that we go back in United States history to the early days of urban growth, and to the days when automobiles were just making their appearance—periods of profound and lasting influence over the future shape of transportation and transportation politics.

CLASS INTERESTS AND CONTRADICTIONS IN TRANSIT DEVELOPMENT IN THE UNITED STATES

One must appreciate the historical development and contradictions of United States capitalism in order to appreciate the role of transportation in the accumulation process, how that role has varied over time, and how transportation reflects basic contradictions within the market economy. This requires that we view transportation as not involving simply a question of technical efficiency, but also being impressed with the stamp of marketplace logic and the needs of the dominant class. I shall argue that the development of transportation, like the development of metropolitan regions, has been greatly bounded and shaped by the unfolding of the capitalist system. As in any system, it is meaningful to look at the links, in this case links among capitalism, classes, cities, and transportation. It is into this broader context that the California transportation cases must be put. It will be argued that transportation in the United States reflects three major (and many lesser) contradictions: (1) lack of social planning, (2) social production versus private profit, and (3) the concentration and centralization of capital.

LACK OF SOCIAL PLANNING. It is held to be the particular virtue of market societies (especially so in the United States) that the state intervenes as little as possible in the private affairs of buyers and sellers. This ideal of the minimalist state is buttressed by the conception of the market as being an essentially self-regulating and efficient allocator of goods and services, an adept employer of labor, and a defender of the universal interests and freedoms of its citizens. The state must, of course, provide those public or collective goods and services that cannot be produced by the market (such as the construction of public highways), but the ideology of free enterprise would leave all else to market forces. Planning then, especially large-scale planning for the society as a whole, has been considered anathema. The relatively free play of market forces has been allowed to shape most of our institutions and social services, including our cities and transportation systems. Within a loose legal framework provided by national, state, and local governments—and with that framework generally reflecting capitalist class interests—private property and private initiative and the logic of the market have largely built our cities and constructed our transportation systems. Government has most commonly been limited to planning that is local, limited in scope, short-range, and ad hoc. Since the state must also function to insure private accumulation and the legitimacy of the political economy (see O'Connor, 1973), its role has been further restricted by these two often mutually contradictory functions. The state has thus not been fully effective in defending and advancing the common interests of capital, and therefore (as has been demonstrated in the case of these transit campaigns) capitalists have been obliged to engage in a certain amount of internal class organization (Whitt, 1979b) to thrash out common interests and actions and to engage in supplementary private planning (see Domhoff, 1979).

In regard to transportation, the most clear example of lack of effective planning is the largely unsystematic, almost accidental, relationship that exists between cities and transportation systems. Instead of comprehensive, long-range, publicly determined goals for city and regional development (with plans for transportation systems that complement and facilitate overall urban development) we have cities that grow haphazardly and transportation facilities that provide inadequate service for many residents of the metropolitan area (see Meyer, Kain, Wohl, 1965). While the structure of urban areas could be planned, for example, to minimize the need for unnecessary transportation of goods and people, the opposite condition has often existed in the United States. To the extent that there has been any urban planning, that planning has involved a surrender to the automobile. As Flink (1975:164) keenly observes, "Thus, instead of attempting to discourage the use of private passenger cars in cities, politicians and city planners adopted the expensive and ultimately unworkable policy of unlimited accommodation to the motorcar. That American urban life would conform to the needs of automobility rather than vice versa was obvious by the early 1920s." Cities have thus grown to the limits allowed by the system of transportation, with suburban commuters becoming evermore removed from their centrally located jobs. As James Vance (1966:307) comments, "Probably few events in economic history have had more fundamental effect on the shape of the city than the physical parting of the residence from the work place." The result has been that transportation has been maximized rather than conserved, leading to an increasing burden of social costs, destruction of urban neighborhoods, and rising fiscal demands on the state. Lack of planning, coupled with the logic of developing capitalism, thus generated long-run contradictions for urban areas. Historically, the roots of the present contradictions go back more than a century. With the transition from what Gordon (1978:37-39) calls the "Commercial City" to the "Industrial City," an event he places between roughly 1850-70, upper and middle classes began to escape from the central city. As Taylor (1970:134) puts it, they were "fleeing from the noise and confusion of the waterfront, the dirt, the stench, and the intolerably crowded conditions of the old central city." The more affluent were trying to escape the effects of rising capitalist industrialization. Other contradictions were in the offing. The industrial city had concentrated factories and workers near the center city. Late in the nineteenth century, however, workers began to assert themselves via increasing strikes and unionization. Gordon (1978:47-49) argues that it was this increasing working class organization and militancy, more than the conventional putative cause of technological changes, that led capitalists to begin moving factories outside the central city: industrial decentralization too had begun. The United States was moving into the stage of the "Corporate City" (Gordon, 1978:47). Once more, these changes were outgrowths of the contradictory evolution of cities under capitalism, not the result of planning. As Gordon (1978:50) notes:

> I do not mean to imply that the sudden construction of the satellite cities [as a response to industrial decentralization, starting about 1898] represented some massively engineered, carefully calibrated classwide conspiracy steered by the new corporate giants. Individual corporations understood the reasons for the implications of their actions, to be sure. . . . But individual corporations were largely acting on their own, without central coordination or suggestions, perceiving and protecting their own individual interests. There were some examples of collective planning, Taylor notes, but "much more usual, if not so conspicious, is the shifting of factories one by one to the edge of the city" (p. 71). The individual corporations did not need to be directed in their flight from central-city labor turmoil. They had little choice.

Industries were following the earlier exodus of affluent residents to the suburbs. The result was more unplanned decentralization of the urban area: "Before, the city had crammed around its center; now, the Corporate City sprawled" (Gordon, 1978:55). As the corporate city developed further, it would become subject to additional contradictions.

Streetcars, and later automobiles, extended differential mobility for the urban population, with the more affluent classes becoming most freed from the restraints of time and distance. The result was an eruption of the city beyond its traditional and formal boundaries. After World War II, suburbanization grew particularly rapidly as the more advantaged groups further removed themselves from their places of work. In the period of economic expansion after the war, the provision of Federal Housing Administration and Veteran's Administration home mortgages, along with the burgeoning of auto production and sales, and the construction of the urban freeways, aided the process of suburbanization. This further, unplanned spreading and decentralization of the urban form also carried within it the seeds of future contradictions and problems. The rough geographical separation of the classes was continuing. The poorer classes, the racial and ethnic minorities, were increasingly being left behind in deteriorating central cities. Eventually, this decentralization and segregation would lead to a situation that has been likened to a colonial relationship between suburbs and cities, where the more affluent and politically dominant suburbs are able to export wealth earned in the central city to the serenity of the greenbelt (O'Connor, 1973). On the other hand, high levels of unemloyment, underemployment, and welfare dependency in the central cities place a substantial drain on city revenues, yet suburban residents can avoid paying taxes to support the needs of the central city population. This structural and fiscal segmentation of the urban population disproportionately confines the problems of poverty, dependency, crime, and physical deterioration to the central city. This leads to accumulation and legitimation problems for capitalists (particularly bankers and corporate headquarters administrators) who have interests in operating from centralized locations in the city and who also wish to defend central city property values and investments. One response on the part of capitalists, operating through the state, has been various "urban renewal" programs designed to destroy the residences of the urban poor and to place new capital investments in cleared areas (Greer, 1965). However, this programmatic response also led to a contradiction. Poor people sometimes resisted displacement, and more recently they have begun to engage in political challenge of central city projects and governments (Piven and Cloward, 1971). As analysis by Friedland (1976:557) shows, there is a direct relationship between the amount of money spent on urban renewal projects in American cities and the severity of subsequent urban riots. Displacement eventually led to violent social outbreaks.

Thus, the unplanned, essentially anarchic, growth of metropolitan areas produced a series of unanticipated contradictions for capitalists and a series of short-range collective responses by capitalists. Decentralization of production and population, and the segregation of poor and working class people in central cities began to be perceived by capitalists as a threat to central city property values and to the continued existence of centralized administrative control of the corporate economy. The automobile was blamed for most of these problems. *Business Week* (1972:60), for example, pointed an accusing finger at the recent construction of circumferential highways and the growth of light industrial and office parks in the suburbs, saying that they had produced ''a disastrous effect on city cores.'' In addition, the journey to work for most corporate executives and middle class white-collar clerical workers (required for corporate office functioning) was becoming increasingly subject to uncertainties and delays caused by urban traffic congestion. The ''renaissance in urban transportation'' that was heralded in the 1960s and early 1970s must be understood in the light of all of these larger factors that impinged on the cities' role in promoting capitalist accumulation. Projects such as BART were one—but not the only—response made by more class-conscious capitalists. As was noted in Chapter Two, big business in San Francisco was concerned after World War II with the likelihood that metropolitan decentralization would result in central city decay and declining prosperity (Zwerling, 1973:15). There was also much worry over the problems of traffic congestion that had become manifest during the war (Scott, 1959:244-49). It was out of these concerns that BART grew.

BART of course did not solve all, or even most, of these problems in the San Francisco Bay Area. Because the system is not an integral part of a larger, long-range, systematic plan for the equitable development of the Bay Area—a plan that would take into account the mobility needs of all people, including those people in the city's largest black ghettoes such as Hunter's Point—BART serves the needs of only a fraction of the urban population, primarily that affluent fraction of corporate executives, lawyers, and accountants who live in the suburbs and who work in the downtown San Francisco area. The system has been aptly called a ''Cadillac Commuter'' system. The corporate leaders who conceived BART were demonstrably more concerned with accumulation-enhancing patterns of urban growth and elite commuting access than they were concerned with fully planned, wide-ranging, socially equitable, mass transportation. Lack of social planning allowed the vacuum to be filled by the more narrow, short-range plans of capital.

Thus, a publicly funded project such as BART was designed to serve essentially private ends. This is, of course, a common occurrence in our society. In the absence of overall planning, nominally public programs and projects are harnessed to the requirements of private capital accumulation. This outcome reflects the second major contradiction to be analyzed here, the private nature of profit and the public nature of production.

THE SOCIALIZATION OF PRODUCTION VERSUS THE PRIVATIZATION OF PROFIT. Increasingly, the process of production is social in character. That is to say (1) production is undertaken within a certain structure of social relationships (what Marx called the relations of production) and (2) production itself has profound consequences for the society. As a result of their position within the production process, individuals are divided into social classes, classes whose existence has far-reaching impact upon their income, health, and life chances. Moreover, production per se requires the construction of an infrastructure of public institutions such as industrial parks, specialized urban areas, transportation systems, communication systems, educational institutions, and so on. Finally, the products of the process of production not only consume natural resources, but often generate social costs in the form of air and water pollution, noise, wasted energy, and safety and health effects. In this sense, production can be said to be social. As our economy becomes more complex and interdependent, production becomes increasingly socialized, being evermore entangled with the functioning of the larger society.

Yet, profit remains essentially private. The profits derived from the process of production are not controlled by and do not benefit all classes and segments of society equally. Profits go mainly to the capitalist class, where a disproportionate share of the national wealth is concentrated. Domhoff (1979:4-5) summarizes a number of recent studies showing that the top one-half of one percent of the United States population consistently has held over 20 percent of all the personal wealth, more than forty times the amount they would have if all wealth were equally distributed.

In the simplest terms: all of society pays the bill for capitalist production, but most of the benefits are reaped by a relatively small class whose members own and control the means of production.

Kapp (1963) demonstrates how many serious social costs are generated by the private process of production. He defines social costs as "all direct and indirect losses sustained by third persons or the general public as a result of unrestrained, unregulated economic activities" (1963:13). Such costs may take the form of immediate monetary losses, damages to human health, deterioration of property values, the premature depletion of natural resources, and the impairment of less tangible human values. Kapp notes that "in order to be recognized as social costs, harmful effects and inefficiencies must have two characteristics. It must be possible [in principle] to avoid them and they must be part of the course of production activities and be shifted to third persons or the community at large" (Kapp, 1963:14).

While there have been notable exceptions (such as Lange, Pigou, and Veblen) Kapp charges that economists have generally treated social costs as if they were insignificant and unavoidable consequences of the process of economic growth: "In fact, for all practical purposes, value theory considers it as axiomatic that entrepreneurial outlays and private returns constitute a theoretically adequate measure of the costs and benefits of productive activities" (Kapp, 1963:6). The fact that entrepreneurs are able to shift part of the costs of production to the shoulders of persons external to the market transaction means that (1) there is an economic redistribution effect, involving questions of social equity, and (2) since the costs borne by third parties are not part of the traditional calculus of the economic value of a productive activity, we may expect that some such activities will be shown to be of reduced or even negative social worth once all social costs are added to entrepreneurial costs. In other words, that which appears desirable and rational to the capitalist may be disastrous for the larger society.

The private automobile is a case in point. On the one hand, automobiles generate high levels of individual social utility. They provide a highly flexible and wide-ranging mode of transport matched by no other. They have proved popular with Americans from the earliest days of automobile production. The possession and use of the private auto conveys to many a strong sense of freedom, power, mobility, and individuality that fits well with

American cultural values and with the imperatives of a competitive, market economy. The essential appeal of the automobile to Americans, coupled with its capability of being sold as an individual commodity, led to a mass market for this form of transport. In turn, the rise of the automobile generated an enormous amount of private profit for auto makers, oil companies, highway construction firms, tire and rubber companies, insurance companies, and so forth. In short, the populace as a whole, as well as specific segments of capital, undoubtedly benefit from private automobile production and use. However, the automobile also imposes great social costs on substantial segments of society. It is an open question as to whether total benefits exceed total costs. In addition, the marketing of the automobile as an item of mass consumption and as the primary mode of urban transportation leads to numerous contradictions for society as a whole and for urban-oriented corporate class members in particular.

Most of the air pollution, or smog, that affects urban areas is due to automobile usage. Hickey (1971:191) estimates that for the nation as a whole—in urban areas the figure would be much higher—the automobile contributes about 60 percent of the total burden of air pollution. This is chiefly in the form of carbon monoxide, hydrocarbons, and oxides of nitrogen, although a total of more than two hundred different chemical compounds have been identified in auto exhausts (Graham, 1970:207). Urban air pollution not only makes urban living less aesthetically attractive, but it also affects property values, does damage to plant life and agriculture, and impairs human health. The United States Council on Environmental Quality (1970:17), for example, reports that "paint deteriorates faster, cleaning bills are higher, and air filtering systems become necessary [on account of air pollution]. Direct costs to city dwellers can be measured in additional household maintenance, cleaning, and medical bills." Lave and Seskin (1970:730) have demonstrated a correlation between levels of urban air pollution and morbidity and mortality due to such diseases as bronchitis, lung cancer, cardiovascular disease, and other respiratory diseases and various forms of cancer. As a rough estimate, they conclude that a 50 percent reduction in levels of urban air pollution would result in a $2 billion reduction in morbidity and mortality costs for the society (Lave and Seskin:730). These enormous auto-related social costs fall on all who live in cities, not just purchasers and drivers of automobiles.

Another social cost of automobiles is the displacement and destruction of urban residents' homes, often the homes of poor and minorities near the central city. The clearing of rights-of-way for urban freeways (like urban renewal) imposes great financial, social, and psychological hardships upon the persons displaced. Neighborhoods and social relationships are disrupted, residents are forced to look for newer and thus more expensive places to live (which they often cannot afford), and they usually suffer serious financial losses (Downs, 1970). Small businesses forced to relocate often simply go out of business (Zimmer, 1964). Historically, many thousands of people have been so displaced. It has been estimated, for example, that during a typical fifteen-month period in the late 1960s, almost eighty thousand people were displaced in the United States (*LAT*, Dec. 25, 1971). Such a massive and costly disruption was bound to lead eventually to resistance by the groups of people (often working and lower middle class) affected. In fact, the increasing resistance of urban residents in the 1960s and 1970s has made additional building of urban freeways much more difficult.

An often overlooked social cost involved in the building of urban freeways and roads has been the stress it has placed on the fiscal budgets of city governments, contributing to a decline in other social services (e.g., schools) that governments must provide. The direct costs of land acquisition and construction for highways are very high (as early as 1973 the costs for an urban freeway were running about $25 to $50 million per mile, with some reported to be as high as an incredible $100 million per mile) thereby putting great strains on the state and national highway trust funds. As a result, the actual construction of such facilities further stresses the budgets of city governments. Some of the highest priced and most highly taxed land in urban areas has been paved over and thereby taken off the city's tax rolls. Gottman (1961:688) calls attention to this problem: ''While parking, freeways, municipal garages, and heavy costs of roadbed maintenance on streets add to the expenditures of the city government, the space taxable by the city is reduced by the area given to streets, municipal parking facilities, freeways, and so on. A cycle is thus started in which the city is required to perform more services, in more onerous fashion while its major resource (taxable land) is reduced.''

A large portion of the city's taxable land is often lost. It has been estimated, for example, that over sixty percent of the land area of Los Angeles is devoted to automobile facilities (Fellmeth, 1973:407; Robinson, 1971:79). In the immediate downtown area, the figure is an overwhelming 85 percent (Snell, 1974:48). In this way, the presence of the automobile in urban areas contributes to local budget crises, its social costs giving rise to another contradiction.

Another major social cost of the automobile involves resource depletion. The manufacture of automobiles uses a huge quantity of raw materials, and to the extent that these materials are nonrenewable resources in limited supply (as many are), their use raises the price, reduces the availability, and tends to foreclose other, nonautomotive uses. For example, it has been estimated that automobile fabrication (in 1968) used the following percentages of the total United States consumption of these materials: steel, 21.0 percent; aluminum, 10.4 percent; copper and copper alloys, 8.2 percent; gray and ductile iron, 19.4 percent; lead (including gasoline additives), 54.7 percent; malleable iron, 40.0 percent; nickel, 14.3 percent; rubber (natural), 68.8 percent (reclaimed), 59.8 percent (synthetic), 64.1 percent; and zinc, 36.5 percent (Automobile Manufacturers Association, 1970:34). In a world of shrinking resources, growing worldwide demand, and international rivalries, such ravenous consumption of resources by United States automobiles is being recognized as constituting a portentous social cost. This is particularly the case in regard to one crucial resource—oil. The current ''energy crisis'' with its scare over the skyrocketing price of oil and its tenuous availability has brought home the significance of the fact that United States automobiles consume a major percentage of domestic petroleum usage. Extreme reliance on the private automobile therefore not only puts a squeeze on mobility as gasoline prices escalate, but also imperils energy availability for other industrial and nonindustrial uses.

The disproportionate usage of energy by automobiles is not unrelated to the efficiency with which autos transport people in urban areas. Autos are very inefficient in two senses: (1) they consume large amounts of energy for the amount of useful work they do, and (2) they cannot move passengers into or out of urban areas nearly as quickly as many other forms of urban transport. Regarding the first point, Professor of Transportation Richard A. Rice (1972) has calculated the net propulsion efficiency (number of cargo-ton-miles or passenger miles per gallon of fuel) of various modes of transport:

Oil pipelines	300
Waterways	250
Railroads-freight	190
Buses	110
Trucks	60
Railroads-passengers	40
Personal automobiles	30
Aircraft	10

As is evident from the above chart, autos burn up a lot of fuel and do not carry many passengers. About 80 percent of a car's fuel energy is wasted through the exhaust pipe (Flink, 1975:232). Not only that, but automobiles on city streets are notoriously inept at moving passengers. In his classic work, *Megalopolis*, Gottman (1961:652) compares the carrying capacity (passengers per hour) of a single lane of various modes of transport:

Passengers in autos on surface streets	1,575
Passengers in autos on elevated highways	2,625
Passengers in buses on surface streets	9,000
Passengers in streetcars on surface streets	13,500
Passengers in streetcars in subways	20,000
Passengers in local subway trains	40,000
Passengers in express subway trains	60,000

It is clear that with respect to either fuel use or carrying capacity, the private auto is the least efficient of the several possible means of urban transport. It has been estimated that in terms of both fuel (in this case, food) use and total capacity, even walking and bicycling are considerably more efficient movers of masses of people than is the automobile (Fellmeth, 1973:409). This inefficiency is a major contributor to urban traffic congestion and delays. The private auto is being required to do a job for which it is most poorly suited: the task of moving masses of people in and out of compact urban areas twice per day, usually at the rate of one or two commuters per vehicle. This process constitutes virtually individualistic—and extremely energy-inefficient—competition for road space, resulting not only in traffic jams but also the waste of roughly one-half to three-fourths of the unused carrying capacity of each vehicle. The arteriosclerosis of urban traffic circulation systems is the result. Reliance on the private auto produces the paradox that urban traffic flows are sometimes slower today than at the turn of the century: Philadelphia, for example, suffers from rush-hour traffic on one of its major thoroughfares that moves at only 4 miles per hour (*LAT*, Dec. 7, 1972).

Other social costs and contradictions arising from automobile dominance in urban areas could be cited. The point is not simply that such costs exist. Nor is it that they are inequitable, falling as they do on the shoulders of persons who do not necessarily buy or drive automobiles. The point is that capitalists (particularly those segments of the class that produce autos, highways, and related products) have historically reaped large profits from the production and use of automobiles. Now, however, the juncture has been reached where the automobile has begun to bite the hand that feeds it. Capitalists are not very concerned about social costs that burden others. Yet, when social costs become so large and pervasive as to threaten the capitalist accumulation process as a whole—or at least substantial portions of it—then it is a different story. In this case the contradiction consists of the fact that the very success and profitability of the private automobile is now giving rise to social costs and contradictions that are beginning to undermine that profitability and to jeopardize the conditions of capitalist prosperity in urban areas. Air pollution, noise, and traffic congestion make urban areas increasingly less attractive, encouraging further decentralization of industry and residences. The fiscal crisis of cities is exacerbated. Costs of local government are increased, threatening to drive up property tax rates. Property owners, particularly central city businesses, feel the pinch and consider leaving the central city. Capitalists in the central city (particularly financial and administrative capitalists) see the center as a necessary location for their activities. Consequently, they regard these trends as threatening, particularly to the value of their often large property holdings in the city. The poor and minorities often organize in the central cities, demanding more social services and challenging capitalist political hegemony, urban development plans, and highway construction projects. Roads become much more costly—in both an economic and a political sense—to build, placing additional strains on local and state highway funds. Capitalists begin to try various programs aimed at dealing with some of the more severe (from the standpoint of accumulation) problems. However, urban renewal programs and BART-like transportation systems—within the context of essentially unplanned cities and the logic of capitalism—have their own inherent contradictions. They may solve certain problems, but inevitably create others.

There is also a second sense—in addition to the social costs of private auto production and use—in which transportation reflects the gain of private profit on the one hand, but the socialization of the costs on the other. Until fairly recently most urban public transportation companies (e.g., streetcar and early bus systems) were privately owned. Due in part to the dominance of the automobile (and the costs that the society as a whole has borne for the automobile), this kind of private investment has become less competitive. The declining profitability of public transport has led to a withdrawal of private capital and the necessity to operate this service (at a loss) by local urban governments. And since such systems do serve (albeit in a limited way) the needs of less affluent persons who will not or cannot pay the market cost of this service, public transportation must often be subsidized by local tax revenues. This, in turn, places additional revenue requirements on local governmental units. Thus, while capitalists were generating plans for new, expensive, accumulation-enhancing transportation systems such as BART, the units of local and federal government that were expected to finance these systems were increasingly feeling the pinch of the modern budget crisis and taxpayer resistance. It became very difficult to finance such costly programs, and the federal government began to promise less and less financial assistance. At the same time, the rising costs of highway maintenance were beginning to provide new political insolation for the state and national highway trust funds.

This new contradiction reflects the essential fact of private profit from social production. Profits from production are the source of capital. This capital is controlled by the capitalist class. Government must rely on its taxing power to gain revenues, revenues that are limited by structural restraints (O'Connor, 1973). Although capitalists see the need for new transportation systems to boost accumulation in urban areas for the cities, they are unwilling to finance them directly, and government cannot afford to pay for them. Plans for BART-like systems have therefore had to be cut back. Currently, large-scale transit plans are caught between the desire on the part of some segments of capital (particularly financial and administrative capital) for the defense of central urban dominance and accumulation functions, on the one hand, and the unprofitability of public transport and the budget crisis of the state, on the other hand.

This contradiction is made more severe by the commodification of transport. Profit is most readily made through the production of material commodities, not through the production of services or ideas. Under the market system, transport has generally been treated as a profit-making commodity rather than a public service. A public service, since it may serve the needs of the less affluent, may require subsidization, or may at least offer low profitability. Hence, historically there has been a robust affinity between capitalism and that quintessential commodity, the private motor car (see Flink, 1970). In time, the highly profitable automobile became the dominant form of surface transport in the United States. It has been estimated for example that there is about one automobile for every two people in the United States—the world's lowest ratio. Approximately 80 percent of urban commuting is by car, and around 90 percent of travel between cities (Automobile Manufacturers Association, 1970).

As a result of the automobile, United States transportation became highly commodified: individual consumers purchased their own means of transportation, bought their own tires and batteries, and paid for their own fuel and insurance. Thus, in order to increase sales, auto makers, oil companies, and insurance companies sought to increase the private consumption of transport—the more driving the better. This commodification of transport is apparent also in the so-called public mode of transit, where proposals are made for billion-dollar, high technology systems such as BART (which can turn a profit for the producers) rather than for alternative modes of transportation (walking, bicycles, etc.) or better design of urban areas to eliminate unnecessary travel (as by reintegrating work and home). In short, steel and electronics come to displace plans, ideas, and new designs. Yet, it is also clear that transportation is in essence a public service, closely related to urban design, that never can be commodified entirely. Plans and ideas will always have a role, and the private market cannot produce every form of transit for a profit. Clearly, there are limits to private ownership and to the commodification of transport. Thus, a minimal form of public transit yet survives in the interstices of the automobile-dominated transportation system.

The final major contradiction to be examined here, the centralization and concentration of capital, is related to private ownership of transportation production and its consequent commodification. Transportation that is privately produced in the form of commodities, like similar industrial products in a market society, becomes subject to the tendency for production to take place in fewer and fewer large productive units.

CONCENTRATION AND CENTRALIZATION OF CAPITAL: THE AUTO INDUSTRY. Marx accurately predicted the rise of oligopolies and monopolies within capitalism. Competition among capitalists would result in the "ruin of many small capitalists," leaving capital and production in fewer and fewer hands. Moreover, as the productive process evolved, there would be "an increase in the minimum amount of . . . capital necessary to carry on a business under its normal conditions" (Marx, 1961:626).

The automobile industry provides a prime example of the concentration and centralization of capital with the rise of market oligopolies. Although the automobile was initially developed in Germany and France in the late nineteenth century (Flink, 1970:12), the first successful commercial automobile production in the United States began in 1893 (Motor Vehicle Manufacturers Association of the United States, 1974:11). At first, the industry was small and consisted of a multitude of dynamic, highly competitive firms. For example, Flink (1970:302) estimates that over five hundred companies engaged in the manufacturing of autos in the United States between 1900 and 1908. However, some firms lost out while their more successful competitors grew, and the industry soon began to show signs of rising concentration. As early as 1912, only seven companies accounted for over half of United States production of autos (Flink, 1970:331). In 1908, there were 253 active automobile manufacturers in the United States; by 1920, there were only 108. Just nine years later, in 1929, there were 44 (Flink, 1975:58). During the intervening decades, United States auto producers have grown dramatically larger in size and fewer in number. Today, an overwhelming 97 percent of domestic auto production is accounted for by just three firms, and with the current financial crisis facing Chrysler Corporation, that number may soon be down to two. As the *Yale Law Journal* notes: "As measured by either of the structural economic criteria [i.e., high market concentration and high barriers to entry by smaller firms], automobile manufacturing is one of the least competitive industries in the American economy. Its structural concentration is unprecedented" (Yale, 1971:570).

It is often asserted that centralization of capital in large productive units simply reflects socially desirable production efficiency, since it is supposed to arise as a result of economies of scale. The data put forth by Snell (1974), however, dispute this contention. While market concentration may well be inevitable under capitalism, it is not at all clear that increased productive efficiency results. Great concentration of capital leads to overweening political and market power, suppression of technological innovations, inflexibility of operations, artificially high market prices, lack of competition among large producers, and tendencies toward coordinated control over an entire industry. Snell documents in great detail these conditions within the automobile industry.

From the point of view of capital, there is no problem as long as these conditions are internal to an industry and do not affect the prosperity of other large segments of the capitalist class and do not threaten either the accumulation or legitimation processes for the class as a whole. Every class segment gets its share of the pie. However, once the concentration and centralization of capital in an industry has developed past a certain point—particularly in an industry such as transportation or energy where the products are central to many production processes—then, the processes of accumulation and legitimation affecting other powerful segments (and perhaps the class as a whole) may deteriorate. The automobile industry has seemingly reached that point. The enormous segmental class power of automobile-oriented capitalists (including the oil industry, insurance, etc.) has produced strains and contradictions for the remainder of the capitalist class. Automobile firms now have a near-monopoly over other forms of transport as well (i.e., buses, trucks, locomotives), and the petroleum industry seems to be well on the way toward establishing an energy oligopoly over nonoil forms of energy (Ridgeway, 1973). Such monopolies threaten the fabric of the industrial and social systems established by the capitalist class. In brief, metropolitan areas remain important centers for all kinds of capitalist production and administration. Yet they are in a state of decline due to the myriad social costs exacted from private automobile use. Cities tend to fly apart under the decentralizing influence of automobiles. Noise and air pollution from autos make city life unattractive. The presence of large numbers of poor minorities in the inner city threatens capitalist and middle class political dominance there. There is alarm that large offices and administrative headquarters may follow industry and desert the central city (Quante, 1976), further damaging central city investments and accumulation functions. Centrally located capitalists fight to defend these investments and centralized functions, using BART-like high technology transport systems as one means. There are, however, conflicts among capitalists over the desired mix of private autos and new transportation systems, and, most importantly, over how to finance these costly new systems given the budget crisis of the federal and city governments, the inability of private capital to do so, and the defense of the highway trust funds by powerful auto-oriented class segments. This rise of capitalist intraclass conflict based on the specific interests of contending class segments is the most important contradiction. It makes overall capitalist class unity difficult and coordination costly.

Intraclass policy and consensus-seeking groups (see Domhoff) try to resolve differences and achieve some degree of unity of purpose. Sometimes it works, sometimes it works imperfectly, sometimes not at all. General class interests sometimes founder on the specific interests of contending segments, and under such circumstances the state is called upon to defend general class interests. Structural Marxist theoretists Claus Offe and Nicos Poulantzas (1973) argue that the state must have some autonomy from segments of the capitalist class in order to deal with conflicting demands of specific segments and achieve the "liberation of the class interest from the narrow and short-sighted interests of the necessities of the capitalist class" (Offe, 1973:111). However, it can be argued that these authors go too far in assuming that a condition approaching internal welfare within the class is always present. Intraclass conflicts do exist, but not to the degree they maintain. The growing centralization and concentration of capital produces powerful class segments that may come into conflict, as has been seen in the empirical studies in this book. For example, I have documented a conflict between administrative and financial capital (corporate headquarters, banks, etc.) desiring preservation of central city dominance, on the one hand, and auto and highway capital desiring the extension of the metropolitan dominance of the private automobile and the existence of the highway trust fund, on the other. However, the evidence here shows that segments of capital are not always in conflict, and even when they are, a number of powerful mechanisms exist for the intraclass resolution of conflicts. To emphasize disunity is to fail to see unity and coordination, just as to emphasize unity is to neglect the often divisive influence of structurally induced contradictions. In short, the evidence suggests that both unity and disunity exist within the capitalist class, varying according to the historical period and the specific issue or contradiction being confronted (see Whitt, 1979b). I would argue that the only political model that sufficiently emphasizes both of these aspects of the organization of the capitalist class is the class-dialectical model. The model emphasizes the conflict-producing aspects of contradictions (such as those that arise as a result of concentration and centralization of capital) within the basic unity of the capitalist class.

THE CLASS-DIALECTIC HYPOTHESES: AN EVALUATION

The goal now is to show specifically to what extent the dialectical model can account for the political phenomena observed during the five transportation campaigns. It is worth recalling the class-dialectic hypotheses.

Class-dialectic hypotheses: If the class-dialectic model is correct, the study of an important political issue should reveal (1) biases of social institutions that favor outcomes beneficial to dominant classes; (2) evidence of latent class conflict (divergent interests) or observable class conflict over the issue, perhaps including intraclass conflicts among the dominant class, but accompanied by attempts to achieve class unity and cohesion; (3) political alliances and stability of power relations that are historically contingent, reflecting the need to respond to inter- and intraclass conflicts and structural crisis; and (4) outcomes that usually favor dominant class interests, but may also reflect the power of opposing classes and the limitations imposed by structural contradictions.

Regarding the biases of social institutions, the first hypothesis, it is clear that many institutions and social processes do favor the interests of the capitalist class. Our whole conception of transportation tends to be privatized and commodified, lending legitimacy and psychic inevitability to the idea that automobiles are the most natural and efficient mode of transport, and also favoring the high technology approach to new, supplemental transportation systems such as BART. The manufacture of costly mass transit facilities and automobiles—particularly the latter—is a powerful producer of profit for the relevant segments of capital. In addition, as Edelman (1967) forcefully shows, the electoral politics sometimes relied upon by capitalists to validate new transit plans (as in Los Angeles and San Francisco) is very much influenced by symbolic appeals at the mass level (e.g., BART would supposedly ease traffic congestion), yet by instrumental issues at the organized interest-group level (e.g., BART would directly profit transit suppliers and downtown property owners). The public gets reassurance, the capitalist class gets benefits.

The second hypothesis predicts the presence of intraclass conflicts among capitalists, accompanied by attempts to achieve class unity. We have seen both phenomena in these campaigns. Potential and actual conflicts existed over the exact balance between the auto-highway system and new mass transit facilities. Auto lobby segments conflicted with central city-oriented capitalists. In addition, there were strong differences over how to pay for new systems, particularly over whether to use some of the highway fund monies. Within the business community, attempts were made to ease conflicts. The highway lobby opposed Proposition 18 of 1970, but by 1974 had decided not to oppose the similar Proposition 5. By the same token, companies that had not given in support of Proposition 18 (e.g., banks) gave a great deal in 1974. Some conflicts had been resolved or accommodated within the local business community. None of the campaigns was allowed openly to divide the business community into contending segments. Behind-the-scenes efforts to promote consensus and cohesion apparently succeeded rather well, in spite of the potential for severe intracapitalist conflict. The ability of general class interests to overlay and mute the conflicting particular interests of class segments was demonstrated.

The third hypothesis, concerning the impact of structural crises and contradictions on the stability of power and political alliances, is also supported by the evidence we have examined. During the early years of auto-highway system expansion in the United States, there was apparently nearly complete capitalist consensus on the desirability of an urban society dominated by cars and roads. Later, however, the consensus began to unravel as urban decline came to challenge the accumulation function of central city location. Decentralization and the rise of poor, minority populations in the central city gave impetus to various urban renewal programs and plans for BART-like radial transit systems to permit elite commuters access to central locations and to augment central land values. The centralized administrative segment of capital began to see that it had certain interests that had to be separated and defended. Their historical alliance with auto-highway interests could no longer go unchanged. Conflicts of this nature were the central feature of the five campaigns herein analyzed. In spite of these contradictions and conflicts, however, the class was able to maintain its essential unity and to work toward preserving the conditions of accumulation and legitimacy in the central city. Unity has not been complete, nor have the problems been fully solved, but the effort has been made. One reason that all has not been resolved is that other classes are not simply passive observers of these processes. This brings us to the final class-dialectic hypothesis.

The last hypothesis predicts that the power of opposing classes— in addition to the effect of structural contradictions—can alter policy outcomes so that the results do not always favor the dominant class. The organized opposition of working class, minority group, and middle class urban residents made it increasingly difficult in the 1960s and 1970s for the continued construction of urban freeways that would displace thousands of people. This was reflected in the San Francisco "Freeway Revolt" that preceded the passage of the BART bond issue. It was the opposition of Los Angeles voters to the increased taxes to pay for the construction of BART-like systems that had much to do with the defeat of transit plans in that city in 1968 and again in 1974. The dominant class must contend with these challenges and, as a result, the class does not always have things their own way, nor do they win every battle. Over the long run, however, dominant class interests generally prevail—BART was constructed, the California and national highway monies were partially diverted to mass transit uses, and the local capitalist class was able to iron out most conflicts among segments and present a united front. Future attempts will be made in Los Angeles and other cities to follow BART's example and build new systems. They may or may not succeed, depending on the severity of local and national budget crises, voter resistance to new taxes, the impact of energy prices, and so on. Such outcomes are ultimately not predictable since they are historically contingent.

These five campaigns therefore fit well the class-dialectic model of politics. I would argue that these political events are best explained by the class-dialectic model, not the pluralist or elite models. Where the pluralist model would see a rough balance of power between a large number of organized, competing interest groups, there was in reality very little political balance in these campaigns: capitalists were dominant and won most of the issues. Some conflicts did exist among contending capitalist class segments, but overall class unity prevailed. The pluralist view is to be faulted most for the neglect of the larger institutional and historical context in which political contests are waged. Yet this case clearly illustrates how the history and context of a capitalist, class-based society strongly conditions the nature of present political and economic struggles. The class-dialectic model emphasizes these crucial factors.

The elite model appears to be closer to the mark than pluralism, but it tends not to use the most fruitful units of analysis (classes rather than elites) and it presents a much too static and overpowering view of elite domination. The class-dialectic model, on the other hand, holds that while a dominant class exists, its power is not monolithic or unvarying. Contradictions persist that bedevil this rule and often make concerted capitalist action and policies difficult and uncertain. While the tendency is for capitalist rule to generally succeed, it is not so in every case. The armor of the capitalist class is not the seamless protection assumed by the elite model; it has breaches and weak spots.

A Final Summary

This book has attempted to demonstrate that although the theoretical features of the three models are often plainly incompatible with one another (e.g., rule by no group versus rule by institutional elites versus class rule), many of the empirical findings of research are not entirely incompatible. In particular, it is argued that much of what is found in pluralist and elitist research efforts can be explained by class-dialectic theory. This suggests that the class-dialectic model is superior to the other two and that it deserves serious consideration by mainstream sociology and political science.

A fully adequate research methodology must include not only an analysis of interest groups and their interactions, not only an examination of the special roles played by elites, but also must include a systemic analysis that places the relevant political, technological, and social events in their proper historical perspective. When this is done, it is realized that political events which may at first glance seem disparate are actually interconnected, and that a higher level of complexity in explanation must be used. Earlier models of explanation in all sciences are often too simple; increased complexity and understanding generally go together as models develop. The class-dialectic model can explain what the pluralist and elitist models can explain and more. It allows us to make better use of the data and sensitizes us to new insights and new sources of data. For example, where the pluralist model sees competition among interest groups to determine transportation policy, and where the elitist model sees elite domination of crucial transit decisions, the class-dialectic model extends the analysis to show that competition at the level of interest groups is not incompatible with elite domination at higher levels. Most importantly, the class-dialectic model demonstrates that one must understand transportation politics as an historical progression of attempted solutions and resultant contradictions. These contradictions arise as a consequence of the nature of our economic system, the calculus of dominant class goals and problems, the technology and conception of transportation, and the nature of urban development. For instance, the innovation of the private automobile permitted greater individual mobility, generated a booming industrial expansion, and transformed the cities. However, within the context of a market economy, it also eventually generated a saturated domestic consumer market, a highly concentrated manufacturing structure, urban decentralization, and decimated public transportation systems. Declining central cities and reduced viability of centrally located enterprises forced recent attempts to rebuild mass transport systems, now rendered prohibitively expensive in both social and economic terms. Corporations headquartered in downtown areas desire new transit systems but will not, and cannot, pay for them. Tax monies are the preferred form of finance. But citizens resist extra taxation, especially since such systems are seen as benefiting mostly downtown businesses. Thus, a series of complex and often self-contradictory political actions are taken to "solve" these systemically generated contradictions. It is in the light of contradictions such as these that the series of electoral campaigns analyzed in the book must be understood.

For the dominant class, to deal with one contradiction often means to exacerbate another. Political actions, which from either the pluralist or elitist perspective must appear strangely inconsistent, are seen as responsive to and limited by these inherent contradictions. Contradictions make class rule more difficult but they generally do not destroy it. The class has the internal mechanisms and the versatility to formulate—despite internal cleavages—new class positions to deal creatively with changed conditions, conditions arising from events the class cannot control. Thus a more complex, yet more vivid and comprehensive view of these political phenomena is made available to us by the class-dialectic perspective.

Pluralistic interest group competition exists, but at the most superficial level: the outer layer of the onion. Pluralist methods and assumptions do not probe the deeper hidden layers of the onion. Elitist methods penetrate farther, uncovering in institutional elites a much more concentrated and stable structure of power. Elitist models, however, also fail in that they do not see elites as components of a larger social class—a ruling social class that is generally able to organize itself and to maintain its internal cohesion and dominance, but which must contend with the contradictory political economic institutions that generate and reproduce that dominance. At the core of the onion, at the heart of politics, there is class rule and the dialectics of power.

No political model (be it pluralist, elitist, or dialectical) can be expected to explain every political event. A model is, after all, simply a useful framework for categorizing events and discussing general tendencies. All of reality cannot be encompassed within any one model or even within the broader realms of politics, economics, or social class. Yet, much is explainable by the existence of capitalism, by the actions of social classes, and by the politics of power and profit. Much of that which is important to us (for example, the shape of our cities, the nature of our transportation systems, the character of political events that affect our lives, and the dynamics of public policy) is, I contend, best explained by the class-dialectic model. It can serve as a model for political understanding, a touchstone for essaying public events, and a method of investigation and discovery. This research confirms what most of us already suspect—political reality is both more historically connected and more complex than our conventional models suggest. Our grasp of political events at the level of the community, as well as at the national and international levels, can be extended by recognizing and using two essential concepts: the concept of class and the concept of the dialectic. These are the core elements of the class-dialectic model of politics.

BIBLIOGRAPHY

Aiken, Michael and Paul Mott (eds.).
  1970. *The Structure of Community Power*. New York: Random House.

Alexander, Herbert.
  1976. *Campaign Money: Reform and Reality in the States*. New York: The Free Press.

Alford, Robert.
  1975. "Paradigms of relations between state and society." In L. Lindberg, R. Alford, C. Crouch, and C. Offe (eds.), *Stress and Contradiction in Modern Capitalism*, pp. 145-160. Toronto: Lexington.

Appelbaum, Richard.
  1978. "Marx's theory of the falling rate of profit: Towards a dialectical analysis of structural social change." *American Sociological Review* 43 (February): 67-80.

Automobile Manufacturers Association, Inc.
  1970. *Automobile Facts and Figures*. Pamphlet by the Automobile Manufacturers Association, Inc., Detroit.

Averitt, Robert.
  1968. *The Dual Economy: The Dynamics of American Industry Structure*. New York: W. W. Norton & Company, Inc.

Bachrach, Peter and Morton S. Baratz.
  1962. "Two faces of power." *American Political Science Review* 57 (December): 947-952.

Bailey, James.
  1966. "BART: The Bay Area takes a billion-dollar ride." *Architectural Forum* 124 (June): 38-60.

Banfield, Edward C.
  1961. *Political Influence*. New York: The Free Press of Glencoe.

Baran, Paul and Paul Sweezy.
  1966. *Monopoly Capital*. New York: Modern Reader Paperbacks.

Barnes, Peter.
1973. "So-so rapid transit." *New Republic*, September 1: 15-23.

Bazell, Robert J.
1971. "Rapid transit: A real alternative to the auto for the Bay Area?" *Science* 171 (19 March): 1125-1128.

Bentley, Arthur.
1908. *The Process of Government*. Chicago: University of Chicago Press.

Bollens, John C.
1948. *The Problem of Government in the San Francisco Bay Region*. Berkeley: Bureau of Public Administration, University of California.

Bonjean, Charles, T. Clark, and R. Lineberry (eds.).
1971. *Community Politics: A Behavioral Approach*. New York: The Free Press.

Buel, Ronald A.
1972. *Dead End: The Automobile in Mass Transportation*. Baltimore: Penguin Books, Inc.

Business Week.
1972. "Attacking the mass transit mess." June 3: 60-65.

California Journal
1970a. "Environmental quality: Key 1970 issue." 1 (January): 8-11.
1970b. "Smog, transit proposition rejected." 1 (November): 308-325.

Chambliss, William.
1979. "Contradictions and conflicts in law recreation." In S. Spitzer (ed.), *Annual Review of Sociology of Law*, in press. Greenwich: Jai Press, Inc.

Cochran, Thomas C.
1957. *The American Business System: A Historical Perspective, 1900-1955*. Cambridge, Mass.: Harvard University Press.

Cohen, Stanley.
1972. "BART makes tracks to the future." *Consulting Engineer*, January 1972.

Council on Environmental Quality.
    1970. *Environmental Quality: The First Annual Report of the Council on Environmental Quality*. Washington: U. S. Government Printing Office.

Crenson, Matthew.
    1971. *The Un-Politics of Air Pollution: A Study of Non-Decisionmaking in the Cities*. Baltimore: Johns Hopkins University Press.

Crump, Spencer.
    1962. *Ride the Big Red Cars*. Los Angeles: Trans-Angle Books.

Defreitas, Greg.
    1972. "BART: Rapid transit and regional control." *Pacific Research and World Empire Telegram* 4 (November/December): 12-19.

Dahl, Robert A.
    1961. *Who Governs? Democracy and Power in an American City*. New Haven: Yale University Press.

Domhoff, G. William.
    1967. *Who Rules America?* Englewood Cliffs, N.J.: Prentice-Hall Inc.
    1970. *The Higher Circles*. New York: Random House.
    1974. *The Bohemian Grove*. New York: Harper & Row, Publishers.
    1975. "Social clubs, policy-planning groups, and corporations: A network study of ruling-class cohesiveness." *The Insurgent Sociologist* 5 (Spring): 173-184.
    1978. *Who Really Rules? New Haven and Community Power Reexamined*. Santa Monica: Goodyear Publishing Co.
    1979. *The Powers that Be*. New York: Random House.

Downs, Anthony.
    1970. *Urban Problems and Prospects*. Chicago: Markham Publishing Company.

Dye, Thomas.
    1976. *Who's Running America?* Englewood Cliffs, N.J.: Prentice-Hall Inc.

Edelman, Murray.

1967. *The Symbolic Uses of Politics*. Chicago: University of Illinois Press.

Engler, Robert.

1961. *The Politics of Oil*. Chicago: University of Chicago Press.

Esping-Anderson, Gosta, Roger Friedland, and Erik Wright.

1976. "Modes of class struggle and the capitalist state." *Kapitalistate* 4-5:186-220.

Ewen, Linda.

1978. *Corporate Power and Urban Crisis in Detroit*. Princeton: Princeton University Press.

Fellmeth, Robert C.

1973. *Politics of Land*. New York: Grossman Publishers.

Flink, James J.

1970. *America Adopts the Automobile, 1895-1910*. Cambridge: MIT Press.

1975. *The Car Culture*. Cambridge: MIT Press.

Friedland, Roger.

1976. "Class Power and the Central City: The Contradictions of Urban Growth." Doctoral dissertation, Department of Sociology, University of Wisconsin, Madison.

Friedland, Roger, Frances Piven, and Robert Alford.

1978. "Political conflict, urban structure, and the fiscal crisis." In Douglas Ashford (ed.), Comparing Public Policies: New Concepts and Methods, pp. 197-225. Sage Yearbook in Politics and Public Policy. Beverly Hills: Sage Publications, Inc.

Galbraith, John Kenneth.

1956. *American Capitalism: The Concept of Countervailing Power*. Boston: Houghton Mifflin Company.

Gordon, David M.

1978. "Capitalist development and the history of American cities." In William K. Tabb and Larry Sawers (eds.), *Marxism and the Metropolis*, pp. 25-63. New York: Oxford University Press.

Gottman, Jean.
 1961. *Megalopolis: The Urbanized Northeastern Seaboard of the United States.* New York: The Twentieth Century Fund.
Graham, Frank, Jr.
 1970. "The infernal smog machine." In Glen A. Love and Rhoda M. Love (eds.), *Ecological Crisis: Readings for Survival.* New York: Harcourt, Brace, Jovanovich, Inc.
Greer, Scott.
 1965. *Urban Renewal and American Cities.* Indianapolis: The Bobbs-Merrill Co., Inc.
Hartman, Chester W.
 1974. *Yerba Buena: Land Grab and Community Resistance in San Francisco.* San Francisco: Glide Publications.
Hawley, Willis and Frederick Wirt (eds.).
 1974. *The Search for Community Power.* Englewood Cliffs, N.J.: Prentice-Hall Inc.
Hickey, Richard J.
 1971. "Air pollution." In William W. Murdoch (ed.), *Environment, Resources, Pollution and Society*, pp. 189-212. Stanford: Sinauer Associates, Inc., Publishers.
Hunt, E. K. and Howard J. Sherman.
 1972. *Economics: An Introduction to Traditional and Radical Views.* New York: Harper & Row, Publishers.
Hunter, Floyd.
 1953. *Community Power Structure: A Study of Decision Makers.* Chapel Hill: University of North Carolina Press.
 1959. *Top Leadership, U.S.A.* Chapel Hill: University of North Carolina Press.
Kain, John F. and John R. Meyer.
 1970. "Transportation and poverty," *The Public Interest* (Winter): 75-87.
Kapp, K. William.
 1963. *Social Costs of Business Enterprise.* Bombay: Asia Publishing House.
Kelley, Ben.
 1971. *The Pavers and the Paved.* New York: Donald W. Brown, Inc.

Key, V. O.
  1959. *Politics, Parties and Pressure Groups.* New York: Thomas Y. Crowell Company, Publishers.
Kizzia, Tom.
  1974. "Los Angeles: Will tracks be back?" *Railway Age* (June): 30-41.
Koenig, Thomas, Robert Gogel, and John Sonquist.
  1973. "Corporate Interlocks and Social Class." Unpublished paper, Department of Sociology, University of California, Santa Barbara.
Kuhn, Thomas.
  1962. *The Structure of Scientific Revolutions.* Chicago: University of Chicago Press.
Lamare, Judith Louise.
  1973. "Urban Mass Transportation Politics in the Los Angeles Area: A Cast Study in Metropolitan Policy-Making." Doctoral dissertation, Department of Political Science, University of California, Los Angeles.
Lave, Lester B. and Eugene P. Seskin.
  1970. "Air pollution and human health." *Science* 169 (21 August): 723-733.
Leavitt, Helen.
  1970. *Superhighway—Superhoax.* Garden City, N.Y.: Doubleday & Co., Inc.
Leinsdorf, David and Donald Etra.
  1973. *Citibank.* New York: Grossman Publishers.
Lewin, Gordon.
  1974. "Rapid transit and the public interest: A case study of the San Francisco peninsula." Stanford Workshops on Political and Social Issues, Stanford University.
Liston, Albert Morris.
  1970. "Regional Rapid Transit Development in the San Francisco Bay Area." Master's thesis, Department of Government, Sacramento State College.
Lowi, Theodore J.
  1969. *The End of Liberalism.* New York: W. W. Norton & Company, Inc.

Lukes, Steven.
    1974. *Power: A Radical View*. London: Macmillan.
McConnell, Grant.
    1966. *Private Power and American Democracy*. New York:
    Vintage Books.
Mankoff, Milton.
    1972. "Power in advanced capitalist society: A review essay
    of recent elitist and Marxist criticism of pluralist theory."
    In Milton Mankoff (ed.), *The Poverty of Progress*, pp. 82-
    93. New York: Holt, Rinehart and Winston.
Mariolis, Peter.
    1975. "Interlocking directorates and control of corporations:
    The theory of bank control." *Social Science Quarterly* 56
    (December): 425-439.
Marx, Karl.
    1961. *Capital*, vol. 1. Moscow: Foreign Language Publish-
    ing House.
Merton, Robert K.
    1968. *Social Theory and Social Structure*. New York: The
    Free Press.
Meyer, J. R., J. F. Kain, and M. Wohl.
    1965. *The Urban Transportation Problem*. Cambridge: Har-
    vard University Press.
Michels, Robert.
    1915. *Political Parties*. New York: The Free Press.
Miliband, Ralph.
    1969. *The State in Capitalist Society*. New York: Basic Books,
    Inc.
Mills, C. Wright.
    1956. *The Power Elite*. New York: Oxford University Press.
Mollenkopf, John.
    1975. "Theories of the state and power structure research."
    The Insurgent Sociologist 5 (Spring): 245-264.
Molotch, Harvey L.
    1975. "The urban growth machine." In William W. Mur-
    doch (ed.), *Environment: Resources, Pollution and Society*,
    second edition. Stamford: Sinauer Associates, Inc., Publish-
    ers.

Molotch, Harvey L.

1976. "The city as a growth machine: Toward a political economy of place." *American Journal of Sociology* 82:309-332.

Molotch, Harvey and Marilyn Lester.

1974. "News as purposive behavior: Or the strategic use of routine events, accidents, and scandals." *American Sociological Review* 39 (February): 101-112.

Moore, Gwen.

1979. "The structure of a national elite network." *American Sociological Review* 44 (October): 673-692.

Mosca, Gaetano.

1939. *The Ruling Class.* New York: McGraw-Hill Book Company.

Motor Vehicle Manufacturers Association of the United States, Inc.

1974. *Automobiles of America.* Detroit: Wayne State University Press.

Mowbray, A. Q.

1969. *The Road to Ruin.* New York: Harcourt, Brace and World, Inc.

Nevins, Jane.

1971. "Proposition 18: A postmortem." *Los Angeles Magazine* 16 (January): 35, 25-29.

O'Connor, James.

1973. *The Fiscal Crisis of the State.* New York: St. Martin's Press.

Offe, Claus.

1973. "The abolition of market control and the problem of legitimacy." *Kapitalistate* 1 (1973).

Pareto, Vilfredo.

1935. *Mind and Society.* New York: Harcourt, Brace, and Co.

Piven, Frances Fox and Richard Cloward.

1971. *Regulating the Poor: The Functions of Public Welfare.* New York: Vintage.

Polsby, Nelson.

1970. "How to study community power: The pluralist alternatives." In M. Aiken and P. Mott (eds.), *The Structure of Community Power*, pp. 297-304. New York: Random House.

1980. *Community Power and Political Theory*. Second Edition. New Haven: Yale University Press.

Poulantzas, Nicos.

1973. *Political Power and Social Classes*. London: New Left Books.

Prewitt, Kenneth and Alan Stone.

1973. *The Ruling Elites*. New York: Harper & Row, Publishers.

Quante, Wolfgang.

1976. *The Exodus of Corporate Headquarters from New York City*. New York: Praeger Publishers, Inc.

Ratcliff, Richard E.

1979. "The command of civic policy and urban disinvestment: An analysis of the impact of capitalist class structure on the decline of older industrial cities." Unpublished paper, Department of Sociology, Washington University, St. Louis.

Rice, Richard A.

1972. "System energy and future transportation." *Technology Review* 74 (January): 37-67.

Ridgeway, James.

1973. *The Last Play*. New York: E. P. Dutton.

Rifkin, Jeremy and Randy Barber.

1978. *The North Will Rise Again*. Boston: Beacon Press.

Robinson, John.

1971. *Highways and our Environment*. New York: McGraw-Hill Book Company.

Rose, Arnold.

1967. *The Power Structure: Political Process in American Society*. New York: Oxford University Press.

Rothschild, Emma.

1972. "The great Transpo expo." *New York Review of Books* 19 (July 20): 25, 28.

1973. *Paradise Lost: The Decline of the Auto-Industrial Age*. New York: Random House.

Schattschneider, E. E.

1935. *Politics, Pressures and the Tariff*. New York: Prentice-Hall, Inc.

Scott, Mel.

1959. *The San Francisco Bay Area: A Metropolis in Perspective*. Berkeley: University of California Press.

Shipnuck, Les and Dan Feshbach.

1972. "Bay Area Council: Regional Powerhouse." *Pacific Research and World Empire Telegram* 4 (November/December): 3-11.

Simmons, Bob.

1968. "The freeway establishment." *Cry California* 3 (Spring): 31-38.

Snell, Bradford C.

1974. *American Ground Transport*. Report presented to the Subcommittee on Antitrust and Monopoly of the Committee on the Judiciary, U. S. Senate, February 26, 1974. Washington: U. S. Government Printing Office.

Sonquist, John A. and Thomas Koenig.

1975. "Interlocking directorates in the top U. S. corporations: A graph theory approach." *The Insurgent Sociologist* 5 (Spring): 196-229.

Stephens, John.

1980. *The Transition from Capitalism to Socialism*. Atlantic Highlands, N.J.: Humanities Press, Inc.

Sundeen, Richard Allen, Jr.

1963. "The San Francisco Bay Area Council: An Analysis of A Non-Governmental Metropolitan Organization." Master's thesis, Department of Political Science, University of California, Berkeley.

Taylor, George Rogers.

1970. "Building an inter-urban transportation system." In A. M. Wakstein (ed.), *The Urbanization of America*. Boston: Houghton Mifflin Company.

Truman, David.

1953. *The Governmental Process*. New York: Alfred A. Knopf, Inc.

Useem, Michael.
1979. "The social organization of the American business elite and participation of corporation directors in the governance of American institutions." *American Sociological Review* 44 (August): 553-572.

Vance, James E., Jr.
1966. "Housing the worker: The employment linkage as a force in urban structure." *Economic Geography* 42:294-325.

Walton, John.
1970. "A systematic survey of community power research." In M. Aiken and P. Mott (eds.), *The Structure of Community Power*, pp. 446-464. New York: Random House.

Whitt, J. Allen.
1979a. "Toward a class-dialectical model of power: An empirical assessment of three competing models of political power." *American Sociological Review* 44 (February): 81-100.
1979b. "Can capitalists organize themselves?" *The Insurgent Sociologist* 9 (Fall): 51-59.

Wright, Erik and Luca Perrone.
1977. "Marxist class categories and income inequality." *American Sociological Review* 42 (February): 32-55.

Yale Law Journal.
1971. "Annual style change in the automobile industry as an unfair method of competition." Volume 80 (January): 567-613.

Zeitlin, Irving.
1968. *Ideology and the Development of Sociological Theory.* Englewood Cliffs, N.J.: Prentice-Hall Inc.

Zeitlin, Maurice.
1974. "Corporate ownership and control: The large corporation and the capitalist class." *American Journal of Sociology* 79 (March): 1073-1119.

Zeitlin, Maurice, W. Lawrence Neuman, and Richard Ratcliff.
1976. "Class segments: Agrarian property and political leadership in the capitalist class of Chile." *American Sociological Review* 41 (December): 1006-1029.

Zimmer, Basil G.

1964. *Rebuilding Cities: The Effects of Displacement and Relocation on Small Business.* Chicago: Quadrangle Books.

Zwerling, Stephen.

1972. "The Political Consequences of Technological Choice: Public Transit in the San Francisco Metropolitan Area." Doctoral dissertation, Department of Political Science, University of California, Berkeley.

1973. "BART: Manhattan rises on San Francisco Bay." *Environment* 15 (December): 14-19.

Library of Congress Cataloging in Publication Data

Whitt, J. Allen, 1940-
    Urban elites and mass transportation.

    Bibliography: p.
    Includes index.
    1. Urban transportation—California.
    2. Local transit—California.   3. Elite
    (Social sciences)—California.   4. Community
    power.   I. Title.
    HE309.C2W48   388.4'068   81-47958
    ISBN 0-691-09398-9   AACR2
    ISBN 0-691-02826-5 (pbk.)

Weakness
Too many lists &
names of Pres + VP